The Guardian Life Insurance Company, 1860–1920

The statue of Germania being lowered from the branch-office building in St. Paul, Minnesota, 1 April 1918, a victim of anti-German feelings during World War I. During the war the Germania Life Insurance Company changed its name to The Guardian Life Insurance Company of America and began to transform itself into a purely American company, thus closing a sixty-year chapter in its history. (Courtesy of Minnesota Historical Society)

The Guardian Life Insurance Company, 1860–1920

A History of a German-American Enterprise

Anita Rapone

NEW YORK UNIVERSITY PRESS
New York & London

Library of Congress Cataloging-in-Publication Data

Rapone, Anita.
The Guardian Life Insurance Company, 1860–1920.

Bibliography: p.
Includes index.
1. Guardian Life Insurance Company—History.   2. German
Americans—History.   I. Title.
HG8963.G942R36   1987   368.3'2'0068   87-7913
ISBN 0-8147-7401-6

Book design by Ken Venezio

Contents

Illustrations

Unless otherwise noted, all illustrations are reprinted by permission from the archives of The Guardian Life Insurance Company.

Frontispiece: Removal of the Statue of Germania from a Branch-Office Building

Illustrations appear as a group following page 80.

Tables

Foreword

Five years ago I discovered that The Guardian had lost track of the first sixty years of its history. The eighty-five-year-old Frank Weidenborner, still a director of the company, could fill me in on events after 1922, but the "German years" that stretched back to 1860 were largely lost to us. We knew that a political refugee named Hugo Wesendonck had been our first president, and we could inspect the names of subscribers to our 1860 stock offering. Our archives also held a few pictures of Hugo Wesendonck with several unnamed family members, but little else—no biographies, no lists of board members, no stories. I convinced myself that it would be a pleasant undertaking to fill the void. Little did I know that there was no history of New York City's once-flourishing German community, or that historians were still sorting out the significance of the Frankfurt Parliament and the German Revolution of 1848–49, or that I would be dealing with political and economic history on two continents. Thankfully, I did proceed, becoming wiser as I went along and thoroughly enjoying every step of the search for information.

Many kind people lent a hand with my phase of the research. Lillian Swanson, Ethel Albert, Herbert Grolnick, Tom DeSanno of The Guardian were a constant support. Genealogist B-Ann Moorhouse assembled sketches of seventy of our directors after I had exhausted the published sources I could think of. Gertrude Schmidt Barber translated from German a biography of Hugo Wesendonck printed in an 1892 collection of lives of prominent German-Americans. I was kindly received by staff members at Lenox Hill Hospital, the Liederkranz Society, the Ottendorfer Branch Library, the Central Savings Bank (formerly the German Savings Bank), and The German Society. Early

Germania directors were active in each. I discovered as a point of interest that Wilhelmina Wesendonck had been the founder of the ladies auxiliary at the German Hospital and Infirmary, which would later call itself Lenox Hill Hospital. Henry Marx, who spent thirty years on the staff of the *New-Yorker Staats-Zeitung* graciously shared with me his extensive knowledge of New York City's past and present German-American community. I owe a major debt to Robert W. Gutman, author of *Richard Wagner: The Man, His Mind, His Music,* for insights into the lives of Otto Wesendonck and his wife, Mathilde, during the Zurich years of Wagner and the Wesendoncks. Clues from the Wagnerian literature ultimately led me to the charming and scholarly Franz von Wesendonk, Otto's great grandson.

Franz von Wesendonk, or more formally Karl Franz Otto Heinrich Sigismund von Wesendonk, I consider a citizen of the Western world. His grandparents were, in equal parts, German, Hungarian, Portuguese, and Italian; Franz and his sister were raised in the Portuguese embassies in Stockholm and at The Hague. He married a German diplomat's daughter, became a military pilot, and spent eight years as a Russian military prisoner. Then came a career as an attorney, mostly with the European Economic Community in Brussels. He is a scholar who speaks and reads eight languages and could not have been kinder to me or more forthcoming with information about his illustrious family. Wiley Wesendonck Borum of Philadelphia, a great grandson of Hugo Wesendonck, repeatedly searched his family's memory in response to my questions.

I must mention Julia B. Bachelder, a gracious neighbor of mine in Greenwich Village. By chance Julia heard my wife Catherine, say that we were going to visit the Franz von Wesendonks in Italy. Then it came out that Julia's great grandfather was Adolf Schniewind, an early director and agency officer of the company. Julia's mother, Julia Schniewind Bachelder, had been a companion of the deaf Tony Wesendonck on several journeys to Europe, and her mementos included a snapshot of Max Wesendonck surveying the scene from the porch of a Swiss hotel.

William Bouwsma, a friend of forty-five years and past president of the American Historical Association, was a valuable confidant and advisor. So was James A. Rawley, another old friend and chairman of the Department of History at the University of Nebraska. I include among Jim Rawley's many kindnesses an introduction to Hans L.

Trefousse, professor of history at Brooklyn College and biographer of Carl Schurz. Hans Trefousse shared extracts he had copied from the Schurz papers that touched on Schurz's service on Germania's board of directors. I should like to recall the kindness and support of John C. Pemberton in this project. John's fifty-three years as an alert and constructive Guardian director ended with his death in 1984 at the age of ninety-one. An attorney by profession, John possessed an unusually keen sense of history and spent years in writing a biography of his grandfather, Confederate General John C. Pemberton, entitled *Pemberton: Defender of Vicksburg*. John's grandmother (the general's wife) was a descendant of Elbridge Gerry, signer of the Declaration of Independence and vice president of the United States under James Madison. John's own line stretched back to Quaker Ralph Pemberton, who accompanied William Penn to Pennsylvania in 1682. Finally there was John's marriage to Catherine Watjen whose father and grandfather had been Guardian directors. The New York branch of the Watjen firm had first been headed by Charles Luling, a founding director of Germania Life, thus creating a remarkable tie to our earliest years.

I also wish to acknowledge my gratitude to Jeffry M. Diefendorf, author of *Businessmen and Politics in the Rhineland, 1789–1834*, for naming archives in Germany that were useful to us. Hans Buhlmann, president of the Swiss Actuarial Association, helped me uncover the origins of John Frederick Entz, our first actuary. Charles E. Brooks of the Swiss Reinsurance Company of Zurich led me to nineteenth-century yearbooks with short biographies of members of our European board of directors.

The time came when I realized that there was a history to be written and that I lacked the time and the skill to do it. In the spring of 1982 I learned of the existence of Key Perspectives, a humanities consulting firm in New York City. Dr. Karen S. Rubinson, Director of Key Perspectives, impressed me with her businesslike approach to project management and with the talent Key Perspectives could supply. So we took the first cautious step, which was to ask Dr. Anita Rapone to make a feasibility study and then to go ahead, without any strings attached, and write a scholarly history of the company. She proved fully equal to the challenge of carving a book out of the mountain of raw material she found in our files. I thank her on behalf of The Guardian for a first-rate piece of work and those from the Institute for Research in History who provided assistance. Half a dozen Guardian People read and criticized a first draft of the manuscript; no one, incidentally, suggested deletions or any sanitization.

I would close with a word to present and future Guardian employees. I urge you to greet with open arms this chronicle of the men and women who carefully built our company. Forgive them their mistakes, just as, one hopes, future generations will recognize our own human failings while acknowledging our accomplishments. Above all, I hope that some of the lessons of the past that you will find in our history may be a useful guide to the future.

John C. Angle
Chairman of the Board
of The Guardian Life Insurance
Company of America

Acknowledgments

I owe thanks and appreciation to the many people who helped me in various ways in the research and writing of this book. I owe a particular debt to John Angle, whose enthusiasm for the history of his company led to this project. Others at the Guardian facilitated my research there, including Herbert N. Grolnick, Lillian Swanson, and Thomas De-Sanno. Karen Rubinson of Key Perspectives organized and managed the project, and four of my colleagues at The Institute for Research in History made important contributions: Terry Collins helped with research and interpretation; Nancy Robertson organized the Guardian Life archives and answered many queries; Dagmar Stern translated the German records; and William Zeisel suggested editorial improvements. Pamela Lehrer at New York Life, Marianne Stolp at Metropolitan Life, and Judith Schwarz and Burkhard Seubert aided in the search for historical documents. Hans Trefousse, professor of history at Brooklyn College and the Graduate Center of the City University of New York, shared research with me, as did the journalist Henry Marx and Lesley Ann Kawaguchi. Valuable suggestions were offered by two faculty members at New York University who read early drafts: Kenan Professor Vincent Carosso and David Reimers, professor in the Department of History. I received many helpful comments also from Deborah Gardner, director of the Center for the Study of Women in Business, Baruch College, City University of New York, and Esther Katz, deputy director of The Institute for Research in History.

Anita Rapone
State University of New York
at Plattsburgh

Prologue

At three in the afternoon on 28 March 1860, twenty-one men sat down at Delmonico's Restaurant in Manhattan on the corner of Broadway and Chambers, to discuss the founding of a company to sell life insurance to German-Americans. Most of the men at that meeting were themselves German immigrants. Some had fled political persecution after the failure in 1848 of a wave of liberal uprisings in Germany and elsewhere in Europe; one such refugee was Hugo Wesendonck, who had called the meeting at Delmonico's. Others had emigrated to seek their fortunes in the rapidly industrializing economy of the United States in the decades before the Civil War. Most German-Americans settled in the northeastern states and in the developing Midwest, where they became important in agriculture, commerce, industry, finance, and the retail trades. They retained a strong sense of their native culture, a fondness for the homeland and German things, and a desire to create and preserve a vigorous community in the New World. This desire to nurture the German-American community was one reason why Hugo Wesendonck and his associates decided to found an insurance company that would cater to the special needs and interests of their fellow emigrants. The name of the company was to be the Germania, and it would open its door in New York City, at that time the major German-American community.

The young company, benefiting immediately from the ready market of German-Americans, soon established itself as an important part of the American life insurance industry. Within a few years of opening, the Germania expanded operations to Europe, where it quickly developed a large clientele, especially in Germany. From the 1870s through the early 1920s the Germania had both domestic and international operations, competing in markets as diverse as Cincinnati, Paris, and Berlin. As with any insurance company, it experienced the ups and downs of the economy and changes in the life insurance industry that altered the conditions of doing business. It weathered a particularly difficult decade from 1898 to 1908, when, in succession, its president and founder retired, it was subjected to a takeover attempt, it underwent internal turmoil involving allegations of personal misconduct by its president, and it was asked to provide testimony in one of the most important government investigations of the life insurance industry, that conducted by the Armstrong Committee. Having moved successfully through these trials, the company entered a period of relatively calm development, which was suddenly disrupted by the First World War. That war divided the home office from its large operation in Germany and, even worse, called into question the company's loyalty to the Allied cause against Germany and Austria-Hungary. Under enormous pressure from agents and policyholders, the directors and officers decided to change the name to the Guardian Life and to pull out of all foreign operations, including the lucrative German market. This decision, made late in 1917 and put into execution the following year, marked the single most decisive event in the company's history since its founding in 1860. After World War I, the Guardian Life Insurance Company began to evolve in different directions from the old Germania, although the full implication of the changes did not appear for many years. Today the Guardian Life is the twentieth largest company in its industry.

When this historical study of the Germania/Guardian was begun in 1983, it seemed possible to encompass the entire work in a single volume. As research and analysis progressed, however, it became evident that the company's name change in 1917 was more than superficial, and marked a new direction in affairs. Moreover, the period from about 1910 to 1920 also marks a change in the historical evidence. Written materials surviving from before 1910 are sparse and often disappointing. Of necessity, for this period the author relied more than was preferred on "official" documents, such as minutes of committees and the board of directors, supplemented, where possible, by stories in the insurance or popular press and material from scholarly studies. For the period after about 1900 there is some oral-history material written down during the 1930s that is especially helpful in giving a sense of personalities and the physical environment of the company's offices. After 1920, however, the source material increases in size and diversity, and for the period after about 1940 it is possible to add the testimony of living persons, some of them still in the company's employment.

The wide divergence in the evolution of the company after about 1920 and the much greater body of source material available for the later period prompted the author to make this book forthrightly into a history of the company's first sixty years, the period when it sold mainly to the German and German-American markets; and to discuss developments after about 1920 only as they affected the process whereby the Germania was transformed into the Guardian. Since even this more circumscribed tale amounts to a substantial book, it seems that the decision to leave the later periods to a second volume was the right one.

No doubt readers will bring their own sets of questions to the book, but for the author there are three in particular that seem especially pertinent. First is the issue of what it meant for the company to identify itself with a single ethnic group and market. In the short run that decision offered the Germania a clear-cut market that it could approach with a bias in its own favor. But what of the long term? Was it not precisely the ethnic issue that split the company apart during World War I? Throughout the text the relative merits of the ethnic orientation will crop up in various guises, and will be considered again in the Epilogue.

The second question is why the Germania did not grow into one of the giant American life insurance companies. In 1920 the Guardian was not among the twenty-five largest American life insurance companies in the amount of policies in force, but in 1880 it had been the ninth largest company. It was older than the Prudential, yet that company, within a few years of its founding in 1875, grew to be far larger than the Germania. Many other companies, such as Metropolitan and Mutual of New York, also grew enormously during the period after 1880, to become industry giants. What factors prevented this from occurring at the Germania? Was it the inherent limitation of the ethnic market, or a business mentality that preferred stability over rapid growth, or some other factor? This issue appears periodically in the text and will also be discussed in the Epilogue.

Finally, there is the question of how the new Guardian Life re-oriented itself to become a truly American company after World War I. What fresh products and ideas helped the company acquire new business that was not related to the German-American community? The question is worth raising here, and again in the Epilogue, even though the present study cannot offer definitive answers.

The Guardian Life was, and is, a medium-sized business enterprise of the sort that forms the backbone of the American corporate scene. The study of how it was created and the way it operated for its first sixty years offers a perspective on the role of ethnicity in the rise of American business, American society, and the development of the life insurance industry.

[1]

Origins

The Germania Life was founded under the impetus of three powerful forces: the development of modern life insurance as a concept, the industrialization of Europe and North America, and the emigration of millions of Europeans to the shores of the United States during the nineteenth century. The first two developments were preconditions for the rise of life insurance companies as major elements in the American economy, and the third development created an ethnic market that attracted many insurance companies and gave the Germania its individual character.

The concept of insuring against possible loss is at least as old as the Greeks and Romans, who applied it to material objects, mainly ships and their cargoes. As the European economies became more complex during the post-medieval period, however, other forms of insurance came into vogue to protect not only objects but abstract concepts like earning power. Travelers began to take out short-term life insurance policies, to protect their estates against loss if they should fall victim to the all-too-common perils of shipwreck, pirates, or highwaymen. Eventually, the idea arose that even people who were not under an immediate risk to their safety might, with an eye to the inevitable future, want to protect the financial security of the family after their death.

Although various schemes of insuring life were tried during the sixteenth and seventeenth centuries, modern life insurance really dates from the eighteenth, with the invention of the level-premium plan. Until this plan, a major hindrance to the development of life insurance as a concept and an industry had been the inability of any insurance company to find a workable method of assessing policyholders for the funds needed to make the venture work. Were policyholders to contribute to the common fund annually or in a single lump sum? And how much? Many life insurance systems simply assessed all policyholders whenever claims were made on the company, but this raised another question: Should all policyholders be assessed equally, or were those of long standing more (or less) liable?

These and other such issues were resolved in the wake of the level-premium plan, created by English mathematician James Dodson. When Dodson was forty-six years old, he applied for a life insurance policy but was refused because of his age. Dodson was one of many individuals who were denied access to insurance on account of age, since the current systems of calculating premiums and claims placed insurers in the position of either charging older people premiums so high they were unaffordable or, if the premiums were set at a lower level, of possibly opening the company to a future loss when the claim came due.

In the face of his rebuff, Dodson devised an averaging system that took account of the risks of older policyholders without driving up the size of their premiums to unaffordable levels. Invented to help older potential policyholders, Dodson's level-premium concept actually benefited everyone, to a degree probably not anticipated. It worked by charging more than was strictly required during the early years of a policy; the surcharge was invested, and its return was plowed back into investment, producing a compound rate of return, so that by the time the policyholder reached his later years an amount had accumulated that would pay the claim he had through the policy. This system made premiums into regular, predictable payments spread over a policyholder's entire life—the "whole life" concept—which was a vast improvement on the earlier arrangements.

In 1762, Dodson and his associates formed the Society for Equitable Assurance on Lives and Survivorships. The company's success made it the model for all subsequent life insurance companies in England, Europe, and America.[1]

The English model was imported to the American colonies during the late eighteenth century, although it found few imitators owing to the relatively undeveloped local economies and the sparse population. The first known American company (as distinguished from English underwriters who wrote insurance in the colonies) was founded in

1759, when the Presbyterian Synods in New York City and Philadelphia decided to make life insurance available to their ministers.

The pace quickened early in the nineteenth century, with the incorporation of the Pennsylvania Company for Insurance on Lives and Granting Annuities in 1812, which began a trend of joint stock companies specializing in life insurance. One of the organizers, Israel Whelen, had been the Philadelphia agent of an English company. The Pennsylvania Company made efforts to develop a scientific basis for its business: it employed an actuary, required signed statements from applicants with information on health, occupation, and residence, and included several restrictive clauses on travel and other high-risk factors.

During the first four decades of the nineteenth century, other important ventures were begun, including the New York Life Insurance and Trust Company, established in 1830, and the Girard Life Insurance Annuity and Trust Company, which began business in Pennsylvania in 1836. The New York Life had remarkable success largely because it employed a network of agents throughout New York State, the only company in the United States to do so at that time. The Girard followed this example and also introduced a mutualization feature by distributing some of the profits to policyholders as dividends. Mutuality was advantageous because it avoided the need to raise large amounts of capital when a company was founded, an important consideration in the booming, capital-hungry American economy. Further, policies that paid dividends were more appealing to many potential customers (although some stock companies paid dividends on policies too).

After 1843, life insurance was further transformed owing to the rise of aggressive salesmanship. Previously the normal practice among companies was to announce their existence and their offerings and wait for customers to appear. In 1843, the president of the Mutual Life, Morris Robinson, needing an immediate infusion of working capital, began actively approaching potential clients and revisiting the reluctant. He urged this method on his budding force of field agents, and the strategy was so successful it became the model for the industry.[2]

As it became evident to companies that aggressive salesmanship could dramatically increase business, it also became clear that various inducements could increase sales. For example, in England, in 1848, the London Indisputable Life put a clause in its constitution that prohibited it from disputing a policy. This contrasted to the practice of the other companies, whose policies were disputable, that is, subject to certain qualifications when claims were made. In America the first companies to offer indisputable policies did so perhaps as early as 1861, and soon all did.[3] Other inducements included the concept of surrender value, which returned to the holder of a lapsed or canceled policy a portion of the accumulated value beyond what was needed to pay claims and the company's administrative costs. Another was the policy loan, which allowed holders to borrow against the accumulated value of their policies.

These and other innovations made from the middle of the nineteenth century onward contributed to the phenomenal increase of life insurance policies written by American companies: more than $100 million in 1851, over $500 million in 1864, and over $1 billion in 1867. Equally impressive was the number of new companies chartered: seventy-five between 1859 and 1867, including, of course, the Germania.[4]

Although the remarkable increase in the popularity of life insurance derived at least in part from techniques of marketing and salesmanship, it rested much more fundamentally on developments in American social and economic life. Not by accident did the growing appeal of life insurance occur at the same time as the industrialization of the United States, which began in the last years of the eighteenth century and was well established by 1860. Between 1839 and 1859, the value of industrial output quadrupled. Agricultural output also rose (with the rise in general population and the westward push of the frontier), but at a slower pace than industrial output. In 1839, agriculture accounted for 70 percent of the value of commodities produced; by 1900 this proportion had declined to 33 percent. In 1820, nearly two-thirds of the 2.8 million in the work force were occupied in agriculture, but by 1880 this proportion had declined to one-half.[5]

Industrialization produced a rapid and continuous rise in the level of general wealth, beyond anything that had been experienced in previous times, when commerce and agriculture had been the main economic activities. In America, as in much of Europe during the early nineteenth century, the new industries and their managers and workers gravitated to the small towns, and later, the cities. Indeed, industrialization spurred the concentration of population in urban centers both through drawing people from rural areas and through drawing immigrants to the centers of manufacturing.

Between them, industrialization and urbanization transformed the nation's economic and social geography. The full impact of these forces was beginning to be felt in 1860, on the eve of the Civil War, as the North continued its rush into the industrial age while the South held to a rural, predominantly agricultural system. The North's victory in 1865 was an economic event of the first magnitude, which confirmed that the nation would continue to pursue industrializing, urbanizing policies. By the turn of the century, nearly half of all Americans lived in urban areas, participating in the world's largest economy.

The move from rural to urban society affected many aspects of life and culture. The pace of everything quickened with the harnessing of steam and electricity, and with the invention of the internal-combustion engine, and the shape of the day was influenced by the pattern of time spent in factories and offices. Even the shape of the year altered, from the seasonal nature of agriculture to the more steady rhythm of industrial work. The westward move of the frontier and the lure of jobs in the towns, as well as waves of immigration from Europe and the Orient kept a constant ferment in the land, as people moved from farm to town, farm to farm, or town to town, always following their perceived economic best interest. The rapid creation of new wealth, both through industrialization and the opening up of the West, enabled large numbers of people to climb the economic ladder.

Upward mobility, however, did not automatically bring security. In most places, times, and cultures, it has probably been the case that the families of middling wealth have had the most to lose. The wealthy are protected by the size and ramifications of their wealth; the poor expect to suffer and many even see social or economic instability as an opportunity to improve their condition. For those in the middle, however, the situation is quite different. They have achieved a level of affluence envied by the poor, yet without amassing the wealth needed to guarantee their lifestyle against catastrophe. This was true for the emerging middle class in England during the sixteenth and seventeenth centuries—the period, not coincidentally, of the first attempts to create a workable life insurance business—and it was true in the United States during the nineteenth century, as Americans became sufficiently affluent to seek protection against loss.

One means of achieving security was to invest part of the family's income as a nest egg. One might buy houses to rent out, or buy land on speculation, or build shops or factories, if one had funds available. One might invest in corporate securities—railroads and steamship companies were becoming popular by 1860—which might (or might not) provide a stable return and guaranteed form of wealth. One might purchase government securities, federal or local.

All of these investments could provide financial security—in good time, perhaps a decade or two—but not immediately. Moreover, the amassing of such wealth required constant attention and considerable risk. A far more appealing option for many people, especially those who could accumulate wealth only slowly, and who were inexpert at financial development, was to purchase a life insurance policy.

The moment it was signed and approved, the insurance policy offered to provide a stipulated amount of financial support to the family upon the death of the person insured, usually the breadwinner. At one stroke, the young father could protect his wife and small children from the specter of sudden decline into poverty should he die prematurely. In its issue of 26 June 1869, for example, the *Pottsville* [*Pa.*] *Standard* published the letter of a recent widow to her insurance agent. (The agent must have had the letter published as a way of drumming up business, which confirms the prevalence of the ideas expressed.) Mrs. Margaret Boehme began by thanking the agent for paying the death benefit stipulated by the policy within one week of her husband's decease:

Being left without any means of support for myself and children, coming as it does in our need, [the $3,000 payment] is truly a blessing; and much of the solicitude and anxiety of the widow and orphan for future sustenance is destroyed by the foresight of my late husband in getting his life insured in your excellent Company.

I can only say to all wives, urge your husbands to secure a policy in the Germania Life Insurance Company.[6]

It is not surprising that, as the American economy took off during the nineteenth century, and as the middle class rose to prominence, life insurance also prospered and bloomed into one of the nation's major enterprises.

Indeed, the life insurance industry and the American economy have been closely related for the past century and a half, each contributing to the other. Just at the time, in the early nineteenth century, when a jump in economic growth suddenly increased the need for capital, the life insurance industry, through its accumulated premiums awaiting investment, developed and provided a large and growing source of money and credit. It would be excessive to say that the life insurance industry and the economy marched in lockstep through the decades, yet even as careful an observer as Humbert O. Nelli, in a recent study, has concluded that there was "a very high degree of correlation between the growth of the G.N.P. and the growth of insurance in the United States for the period [1869–1966]."[7]

Part of the rapid development in the economy was due to the great influx of immigrants during the nineteenth century. Not only did they provide much-needed labor in a country still underpopulated, not only did they help settle the lands opened up as the frontier moved west, but they also carried with them a powerful desire for economic betterment that was a spur to the creation of new wealth. The immigrants, by self-selection, were those who were dissatisfied with the social, political, or economic conditions of their homelands, or those who were denied access to the growing wealth of Britain and Europe and sought their fortune in a newer, more open society.

Germans began to settle in America by the seventeenth century, and became a significant part of the immigrant stream by the eighteenth, William Penn's colony providing an obvious early example. The influx rose sharply during the middle decades of the nineteenth century, especially after 1848, with the arrival of thousands of Germans who were fleeing political persecution. The years 1848 and 1849 were a period of political turmoil in Europe, the so-called revolutions of 1848, in which politically liberal middle-class groups and parties, often with a strong nationalistic tendency, tried to gain a share of power in several states, including France, Italy, and Germany. The failure of these attempts produced refugees from many parts of Europe, thousands of whom settled in the United States. They were not the huddled masses of Emma Lazarus's famous poem, but members of the rising middle class: educated, cultured, affluent, extremely ambitious. They were ideally suited to achieving success wherever they settled, and wherever they settled they immediately began to contribute to the social and economic life around them.

Later waves of German immigrants would alter this picture, but it remained true that, on the whole, the German-Americans were among the most educated and successful of nineteenth-century immigrants to the New World. When those twenty-one men gathered at Delmonico's Restaurant on 28 March 1860, to found an insurance company for German-Americans, they were by no means pursuing an unrealistic or foolhardy venture; on the contrary, they must have seen the business opportunity that awaited anyone who could sell effectively to German-Americans (see table 1).

Of all German-American communities in the United States in 1860, New York City's was the largest and wealthiest. Fifteen percent of the city's residents were German-born and an estimated additional 10 percent were of German descent. Between 1855 and 1880, the only cities to have a larger German population were Berlin and Vienna.[8] Not only was the German community large, but it was also stable. During the 1860s, for example, with a rate of persistence of 70 percent, Germans were almost twice as likely to remain in the city as the Irish were.

TABLE 1

German-Born Population in Selected Cities, 1860–1890

	1860	1870	1880	1890
Baltimore	32,613	35,276	34,051	40,709
Boston	3,202	5,606	7,396	10,362
Buffalo	18,233	22,249	25,543	42,660
Chicago	22,230	52,318	75,205	161,039
Cincinnati	43,931	49,448	46,157	49,415
Cleveland	9,078	15,856	23,170	39,893
Davenport	—	—	—	6,154
Detroit	7,220	12,647	17,292	35,481
Duluth	—	—	—	1,657
Milwaukee	15,981	22,599	31,483	54,776
Minneapolis	—	—	2,334	7,719
Newark, N.J.	10,595	15,873	17,628	26,520
New York	119,984	151,216	163,482	210,723
Philadelphia	43,643	50,746	55,769	74,971
Saint Louis	50,510	59,040	54,901	66,000
Saint Paul	—	—	4,956	16,250
San Francisco	6,346	13,602	19,928	26,422

Source: U.S. Census Reports, 1860–1890.

New York's Germans had almost no tendency to assimilate through intermarriage.[9]

German ethnicity was further reinforced by flourishing community institutions and the prosperous business elite. The key social organization was the city's German Society, founded in 1784 to provide aid to German immigrants. As in other German-American communities, a spurt of growth and activity was generated by the arrival of the forty-eighters, the liberal political activists and their families who had fled after the collapse of the revolution of 1848–49.[10] By 1860, the German Society, the primary relief agency and the central structure for integrating new immigrants into the German community, provided health care and legal services administered by German-speaking professionals, and assisted new arrivals in finding housing and jobs. In addition to providing services to its community, the society was instrumental in founding social service institutions, including the German Hospital in 1857 and the German Legal Aid Society in 1876, which provided legal assistance to deserving but poor New Yorkers of German birth.[11] During these years, the German Society was also influential in establishing community financial institutions. In 1859, with the assistance of the society, the German Savings Bank opened. By the 1880s, the bank had accounts with some fifty-nine thousand people.[12]

At the center of the social life of the New York City German upper class was the Liederkranz, founded in 1847 and incorporated in 1860 to promote the arts, particularly vocal music. In addition to sponsoring community events, such as evening festivals, formal concerts, and fancy dress balls, the Liederkranz clubhouse was a social center for its members. It provided noon meals to members and their families, and offered both cultural facilities, such as a library, and recreational facilities, such as billiard and card rooms, bowling alleys, and a bar.[13]

The German community was served by an extensive system of bilingual and German-language schools. By the 1860s, for example, six of the eight German Catholic churches in New York City had established parochial schools. As a result of efforts by several forty-eighters, a secular free German school opened in 1859. So important was this institution to the community that some seven hundred people participated in the election of the school's first board of directors.[14]

One of the most important institutions preserving immigrant culture was the foreign-language press. In the 1880s New York City had eight monthly, six semi-weekly, twenty-four weekly, six Sunday, three bi-weekly, and seven daily publications in German. Perhaps the most important of these was the *Staats-Zeitung*, which had started as a weekly in 1834 and by the 1880s had a daily circulation of about seventy thousand.[15]

The integrity of the German-American community was further sustained by the interests and activities of its businessmen, many of whom maintained strong ties with their native country. An estimated one-third of the New York German upper class in the late nineteenth century had begun their American careers as New York agents for German trading houses, and they often remained dependent on their German connections. A second group had achieved financial success through the American-German import-export trade.[16] Others were entrepreneurs who established businesses, such as the German-language newspapers, specifically for and therefore dependent upon German-American patronage.

The members of the German-American business community, including those with transatlantic business connections and those catering to the German-American community, were economically tied to the survival of a German identity. Many of them traveled often back to Germany on both business and pleasure trips. Frequently, they sent their children back to Germany for schooling; Hugo Wesendonck's son and granddaughter were partly educated there.[17]

The members of the Germania's founding board of directors participated actively in the life of the German immigrant community and strongly supported its organizations and institutions. Nine members of the original board, for example, were among the original incorporators of the German Hospital in 1857. Two board members were very active in the German Society. They were also involved in the society's founding of the German Savings Bank in 1859, and other members of the Germania board served as bank directors. Hugo Wesendonck and others involved in the creation of the Germania had played an important role in founding the Free German School in New York in 1859, and were speakers on its dedication program.[18]

Germania board members were prominent in social organizations as well. Two were listed as incorporators for the Liederkranz in 1860. From time to time, others served as officers in the organization. When Hugo Wesendonck died in 1900, his funeral services were held in the Liederkranz Hall.[19]

Through their social and cultural links the members of the German-American business community maintained strong relations with each other, in a way that interwove economic and personal interests. Their personal efforts and financial investments helped create and support the institutions that made German-America viable for decades. One of those institutions was the Germania Life.

Although the idea of founding a life insurance company oriented toward German-Americans seems to have attracted considerable support from members of the German community, as indicated by the many prominent German-born members of the Germania's board of directors, the major role in actually forming the company and steering it through its formative years was played by Hugo Wesendonck, the company's first president.

Hugo Wesendonck was born in 1817 in Elberfeld, a textile manufacturing center in the Wupper valley on the Rhine, where his father, August, owned a silk-dyeing factory. Elberfeld was one of the new manufacturing centers that were beginning to spring up in the German states with the advent of industrialization, and members of its business elite soon became prominent in fields such as banking, international commerce, and insurance. (The Wesendonck family, a part of this elite, is perhaps best known today because Mathilde Wesendonck, the wife of Hugo Wesendonck's brother, wrote some poems that were set to music by Richard Wagner.)

Following his grandfather's profession, young Hugo Wesendonck trained in law at the Universities of Bonn and Berlin. He served a legal apprenticeship at Elberfeld, and, in 1842, was accredited as a lawyer. Upon establishing a practice in Düsseldorf, Wesendonck became active in progressive politics, helping draft many civil rights petitions.[20]

Like many liberals of his day, Wesendonck participated in the revolutions of 1848–49; he was a member of the Frankfurt National Assembly, which was convened in 1848 to draft a constitution for a united Germany. He was elected to represent Düsseldorf as a member of the democratic left at the assembly. When, in the spring of 1849, Friedrich Wilhelm IV of Prussia refused the offer of the assembly to become kaiser of a united Germany, several states recalled their delegates, thereby stymieing the assembly. Those remaining voted to move to Stuttgart. Because of his participation in this rump session, Wesendonck was accused of treason and forced to flee Germany. He was later tried and convicted in absentia and sentenced to death.[21]

With his wife Johanna Wilhelmine Schramm, daughter of a Krefeld industrialist, and two children, Wesendonck arrived in New York City in December 1849. His brother Otto, who had been in New York intermittently during the 1840s as an extremely successful import agent for Elberfeld textile firms, provided some assistance to the family. He undoubtedly eased Hugo Wesendonck into the commercial world, for after a short while, the family moved to Philadelphia where Hugo Wesendonck established himself as a successful importer.[22]

Immigrant German forty-eighters such as Wesendonck quickly assumed social and cultural leadership in the German-American community in Philadelphia and helped reassert its Germanness. As a result of their influx into the German Society, for example, which Wesendonck joined in 1852, the organization reestablished German as its operating language. Wesendonck joined other social organizations such as the exclusive Mannerchors, a German music society, as well.[23]

Affluent German-Americans took responsibility for meeting the social needs of their community. In 1853, for example, Wesendonck joined with other prominent Philadelphia Germans in a move to establish a hospital for the German community. Their efforts succeeded, and the German Hospital was chartered in 1860.[24]

In addition to his participation in social and cultural organizations, Wesendonck was also active in Philadelphia politics. Like other forty-eighters, such as his friend Carl Schurz, Wesendonck joined antislavery organizations. In 1856, radical Germans in Philadelphia founded the antislavery German Republican Central Club and elected Wesendonck president. As head of the club, he was prominent in the public debates that accompanied the presidential election that fall.[25]

In 1859, the Wesendoncks moved from Philadelphia to New York City.[26] The reason for the move is unknown. Perhaps, Hugo Wesendonck felt his ambitions were cramped and required the larger German-American forum in New York. Whatever the reason, the move came barely a year before the events that led to the founding of the Germania Life.

[2]

Opening Moves

The discussion that led to the founding of the Germania must have begun late in 1859 or early in 1860, for on 28 March 1860, Hugo Wesendonck was able to present a draft corporate charter to the first meeting of the board of directors, at Delmonico's Restaurant. According to the charter, the company would be incorporated to issue "insurance upon the lives of individuals and every insurance appertaining thereto or connected therewith, and to grant, purchase or dispose of annuities."[1] The directors approved the charter unanimously, which suggests that the matter had been worked out ahead of time, and then took two steps that gave the new venture its financial and administrative shape for the next several months. First, the directors authorized the sale of stock, and second, they established three working committees to develop the premium tables and the sales-agent system and to write the bylaws.

The Germania was established as a mixed company; that is, it would be a stock company paying dividends to policyholders and stockholders both. Initial capitalization was set at two hundred thousand dollars, twice the amount stipulated by the New York insurance law of 1853, which required every new life insurance company to have capital of one hundred thousand dollars invested in government bonds or real estate mortgages, deposited with the state comptroller.[2] This law was one of many that the state had passed since 1814 in an effort to regulate the rapidly evolving life insurance industry, many of whose largest and most ambitious companies were then headquartered in the state. The Germania's charter limited stock dividends to 7 percent a year, and provided for the division of the net profits in every third year, beginning in 1864, with 20 percent to be divided among the stockholders and

80 percent among the policyholders who held "participating" policies.[3]

The dividends to shareholders were meant to make the Germania attractive to potential policyholders, who would benefit both through the security provided by their policies and through regular, additional payments in the form of dividends. In this, the Germania was following the common practice. Some of the American companies founded during the 1840s—the mutuals—had no stockholders and were able to pay all their "surplus" funds out as dividends to policyholders. This approach was not available to the Germania, however, because the increasingly stringent New York State insurance laws required an immediate, up-front capitalization of one hundred thousand dollars, which Wesendonck and his associates evidently could raise only through the sale of stock. On the whole, the Germania's 80-20 split of dividends to policyholders and stockholders worked well at first, but when the company began to encounter stiffer competition, for example, in the New York City market, it suffered somewhat because it could not always offer as attractive dividend plans to potential policyholders as could some other mutual companies. This problem was discussed in a meeting of the Committee on Agencies on 30 September 1863.[4]

The Germania stock consisted of four thousand shares sold at fifty dollars each. A large portion was bought by the Wesendoncks and their business associates. The largest single purchase of Germania stock was made by Hugo Wesendonck's brother Otto. This block, combined with the founder's own stock purchase and additional subscriptions tendered through the New York City agent of Otto Wesendonck's firm, totaled nearly 25 percent. The Wesendoncks also drew upon individuals who were known for their participation in the political events of 1848–49 and were now successful in New York. Edward von der Heydt, for example, like Wesendonck, came from a prominent Elberfeld family and served with him in the Frankfurt Assembly. Other notable forty-eighters included Frederick Kapp, a lawyer in New York and an active Republican, and Oswald Ottendorfer, the publisher of the Staats-Zeitung. Another forty-eighter, Wilhelm Loewe aus Calbe, the president of the radical rump assembly that met in Stuttgart after the dissolution of the Frankfurt Assembly, agreed to be the company's first medical director. A third group consisted of other prominent members of the German-American community, such as C. Godfrey Gunther, a fur merchant who was elected mayor of New York City in 1864, and the investment financier Joseph Seligman, who had emigrated from Bavaria in 1837.[5]

While the sale of stock proceeded, the three working committees established at the first meeting of the board began their work. On 21 April the Working Committee on Agencies authorized Wesendonck and Frederick Schwendler to correspond with prospective agents and physicians in various cities, and to visit Philadelphia, Baltimore, and other nearby cities in order to make preliminary arrangements for establishing agencies. The committee further authorized Frederick Kapp, another director, to do the same during his anticipated travels in the west.[6]

Within the next few days, Wesendonck and Schwendler prepared a form letter to solicit agents and physicians for prospective branch offices to be established outside New York City. The letter made very clear the company's orientation:

The Germania Life Insurance Company . . . intend to establish a Branch-Office in your city, where they will require for this purpose an Agent and a Physician. Both ought to be Germans of the highest respectability, popular, active and responsible men, and in daily contact with the substantial middle classes of the Germans, as the Company will chiefly rely for business on the patronage of this population.[7]

The directors met again on 6 June. At that time, both the Working Committee on Agencies and the Working Committee on Premiums reported on their progress. Wesendonck and Schwendler had begun correspondence with prospective agents and physicians in thirteen cities that had large German populations: Philadelphia; Baltimore; Boston; Cincinnati; Chicago; St. Louis; Milwaukee; Louisville; Buffalo; Detroit; Albany, N.Y.; Pittsburgh; and Cleveland. They had received many favorable responses. In addition, Frederick Kapp was at that time making inquiries on the company's behalf in the western cities he was visiting.[8]

The Working Committee on Agencies had also begun to gather information on the legal steps and costs involved in setting up branch offices. For the most part, it projected very few expenses. Except for Pennsylvania, which required 3 percent of all premiums collected in addition to a two hundred-dollar license fee, the state-imposed fees were minimal. Furthermore, the committee anticipated that the company would avoid most expenses other than advertising "by making convenient arrangements with agents in such places, where an agency would turn out to be a great gain to the agents."[9]

The Working Committee on Premiums presented eight blank forms, prepared in both German and English. The committee also announced that it had drafted a pamphlet, again in both languages, and recommended ordering twenty thousand copies for distribution. It informed the directors that the printing would cost between five hundred and six hundred dollars, and that most of that cost could be covered by selling advertising space at the end of the pamphlet.

The committee also presented and recommended for adoption fourteen tables of premiums prepared by the company's actuary, John Frederic Entz. Born in Appenzell, Switzerland, on 16 February 1798, Entz had migrated to the United States by 1847, when his publications began to appear in American magazines and periodicals. In 1859 he was elected honorary member of the American Life Underwriters' Convention, when he was associated with the New York Life Insurance and Trust Company. He left that company to become Germania's actuary, and held the post for several years, before returning to his previous firm. Entz died in November 1872.[10]

The Germania engaged Entz at an annual salary of twelve hundred dollars, with a bonus due should the company derive the "great advantage" from his actuarial tables that he predicted. The tables listed premium rates for whole-life insurance, with and without participation (i.e., sharing in the company's dividends); limited-term life, with and without participation; endowment with single or annual premiums; children's endowment with single or annual premiums; and six types of annuity insurance.[11] On 6 June, when it received the report of the Working Committee on Premiums, the board of directors requested additional information, including a comparison of the proposed tables with those of four leading insurance companies. In addition, the board requested a report on the principles used by Entz in calculating the tables.[12]

The first official meeting of the board of directors of the newly organized Germania Life Insurance Company was held a week later, on 14 June. With nineteen of the thirty directors present, the board elected the company's officers and then drew lots, as required by the charter, to divide the directors into five equal classes with staggered terms of office. The board appointed members to the standing committees specified in the bylaws: finance, insurance, agencies, and auditing.[13]

The Finance Committee, composed of six board members and the president, was to "superintend and direct all the investment that shall be made of the funds of the Company" and to "consult and advise with the officers in all matters connected with the finances of the Company and the declaration of dividends."[14] The Committee on Insurance, consisting of four directors and the president, was to "consult and advise with the officers in all matters relative to insurance, and to the settlement of claims for losses."[15] The Committee on Agencies, with four board members and the president, was directed to "consult and advise with and assist the officers in all matters relative to Agencies."[16] The last committee, the Auditing Committee, consisted of three directors who were to "examine each Quarterly Statement submitted to the Board."[17]

After appointing the standing committees, the board adopted the tables of premiums prepared by actuary Entz for whole-life insurance, with and without participation. As the final item of business at its first meeting, the board unanimously approved the salaries for the president and vice president at $3,750 and $3,250, respectively.[18]

Open for Business

The Germania received permission from the New York State Insurance Department to begin business on 10 July 1860. Months before, the company began to make provision for its office, located at 90 Broadway, on the corner of Wall Street. The Germania opened for business with a working staff of six: Hugo Wesendonck, its founder and president; Frederick Schwendler, vice president and secretary; two staff members, J. Fenneberg and Cornelius Doremus, the latter of whom became the company's second president in 1898, when Wesendonck retired; John F. Entz, actuary, and Wilhelm Loewe aus Calbe, resident medical examiner.[19]

The company got off to a positive start when it issued its first life insurance policy on 17 July 1860, followed by twenty-three more policies during the next two weeks. By 31 December, the company had

sold 170 policies, including 152 whole-life policies, 10 short-term policies, 5 endowments, and 3 children's endowments—policies worth a
total of $500,979.[20]

Even while the first premiums arrived, the company was defining its
administrative organization and procedures. Regarding insurance policies, for example, the whole-life plan had been approved by the board
at its 12 June meeting, but the term life and endowment plans remained for consideration. The Committee on Insurance continued the
work begun by the Working Committee on Premiums, which had
presented fourteen tables calculated by the actuary, John Entz, to a
meeting of directors on 6 June 1860. At that time, the directors had
requested additional information, including a comparison with other
life insurance companies and a complete explanation of the method of
calculation. On 15 June 1860, just three days after its appointment at
the first meeting of the board of directors, the Committee on Insurance
considered and adopted the premium tables prepared by Entz for term
life insurance, with and without participation in the company's profits,
and requested Entz "to make further explanation in writing at their
next meeting."[21]

At the committee meeting of 9 July 1860, Entz discussed his rate
tables for children's endowments and for immediate annuities. His
tables for children's policies were based on those compiled by English-
man Dr. Farr, and those for immediate annuities on work done by a
man named Mr. Neison. Both, he believed, would "show the largest
profit to the Company."[22] After comparing Entz's rates with those of
other life insurance companies, the committee agreed to submit these
tables to the board of directors for adoption. They then discussed with
Entz the preparation of the remaining premium tables for endowments
and deferred annuities. Entz explained that in order to calculate the
rates for deferred annuities it was necessary to use a complicated three-
table, three-step process. The committee, after an extended discussion
of the issues, voted unanimously to request Entz to prepare the tables.[23] Several weeks later, Entz presented six rate tables for endowments and deferred annuities. The committee discussed the merits of
the tables, compared them with other tables prepared by Entz, and
finally voted unanimously to recommend them to the board of directors for adoption.[24]

Associated with matters involving policies was the question of how the money received as premiums from policyholders should be invested by the company. This became especially pressing once the Germania opened its doors and began accepting money from policyholders. The two hundred thousand dollars raised by the initial sale of stock was invested by the directors of the Germania in U.S. bonds of the loan of 1858, which paid 5 percent interest. This was a temporary expedient, however, for, like other insurance companies, the Germania planned also to invest in mortgages, which often paid as much as 7 percent. At a meeting of 27 June 1860, the Finance Committee charged the officers to report on the value of all property on which applications were made for bonds and mortgages, and, when necessary, to consult experts.[25] At its next meeting, on 11 July, the committee considered its first two applications for mortgages. It rejected the first, a request for $17,350, and accepted the second, a request for $6,000 on buildings at 357 and 359 West Twelfth Street, with the "provision that part of the money shall be used for putting the buildings in good order."[26]

During the next several weeks, the committee considered a few applications at each meeting, approving about 40 percent of them. By the end of 1860, however, with thirty-nine thousand dollars invested in mortgages, the committee found itself strapped for funds. Evidently the money invested to date in mortgages had come from premiums received, not from the initial stock capitalization, which was still invested in U.S. government securities. Since mortgages were now offering a better return than government securities, the committee wanted to liquidate some of its Treasury holdings to obtain cash for mortgages (a New York State law of 1849 allowed the stock-offering funds to be invested in New York real-estate mortgages worth double the amount loaned). But the government securities had declined in price since their purchase, a result of the growing secession crisis that would lead the nation into civil war the following year. The losses incurred in selling off the depressed securities would have been unacceptable, and the committee decided to sell only twenty-five thousand dollars' worth. With the nation well on the road to war, the issue of securities versus mortgages was to remain unsettled for the next five years.[27]

Civil War

The Germania Life Insurance Company came into being at a time when the nation seemed on the verge of dissolution. The evident reasons for the Civil War were tied to slavery and states' rights, but there were also sectional and socioeconomic elements at play. North and South had been evolving along quite distinct lines for decades, especially as cotton became the leading cash crop during the early nineteenth century. Various economic differences, which were often debated in terms of tariffs and the banking system, became important in the growing tension. But the passions of debate ran highest over the issue of slavery, which set North and South apart with a vehemence that other issues of the disagreement lacked. By 1860, many southerners became convinced that only a radical change in the nature of the Union could protect the continued existence of slavery in the South and border states. The rise of abolitionism as a major plank of the Republican party—a party strongest in the North—sharpened southern fears that antislavery views would soon control the White House.

In February 1860, the Alabama legislature resolved that the state should secede from the Union if Abraham Lincoln won the presidential election in November. This was only one month before the first meeting of the Germania's directors at Delmonico's in New York. In April, while the Germania's three working committees were establishing the broad outlines of the company, the Democratic party was trying unsuccessfully to nominate a presidential candidate who would be able to unite the party's southern and northern wings. In June, when the Germania's working committees reported to the board on their activities, the Democrats were electing two presidential candidates—Stephen Douglas in the North and John Breckinridge in the South. As many observers then perceived, Douglas and Breckinridge would split the national Democratic vote and thus assure the victory of the Republicans, who in May had nominated Lincoln. When the Germania opened its doors for business, in July, the presidential campaign had moved into high gear, and apprehensions grew that the choice of president was going to have momentous consequences.

Lincoln's victory in November confirmed the worst fears of those southerners who viewed the North with suspicion. Months before the president-elect assumed office, events unfolded that brought the country to open secession and threw the economy into a deep recession that lasted well into 1862. The first state to secede, South Carolina, made its decision in December 1860, and by February 1861 the other states of the lower South had followed.[28]

The magnitude of the crisis that impended, and the obvious inability of President James Buchanan's administration to take any effective action before leaving office on 4 March 1861, no doubt contributed to the fall in value of the government securities that the Germania held and was trying to liquidate. Unfortunately for the company, events of the next two years gave little reason for the price of the bonds to rise. The government had no machinery in place to raise the enormous sums of money needed to pay for the vast military establishment that was created out of almost nothing. The succession of federal defeats at Lee's hands in the East kept alive southern hopes for diplomatic recognition and financial assistance from abroad. The strong likelihood that the government in Washington would not have the resources, the will, or the popular support needed to reestablish the Union cast doubt on the ability of the government to pay what it had borrowed.

On the other hand, the value of tangible goods rose, especially real estate and gold, since they would retain value even if greenback dollars and Treasury war bonds proved worthless. In these circumstances it is understandable that the Germania Finance Committee sought eagerly to sell its government bonds—but not at too great a loss—and buy mortgages. By the end of 1861, the company held only $120,000 in U.S. securities, an amount that fell to $70,000 a year later. The sale of securities often involved spirited discussions on the Finance Committee and on the board. Since the value of the securities fluctuated over time, timing was important in the sales, but another question was how much of a loss would be acceptable to take. At a meeting of the Finance Committee on 13 May 1862, for example, William Aufermann, acting as president *pro tem* in Wesendonck's absence, and evidently representing the position of the board, advocated selling $20,000 of government securities at no lower than 96.5 percent. His motion did not receive a second. Instead, Louis Jay moved that "in consideration of the present state of the affairs of the country and of the difficulty of placing money," the Germania not sell government securities at a loss. Apparently, even mortgages were not attractive investments that May. Jay's motion carried in the committee.[29]

Four days later, the board considered the same question. The value of the government securities had risen considerably during the intervening period, which encouraged the board to vote for selling $20,000 to $50,000 worth at the current price. An amendment that the securities not be sold below par failed to receive a second. The board's decision caused the Finance Committee to meet again a few days later. After considerable debate, and acting under duress, the committee voted to sell $25,000 worth of the securities. That same day, $20,000 worth was sold at 94 percent.[30]

Under the prodding of the board, the Finance Committee continued to sell off government securities at a gradual pace. In June 1862, the committee voted to sell $20,000 worth at no lower than 98 percent. In July, the board of directors voted to replace the $100,000 of government bonds on deposit with the New York State Superintendent of Insurance with mortgages and nonfederal securities. That would allow the Finance Committee to sell the federal securities as occasion permitted. The committee implemented this board resolution at its next meeting.[31]

By the end of the year, the committee had converted $50,000 from federal securities into mortgages and nonfederal securities, leaving only $70,000 invested in Treasury offerings. By the end of 1863, Treasury holdings had fallen even further, to $55,000. This sum amounted to 16 percent of the Germania's total investments. By contrast, most New York life companies held at least 30 percent of their investments in federal securities, and one as much as 68 percent.[32] The disparity is puzzling on business grounds, since the other companies were not suffering unduly as a result of holding the federal offerings. It is also remarkable considering that Hugo Wesendonck's political sympathies as a staunch Republican (president of the Republican Club of Philadelphia in 1856) must have been firmly pro-Union. It is true that not every member of the Germania's board had shared Wesendonck's political view—August Belmont, for example, was a chairman of the national Democratic Party—but against these may be set such prominent board members as Frederick Kapp, who had attended the Republican convention in Chicago that nominated Lincoln, and Joseph

Seligman, who, among other services to the Washington government, helped place $200 million of U.S. bonds in Europe. Moreover, during the Civil War the government in Washington successfully persuaded numerous northern financial institutions, especially those in the nation's financial capital, New York, to invest heavily in the issues and Treasury notes that financed most of the war effort. Under the combined pressure of patriotism and government urging, the Germania would have seemed likely to hold a high proportion of its investments in Treasury offerings.[33]

That it chose to move in the contrary direction suggests some deep, overriding concern on the part of those company officers and directors who controlled the board, for the board was the citadel of the move to sell federal securities even at a loss. Given Wesendonck's preeminence on the board, we must see his hand in those efforts. Evidently, the economic woes that attended the first two years of the war were so serious that in Wesendonck's view they threatened the new company's survival. This called for drastic measures that overrode matters of short-term loss: after all, no one in 1862 could be sure the Union would triumph, and if it had not, the war bonds would have been scraps of paper. To the argument that by refusing to purchase war bonds the company was acting against the interests of the Union, Wesendonck might have responded that the company also had an obligation to its policyholders, who would have suffered serious loss if the company had failed. Perhaps Wesendonck and his German-American colleagues felt a stronger tie to their fellow German-Americans than to the nation as a whole, especially if they took the viewpoint that a successful secession by the South would not destroy the North but simply reduce its reach.

All this is speculation, however, and the facts reveal that after 1863 the Germania's investment portfolio began to increase its share of Treasury offerings. By December 1864 these holdings rose to sixty-six thousand dollars' worth. On the face of things, it is easy to correlate the rise to the major war successes by Union forces. Gettysburg had been fought and won, and even contemporaries knew it was a turning point. Grant, having cut the South in two during his western campaigns, had come east to assume command of the Army of the Potomac. The naval blockade of southern ports, and the taking of some of the ports, was beginning to exact its toll on cotton and tobacco exports and on imports of badly needed war materiel. The North too, however, was feeling the drain: the most severe financial strain on the Treasury occurred late in the war, during 1864 and 1865, after the accumulated weight of war expenses began to undermine government credit, devalue the securities and greenbacks, and call into question the whole massive structure of federal debt. Treasury Secretary Salmon P. Chase resigned in the spring of 1864, and his successor, William P. Fessenden, faced the need to finance the spiraling war costs with issues that seemed to have little appeal in the marketplace. At about the same time, in mid-1864, the Germania's Finance Committee, still committed to investment in U.S. securities, decided to bid on a new federal issue, the so-called 10-40s of 1864 which carried a nominal annual yield of 5 percent.[34] The board, still reluctant to hold federal securities, asked the committee to reconsider its decision and to invest instead in state or city instruments. Meanwhile, the Treasury had accepted the Germania's bid for $120,000 of the new offering. The Finance Committee discussed the investment situation and the board's recommendation, but did not change its position. A motion to sell $25,000 worth of the newly purchased securities was defeated. A month later, however, the committee softened its position and authorized the sale of some of the securities if the funds were needed for mortgages.[35]

Despite the new offerings, the credit standing of the Washington government continued to decline. In October the Treasury temporarily stopped issuing monthly statements of federal finances, and the potentially disastrous situation did not improve until after December, when additional securities sales restored public confidence to some degree. The improvement may have contributed to the Germania's willingness to purchase more federal securities in 1865. By the spring of that year, when Grant and Lee were nearing their final rendezvous at Appomattox, the Germania's monthly cash receipts were averaging a healthy $25,000. The Union, it was clear to all, would survive, and so would the national economy that the Germania was seeking to exploit. With the worst behind them, Wesendonck and his associates could take a more relaxed view about the risks of federal paper, for losses that might occur, if any, would be unlikely to threaten the company's existence.

At its March meeting, the Finance Committee considered the suggestion of the company's officers to invest part of the cash receipts in federal securities whenever prices were good. The officers noted that federal offerings were exempt from state and city taxes and were more convenient than mortgages for depositing with the state insurance department, reasons which had not prevented the board from seeking to sell federal securities two years before. The committee, acting no doubt on its experience in previous years, voted not to buy U.S. securities without the board's prior consent.[36]

The resolution split the board. Some members thought the board should not retract its position that the Finance Committee should not buy U.S. securities, even though the committee considered that position a restriction. Another view prevailed, however, and the board finally voted to allow the committee to buy federal securities if it considered them the best investments for the company. The committee voted at its next meeting to invest up to $100,000 of revenues in Treasury offerings. This investment pattern continued over the next two years, and by the end of 1867, the company owned $455,898 in government paper.[37]

Peace Returns

The end of the Civil War was the beginning of a new era for American insurance companies. The nearly five-year span of hostilities had deeply affected those companies that had enjoyed a substantial southern business, although the development of new markets in the Midwest and West, which were under Union control, compensated for much of the loss. Once peace returned, these companies, having benefited from the robust Union economy during the later years of the war, found themselves ideally poised to reenter the South, and even to expand abroad.

The same opportunities beckoned to the Germania. The company's heavy reliance on mortgage investments must have returned it a handsome profit during the war years, providing the capital needed for expansion into the South, and, eventually, abroad. But before the company could begin to move, it had to reorganize its agency system, which was the backbone of its whole way of doing business. In theory, the agencies fell under the purview of the Committee on Agencies, one of the four committees that the board had established at its meeting of 12 June 1860. In fact, although the committee started its life with a certain vigor, producing a wide array of ideas about how the company would acquire business through its agents and brokers, the presence of Hugo Wesendonck in these matters soon became overwhelming. The origins of this situation go back to the summer of 1860, when the agency system was created.

[3]

Creating an Agency System

From its founding, the Germania looked toward building up a national field force in cities with sizable German communities. Inquiries about potential agents and other personnel began even before the company had been incorporated, and, once in business, the company immediately set up agencies in several cities across the country. It was Wesendonck's contention that "in small cities the German population can be easier secured to this Company, if they can be made willing to insure at all, than in the City of New-York and some other large cities." He therefore "made particular efforts to establish Agencies and to make them work."[1] Within a few years of the company's founding, it was clear that the agency system throughout the country was vital to the Germania's survival, whereas the New York market, although sometimes lucrative, was not. This did not mean that the company would ignore the New York market, however, and during the first two years of operation the city's German-American community provided most of the customers for the new firm.

Nearly a month before the Germania opened for business, the Committee on Agencies began meeting to discuss the creation of a national agency system. The first meeting was convened on 20 June 1860. In frequent meetings during the next few months, the committee elaborated the structure for a system consisting of brokers and agents, and also appointed field personnel in several major cities across the country.

As board members often did when developing policy, the committee first considered the practices of other life insurance companies. They found that most companies had adopted the general-agency system, which had evolved during the past decade. The earliest insurance companies had required that a prospective policyholder come to the company's headquarters to take out a policy. Soon, however, most companies also began taking clients on the recommendation of trusted men in areas outside the reach of the home office. This was both a convenience to clients who did not have easy access to the town where the headquarters was located, and an aid to increasing the number of policyholders. Gradually there grew up a system whereby insurance companies made formal arrangements with men who could represent them in other towns and areas; by the 1840s, in the United States, some of these representatives were so closely bound to the company that they were looked upon as its exclusive agents. Inevitably, some of these agents extended their influence over broad regions. When they acquired the right to bestow subagencies within their regions, the general-agency system was born. The first person known to have carried the title of general agent was H. H. Hyde of the Mutual Life of New York in 1853.[2]

This was the system that prevailed when the Committee on Agencies began its work on the Germania's field force. The committee decided first to define the role of the broker, a title referring to a representative who was not so closely bound to the company as was the agent. It seems likely that the committee members hoped to gain quick entry to the insurance market in New York by engaging various individuals to act as nonexclusive representatives, while the force of agents was being developed.

The committee defined the broker as one who introduced applicants for life insurance to the Germania. If such an introduction resulted in the purchase of a policy of more than five years, the Germania would pay a brokerage of not more than 25 percent of the first year's premium. For policies issued for only one or five years, the broker would receive the policy fees charged on such contracts, rather than a brokerage. Brokers were not authorized to act in the name of the company, nor did the company assume any responsibility for their actions. In some cases, the company might negotiate an individual agreement that would guarantee a minimum amount of business to a broker. Those who agreed to "keep office-hours convenient to the Company, and engage themselves to canvass for the Company, to the exclusion of every other life insurance company" might be allowed signboards identifying them with Germania, a minimum brokerage, and/or inclusion in the company's advertisements.[3]

At its meeting on 6 July 1860, the Committee on Agencies adopted a set of rules and regulations for agents, the backbone of the company's sales system. As the Germania's field representative, the agent was to evaluate the desirability of applicants for insurance or annuities, notify policyholders when premiums were due, collect premiums, provide necessary proof of death when claims were filed, and remit monthly reports and payments to the home office. The company retained the right to issue policies and grant changes or modifications, such as permission to travel, in existing policies. Unlike the broker, the agent would be closely tied to the company by a set of mutual responsibilities. Basic to the agreement with agents was exclusiveness; the Germania would grant the agent the right to represent the company in a defined territory, ranging in size from part of a city to one or more states, and the agent would agree to represent no other life insurance company. In addition, the agent would be required to give security and possibly one or more sureties to the company as well as whatever security was demanded by the state and/or county.[4]

The agent was responsible for learning about life insurance in general, and about the Germania and relevant state and local insurance laws in particular. The agent and the Germania were to share business expenses. The company would pay for advertising, pamphlets and other materials, licensing fees, other fees required by state or county governments, and postage. Unless other arrangements were made, the agent was to cover all remaining expenses, including office rent, stationery, and signboards.[5]

As was common in the business, agents were to be paid on a commission and fee basis. On life insurance policies issued for more than five years, agents would receive 10 percent of the first premium and 5 percent of renewal premiums as long as they were agents of the company. They would receive no commission on life insurance policies issued for one or five years, annuities, and endowments because the company's profits would not justify it. Instead, the agent would be paid a policy fee of one dollar, which was to be charged to the insured.[6] A few weeks after its 6 July meeting, the Committee on Agencies changed the compensation on endowments and annuities from a simple fee to a commission of 10 percent of the first year's premium, or 1 percent on single-premium policies. This increase in remuneration was based on the opinion of the company's actuary, John Entz, that such a commission was affordable.[7]

In adopting rules and regulations for agents, the committee kept in mind the anticipated German clientele. It stipulated that agents distribute the pamphlets and other written materials to be provided by the company with particular attention to the middle classes of the German population. Agents were to employ German as well as American brokers as needed, and physicians who were "well acquainted with the German population."[8]

The Committee on Agencies also passed resolutions concerning the employment of medical examiners. Since the success of the company depended heavily on identifying bad risks before they were issued insurance, the committee carefully discussed the procedures used by the examiners. These physicians were urged to act cautiously regarding the condition of chest, heart, and pulse; to note the role of genetic predisposition and geographical locality in predicting disease; and to be particularly wary in accepting "persons under 30 years of age, or even somewhat older, all those who are either very tall or very fat or otherwise in any respect differing from a normal condition, and women generally."[9] The warning against insuring those under thirty may reflect the same views of youth that today assign higher risks to young automobile drivers. The reluctance to insure women because of the high risks attendant upon childbearing was common to the insurance business during most of the nineteenth century.[10] Interestingly, one early attempt to reconsider the biases against insuring women came from John Entz. In a report he wrote in 1872 for the New York Life Insurance and Trust Company, Entz suggested that the "repugnance" of companies to insure females was based on an erroneous opinion that the mortality rate for women under fifty (before menopause) was higher than that for men. That idea, Entz noted, was based on the table of expectation, which he regarded as an unfair criterion. He offered in its place his own comparative table of mortality data and through it demonstrated that for women the turning point was at age thirty-seven or thirty-eight. "Firmly believing," Entz continued, "that the time would come when the importance of offering more liberal and equitable terms to the female sex would be fully appreciated, I have undertaken the laborious task to calculate all the tables for both sexes."[11] It is hard to say what effect, if any, this pioneering effort had on New York Life and Trust, but the Germania did not liberalize its ordinary life policies regarding women until the 1890s. Somewhat before then, the

Germania offered policies to both sexes through its industrial insurance branch, but in this it simply followed the lead set by Prudential and other major issuers of industrial policies.

While the Committee on Agencies was developing practices and guidelines for its field force, it was also establishing the Germania in several cities by soliciting applications and appointing agents and other staff. On 10 July 1860, the committee voted to establish agencies outside New York City and made initial appointments in Baltimore, Philadelphia, Boston, Cincinnati, Cleveland, Milwaukee, Chicago, Detroit, Buffalo, and Davenport. Each of these cities had substantial German-American communities, as may be seen from table 1. By the end of the month, the committee had made further agency appointments in St. Paul and Newark. During the following weeks, the committee appointed medical examiners for these agencies, usually at the recommendation of newly appointed agents.[12]

In addition, the committee appointed boards of reference in areas where it established agencies. The committee had decided to appoint such local boards as a means for enabling the public to obtain information about the company. Financial records of both the local agency and the company as well as copies of all documents published by the company were to be made available to members of these boards.[13]

After the first few months, during which the Committee on Agencies met frequently to consider both persons and the terms of appointments which were submitted by the president, the committee conveyed its decision-making power directly to Hugo Wesendonck by authorizing him to appoint agents and medical advisers as necessary and within the terms adopted by the committee. The amount of required security bonds and the expenses covered by the company for advertising were left to the discretion of the president, who "would from time to time inform the Committee of what had been done."[14] After this decision, the Committee on Agencies met less often.

The efforts of Wesendonck, a tireless traveler in the search for new business, were pivotal to the success of the field agencies during the first few years. During the company's first year and a half, for example, the largest number of policies sold through agencies—41 percent of total agency sales—came through the Philadelphia office, a feat which the annual report for 1861 attributed principally to "the personal exertion of the president, who went several times to Philadelphia."[15] A committee report dated 4 April 1863, noted an "unexpectedly large business which has rushed in—owing in part to the successful travels in the west of the President during the last six weeks."[16] Wesendonck seems to have owed his selling success partly to a skillful interweaving of German patriotism and his own repute as a champion of the cause of 1848. According to the testimony of Carl Heye, preserved in a history of the Germania's operations in the St. Louis area during the 1860s, Wesendonck relied heavily on sales pitches that he made in person to large audiences:

Not being able to afford a press agent, he [Mr. Wesendonck] wrote to some of his numerous friends in Chicago, Cincinnati, Philadelphia, St. Louis, and other large cities, particularly to those who had taken part in the Revolutionary movement in Prussia in 1848. He had it made known as widely as possible that Hugo Wesendonck, one of the great "Forty-eighters," and an intimate friend of Carl Schurz . . . would be in town on a certain day and would make a very interesting address on the Revolution of 1848. No hall was hired for the purposes of this meeting. Any place sufficiently large to hold the crowd that assembled sufficed. Tradition has it that Mr. Wesendonck climbed on a table and spoke very interestingly in his forceful manner about the Revolution. He then skillfully switched over to the subject of life insurance, but little known at that time, possibly to him also, but in any event handled by him with such finesse and conviction that his listeners, not understanding it anyway, thought it would be a good thing and placed their signatures on the dotted line.[17]

Wesendonck also took control over marketing and the development of the field force. On the basis of his experience during the early months in business, he concluded that much more was involved in the success of the field than simply making agency appointments. Commissions were usually so small that it did not pay for agents to seek business. Yet the insurance business, if it were to be pursued successfully, required a full commitment of one's time and energy, for it was a complicated business. Persuading potential policyholders to buy was not easy, since no one took insurance on the first sales effort, and continuous solicitations were required. As a result, an agency could not be expected to function effectively unless "particular levers" were applied.[18]

During the first year of business, the officers of the Germania concentrated their efforts on the local New York City market, which had the largest German-American community. Hugo Wesendonck observed that the "nearest friends" of the Germania were being solicited and that the majority of them had taken policies, "most of them in pretty large sums."[19] Wesendonck knew, however, that when this relatively accessible and friendly market was fully developed, the company would have to turn to the broader German-American community, not only in New York but around the country. After 1860, competition with other insurance companies began to reduce the sales made by Germania through its home office, while those secured through field agents outside New York grew rapidly. Whereas in 1860–61, the home office had been responsible for $739,700 in policy sales, in 1862–63 it solicited only $443,200. Its proportion of total company sales for that period declined from a high of 80 percent to only 18 percent. The relative decline in home office sales and the rise of the field force was rapidly making the Germania into a company of national scope.[20]

Wesendonck's marketing efforts met their sternest test in competitive New York City. In June 1860, the Committee on Agencies had resolved not to employ any agents for the city and county of New York and its immediate neighborhood, but to engage the services of brokers.[21] The committee probably did this to save money, since according to the committee's own plans brokers would receive substantially lower commissions on sales than would agents. The committee failed to consider the competitive nature of the New York market, however, which gave both brokers and agents an advantage in making arrangements not only with the Germania but with other companies as well. The committee may also have underestimated the skill and persistence of other insurance companies in pursuing the German-American market in the city. Many companies were already using German agents in the city. National Travelers, the precursor to Metropolitan Life, for example, employed two German agents who were so successful that by 1867 about half the company's policyholders were German. In addition, while the German population may have been predisposed to buy from Germans, non-Germans seemed to prefer American or English companies. "The Germania," Wesendonck warned the Committee on Agencies, "can indeed hardly expect, that any considerable share of the business, other than German will ever be absorbed by it."[22]

As a result, when the Germania's Committee on Agencies began seeking brokers in New York on the terms approved in early July, it discovered it would have to offer additional benefits. First, the committee offered to include "Germania" on their signboards and to list these brokers in company advertisements. In one case, that of Franz Malignon, the committee offered to guarantee a minimum annual brokerage.[23] When the brokers requested additional concessions, the committee yielded. Brokers could call themselves agents or general agents on their signboards and would be so styled in pamphlets and other materials; like agents, they could collect premiums directly, rather than merely recommend the client to the company. (This concession gave the brokers control over large amounts of money, since premium payments were forwarded to the company headquarters only at intervals, and during a period of weeks considerable sums could accrue.) The committee then debated whether these concessions had transformed the brokers into agents, thereby conflicting with the resolution previously adopted not to employ agents in New York City. The committee unanimously decided that, even with the additional privileges, these persons "would remain brokers of the Co., having but the name of Agent or General Agent, which name was considered necessary to do business through them."[24]

Evidently the company continued to have problems with its brokers in New York City, for in November the committee again considered the terms of these contracts. According to Wesendonck, experience had shown the necessity of allowing city agents or brokers the same commission on endowments and annuities as the company was paying its field agents. The committee then authorized Wesendonck to grant such commissions as required.[25] By January 1861, the difficulties in appointing brokers in New York City had become so severe that Wesendonck was compelled to offer them all the privileges of general agents and other favorable terms. After discussing the situation, the Committee on Agencies, considering that the competition "between Agents of other Companies of this City and between the various Agents of the 'Germania' besides is very great, while foreign [out-of-state] Agents have a circuit of their own," authorized Wesendonck to make the best terms available without any restriction by former resolutions.[26]

By 1863, the Germania had engaged a number of agents in New York City with varying commission agreements. The most common arrangement was a 20 percent commission for the first year and 5 percent on renewals. In three cases, agents received advances of fifty dollars a month. The extra allowances were thought essential to maintain even the declining amount of business in New York City.[27]

Whereas in New York Wesendonck used the lever of increased commissions to improve the sales performance of brokers and agents, elsewhere he relied more heavily on the other two levers of his approach—special agents and traveling agents. In areas where the general agents were having great difficulty selling policies, he hired special agents to support their work, and raised the commission scale in these instances, for division between the two agents. The general agent in Chicago, for example, seemed unable to make many sales. After a special agent was hired for him in 1862, the agency quickly became one of the Germania's best. Special agents were used with similar results in other cities, such as Cincinnati, Philadelphia, St. Louis, and Detroit.[28]

The third lever, traveling agents, was necessary, according to Wesendonck, to secure the German business in many small cities. It was the company's experience, he argued, that in those places, the appointed agents did nothing without an officer of the company or a traveling agent's coming to their support. Consequently, Wesendonck made numerous trips to visit agents and solicit policy applicants, and he also appointed individual traveling agents. The first was Mr. I. Weydemeyer, engaged to canvass New York state and the West, at a fee of $150 per month, to propose individuals for appointment as agents and medical examiners, to lecture on life insurance, and to take applications for life insurance, for which last duty he was promised extra compensation.[29] By the end of 1863, Wesendonck had hired six travelers, who individually covered large geographic areas. One agent, for example, handled Pennsylvania, Ohio, Indiana, and Kentucky; another covered New England, Maryland, and the District of Columbia. In addition to soliciting, traveling agents also provided the home office with reports on local agents and medical examiners. The financial arrangements with traveling agents were fairly uniform: the Germania usually paid actual fares and four dollars a day for expenses plus a 10 percent commission on the first year's premium.[30]

Wesendonck and his corps of traveling agents were crucial to the early success of the company. Without them field sales would have been much lower. In 1862, for example, the sales of nearly $1.5 million generated by the travelers accounted for about 60 percent of agency sales and about one-half of the Germania's total sales. The rapid increase in sales from the field outside New York City, therefore, contributed a great deal to the economic growth of the company and may well have been the deciding factor in its survival.

From time to time, the Committee on Agencies thought it necessary to increase commissions and other payments in order to hire or keep agents in the field. In February 1862, after a full discussion of agency effectiveness with President Wesendonck, the committee agreed to liberalize terms in cases where it was deemed essential. These terms, to be negotiated on an individual basis, allowed for larger commissions, reimbursement for office expenses and subagents, and fixed salaries for full-time agents. In order to hire an effective agent for the West Coast, for example, the committee agreed to raise the commission on the first year's premium from the Germania's usual 10 percent to 12 and the renewal commission from 5 percent to 6. The following year, the committee agreed to raise the commission for the West Coast agent even higher, to 20 percent of the first year's premium and 7.5 percent of the renewals. The Germania's attempts to adjust the commissions reflect a common problem among insurance companies during the 1850s and 1860s. The increase in competitive pressure forced every company to resort to various strategies to make agents more productive and to prevent the most successful ones from bolting to competitors. In theory there was a generally accepted commission rate among companies during the early 1860s. The Equitable, for example, said it had a 10-5 percent arrangement, and the trade journals also cited that as the industry scale, but in fact some rates were much higher.[31]

The Committee on Agencies, which played only a small part in directing the development of the field, met infrequently and then usually to hear reports from Wesendonck and approve his recommendations. The Special Committee, appointed each year to verify the final accounts, on the other hand, used its annual reports as a forum for evaluating operating procedures and managerial decisions.

In the reports for the first three years, 1860–62, the Special Committee generally approved of the direction of field development, even when expenses seemed high. In the 1860 report, the committee remarked, "The expenditures stated above include those always connected with the organization of a new company, and it is safe to expect that in future, the expenses will be much smaller comparatively as experience will also teach, which can be avoided and which are necessary for the working and development of the business."[32] As Wesendonck pointed out to the board the next year, expenses in the initial period were necessarily higher than they would be in future years. As its reputation grew, the Germania would become more competitive; therefore, these extraordinary and expensive efforts would no longer be as necessary as they had been in the beginning. Furthermore, since most of the costs of selling a policy were charged to the first year's premium, as renewals increased, net income would also increase.[33]

In 1864 the Special Committee took a more critical stance and asked Frederick Schwendler, the vice president and acting secretary, to prepare a table showing income and expenses for each year of operation (see table 2). The committee was particularly concerned about commission and agency expenditures. For the year 1863, these expenses

TABLE 2

Income and Expenses, 1860–1863

	1860	1861	1862	1863
Income				
Interest	$646	$9,508	$11,635	$18,549
Premiums	9,111	30,063	46,691	118,585
TOTAL	$9,757	$39,571	$58,326	$137,134
Expenses				
Death	—	$500	$7,000	$18,500
Annuities	—	—	175	175
Interest	—	—	—	21,000
Surrender	—	726	305	854
Expenses	$12,944	20,867	20,944	51,879
TOTAL	$12,944	$22,093	$28,424	$92,408
Income/Expense Ratios				
Commissions	$427	$2,374	$3,570	$13,069
% of Commissions to Premiums	4.7	7.9	7.6	11.0
Commission and Agency Expenses	$1,102	$5,315	$6,107	$24,470
% of Commission and Agency Expenses to Premiums	12.1	17.7	13.1	20.6

Source: Annual Report for 1863.

amounted to 20.6 percent of the income from premiums, as compared to 13.1 percent for the preceding year. The committee thought this proportion dangerously large and implied that Wesendonck was perhaps overambitious. They did not want to impede the "proper advancement and prosperity" of the company, yet they wondered if "too eager competition for business should not lead it into an extravagance of expenditure which would be interpreted by the community as a sign of loose management and insecurity."[34] The committee recommended, therefore, the creation of an ad hoc committee to look into the matter and advise the board on a system of regulation for controlling expenses. At the same time, the committee was careful that this recommendation not be interpreted as a rejection of Wesendonck's leadership:

Too much praise can not be accorded to the officers of the Company for the zeal and efficiency displayed by them in the management and development of its increasing business, the happiest results from which are demonstrated by the accounts exhibited in this Report. Your Committee are also much indebted to them for active and obliging cooperation in the performance of the duty.[35]

As the Special Committee recommended, the board appointed an ad hoc committee to consider a system of regulation to keep expenses under control. In its report to the board, dated 13 July 1864, this ad hoc committee accepted the explanation of expenses given by the company's officers. "The increase of expenses," the report read, "has been caused by the introduction of travelling [agents] and by the establishment of the Company in places where the same was not known. [The officers] have shown that a very large amount of business has been secured by the Company by this system, in fact that the Company's business has been trebled since the introduction of it."[36] Another reason given for the high expense rate was really an accounting matter having to do with the practice of deferred premium payments. According to this report, Germans were predisposed to pay premiums on a quarterly basis rather than annually or even semiannually. Since premiums could not be entered as income until they were received, those deferred portions of premiums were not included as income and therefore did not offset expenses in the expense/income ratio. But most convincing of all to the ad hoc committee was the drop in the ratio for the first three quarters of 1864. The report of the ad hoc committee did not address whether the rate of growth was being pushed too fast, as the Special Committee had suggested. Rather, the committee advised against introducing any new controls other than those already in place through the standing committees. It did, however, recommend that the company's officers "use the utmost economy compatible with a proper advancement of the Company."[37]

After this confrontation in 1864 over expansion and expenses, the Special Committee stopped including critical evaluations in its reports. The 1864 annual report noted that the "Committee was much pleased to find a decrease of the percentage [of expenses] . . . and has no doubt that with the increase of business they will show further steady decrease in future years."[38] In its report for 1867, the committee again reported a decrease in the cost of doing business.

In late 1864, perhaps as a result of the self-evaluation initiated by the Special Committee, the Committee on Agencies began to discuss field costs on a regular basis. At its meeting in October, it considered the possibility of reducing agency and commission expenses, and concluded that it could not do so at that time. The committee approved the continued employment of traveling agents, although it could not reduce the expense of travel. The committee did note, however, that the ratio of expenses to income for traveling agents was decreasing, and the committee looked forward to "further decrease until the Company will be so firmly established all over the country, that future business may be expected by less extraordinary efforts, through local agents principally."[39]

In the spring of 1865, Wesendonck reported to the Committee on Agencies that the average expenses of all agencies, exclusive of traveling expenses, were declining.[40] Despite this decrease, the committee decided a few weeks later to change the terms for traveling and local agents to make them cheaper. The committee voted to reduce the commission for local agents from 20 percent to 15 on policies which they sold on their own, and to only 10 percent when a traveling agent or an officer of the company had been involved. The committee also voted to allow traveling agents a commission only of 25 percent on the first year's premium. Rather than the four dollars a day that the company had paid for travel, the agents were now to pay their own expenses, although they would receive an advance of five dollars a day during their travels. When the company's agents objected to the reduction in the first year's commission, the committee agreed to a compromise of 15 percent of the first year's premium whether or not an officer or traveling agent had been involved. No modification was made on the new terms for traveling agents, however.[41]

Over the next two years, the ratio between agency expenses and receipts continued to decline, and for the most part sales went well. In 1866 Wesendonck reported that "a great number of agencies now seem to do a regular business without incurring any extra expenses, and the whole system of agencies seems to have improved upon the past." The drive by the Committee on Agencies to cut costs by reducing commissions, however, did cause some problems, particularly in the highly competitive New York City area, as some agents, who were "attracted by the higher commissions offered by other companies," left the Germania.[42]

By 1868, the system of traveling agents was no longer working satisfactorily, either for the company or for its agents. Although the nature of the dissatisfaction is not documented, it probably involved complaints from the company about poor sales and from the agents about insufficient commissions, since the changes that were made subsequently involved an increase in commissions. At Wesendonck's urging, the Committee on Agencies divided the states into districts whose net sales income in 1867 had been about fifty thousand dollars. For each district the company would appoint a traveling agent, compensated on a sliding commission scale against net sales income: 4 to 5 percent of the first one hundred thousand dollars, 2 to 2.5 percent of the net income over one hundred thousand dollars, and 1 percent of the net income over two hundred thousand dollars. In addition, the company would advance the agent traveling expenses and agree to a moderate terminal payment should the company dismiss him.[43]

Geographic Expansion

Despite problems with the agents, the Germania rapidly penetrated the markets it had targeted in the East and Midwest—testimony not only of the skill of Wesendonck and his colleagues, but also of the rapidly improving network of rail and steamboat lines east of the Mississippi. In 1862, only its second year of operation, the company began arrangements to establish an agency in San Francisco, which was intended to be the center for business throughout the West. At that time, the West was far less accessible from New York than the rest of the country was. Travelers from the East Coast, including thousands of goldseekers, adventurers, and other settlers, could reach the Pacific Coast only via ship around Cape Horn, a journey of twelve thousand miles and not without its hazards, or by wagon train, a journey shorter in miles if not in dangers. Even after the opening of the transcontinental rail link in 1869, the journey across the western plains retained an air of adventure and risk well into the 1870s. What drew the fledgling Germania to leap across the continent so boldly was, of course, the presence of a community of German-Americans in San Francisco: 6,346 in 1860, which grew to 13,602 in 1870 (see table 1).

As usual, the company began by surveying the practices of its competitors. Most companies assessed a surcharge on policies written in the West, to cover the higher risks associated with living and traveling to these newly opened areas. Accordingly, the Germania's Committee on Insurance established a surcharge rate of .5 percent of the face value of each policy, and another .5 percent for each trip made between the West Coast and the East. The committee also decided to appoint a five-member board of reference, composed of persons prominent locally, responsible for approving each insurance application. Their approval had to be seconded by the home office, however, a process that could take a considerable amount of time owing to the long trip East. An interim policy signed by three members of the board of reference would be valid until the home office approved the actual policy. (The Germania developed its interim policy system from the practice of English companies that did business in the United States.)[44]

In the spring of 1862, the Germania's West Coast agent, Bernhard Gattel, reached San Francisco and began surveying the prospects there. He sent the home office the names of the members of the board of reference, which included Henry Seligman, brother of the famous financier Joseph Seligman, who was a member of the company's board of directors. Over the next few months, Gattel recommended that the company change some of its original plans for the West Coast, to improve sales. At his urging, the Committee on Insurance agreed to eliminate the premium surcharge for California business.[45] Again at Gattel's request, the committee rescinded its rule that at least one member of the board of reference approve each policy application.[46] The willingness of the committee to take Gattel's advice may have arisen in part from the patently warm relations between the West Coast agent and the company. At a board meeting on 8 October 1862, Wesendonck announced that Gattel had sent a dozen bottles of California wine, and "by acclamation" the board passed a vote of thanks to the donor.[47]

The first death benefit paid by the Germania on the West Coast went to the widow of an engineer who was killed in a boat explosion in Monterey Bay during the late 1860s.[48]

The decision to expand operations into the West raised the possibility of entering other regions as well, but this required a consideration of the various residential prohibitions that had been adopted in 1860. Like other insurance companies, the Germania preferred to do most of its business in those areas of the country that carried the lowest health risks to policyholders. The most desirable regions were the Northeast and Midwest. Least desirable were the Deep South and the Far West because of the hazards of living in very hot, presumably unhealthy climates: water-borne diseases that were prevalent in states along the Mississippi and Missouri rivers; the risks of frontier life; and the hazards of travel in sparsely settled regions. Companies that did business in the less desirable regions typically added a surcharge to policies, as the Germania tried to do in California.

Although the residence prohibitions reduced a company's policy risks, they also limited the potential markets, and as living conditions gradually improved and travel became less hazardous, insurance companies began revising their prohibitions. For the Germania, this revision began with Wesendonck's trip to the Midwest in May 1862, where he discovered that restrictions on policyholder residence within ten miles of the Mississippi or Missouri river were excluding the company from writing policies in the rapidly developing markets of southern Illinois, Missouri, and Kansas. At his urging, the Committee on Insurance dropped the offending restrictions as far south as the 36°30' north latitude, and extended the southern boundary of the insurable area to include Missouri and Kansas. In doing this the committee was following the lead of numerous other insurance companies, including the Equitable.[49]

Another liberalization of residence prohibitions occurred in 1865, with the end of the Civil War. Between 1861 and 1865, while the war raged, the Germania had restricted its business efforts to regions controlled by or friendly to the government in Washington. This was only prudent for a New York-based company, and was not a great hardship since the Germania had not, hitherto, done any business in the South. The company was now in a mood to expand, however, and could no doubt see that some good business was available in the newly opened states of the former Confederacy. Wesendonck knew about the activities of other life insurance companies, many of which had done a considerable business in the South before the war and were resuming southern operations with the advent of peace. The first steps taken in a southerly direction by the Germania involved shifting its southern jurisdiction line so as to allow residence and travel without special permits in North Carolina and Tennessee, and to allow travel and residence in the settled parts west of 100° longitude (i.e., from the middle of Texas). Evidently the Germania was here following the model of other companies, such as the Mutual Life, which some years earlier had adopted similar measures regarding Tennessee, North Carolina, and 100° longitude.[50]

The next step by the Germania came several months later, in October of 1865, when Wesendonck asked the Committee on Insurance to consider opening business operations in the rest of the South. To do this, however, the company first had to reconsider its prohibition on traveling or residing in that area during the summer months. Wesendonck proposed that the company drop the prohibition but charge an extra premium. He argued that sanitary conditions in most areas of the South had improved substantially, so that the increase in premium rates would more than offset the potential additional risk. In support of his proposal, Wesendonck presented letters from three southern businessmen. When some reservations about this were raised by the board of directors, Wesendonck responded that the officers intended to establish agencies in the southern states only in places where the social and sanitary conditions were satisfactory, and that applicants would have to answer supplementary questions referring to their antecedents and acclimatization. Wesendonck's arguments were augmented by the feeling on the part of some board members that the Germania should take advantage of the renewing of business with the South and that the company should do so before its competitors did. The board, with one dissenting vote, approved Wesendonck's proposal.[51]

Having decided upon the move into the South, the company proceeded with its usual caution. At a 21 October meeting of the Committee on Agencies, the members considered a letter from a Dr. Kesler summarizing his nine-year experience as a physician in Mobile, Alabama. After discussions with Dr. Charles Bernacki, the resident physician, the committee voted not to establish agencies within the tidewater region except in Charleston, Savannah, Mobile, and New Orleans, which seemed safer because of their long settlement and their sanitary regulations. The committee also recommended that the officers draw up a set of questions to ascertain, among other things, if applicants were acclimated to the region (there was a widespread belief among insurance companies that newcomers to the South were more likely to suffer health problems than residents of long standing.) Several months later, Wesendonck traveled through the Southern states to set up new agencies. He reported back to the board that he had successfully established agencies in Charleston, Savannah, Augusta, Atlanta, Montgomery, Mobile, and New Orleans, and that they had begun doing business. On a trip a few months later, Wesendonck investigated additional cities for their agency potential. On the basis of that trip, the Committee on Agencies voted to set up new agencies in Galveston, Texas, and Fernandina, Florida.[52]

After the Germania had been operating in the South for two years, its agents there raised questions about the extra premium of .5 percent charged to southern policyholders. Other life insurance companies had dropped this practice, which put the Germania's field force at a competitive disadvantage. The board of directors unanimously voted to insure acclimated persons throughout the South and unacclimated persons in any part of the South except the Gulf Coast at the northern rates.[53]

As an extension of its southern business, the Germania soon expanded beyond the American border into the Caribbean and Central America, areas previously avoided because of health risks. In January 1867, the Germania's traveling agent for the southern states requested permission to establish an agency in Havana. In support of this request, Wesendonck cited the successful experience of the Equitable, which was then issuing policies in Cuba at their northern rates. He recommended, however, that the Germania accept only native-born Cubans and others who had had yellow fever and were fully acclimated and that they be charged the company's southern rates. The board voted to follow Wesendonck's recommendation and shortly thereafter also appointed an agent, Francisco Kurtze, in Costa Rica. The following year, the Committee on Agencies authorized the establishment of an agency at Valparaiso, Chile. While the area's climate was considered healthy, the committee demonstrated caution by applying its southern rates.[54]

The Germania's expansion into the western United States and regions of Central and South America, only seven years from the company's inception, was a remarkable achievement, aided greatly by the improvement in long-distance communications that occurred during the third quarter of the century. Ships were growing larger, more comfortable, and safer, and some were equipped with steam engines to supplement sailpower. Shipping companies were beginning to establish frequent, regular service from New York to major cities abroad, and sea travel was losing some of its former terror. In 1865, the Germania decided to allow policyholders to travel to and from Europe without special permit.[55] The possibility now arose of extending the company's international business to a market far larger than that in Chile, or Costa Rica, or even the United States—the market in Europe.

[4]

Return to Europe

The expansion of the Germania throughout the New World was governed by the dispersion of German immigrants. The company's marketing strategy was to single out this group from the general population and approach it through an aggressive sales policy. It was only logical that, eventually, the company would cast its eye on the largest potential market of all for its services—the Germans in Germany itself. The men who directed the Germania, although choosing to reside in the United States, retained strong ties to the home country, often, as noted earlier, sending their children there for education. Aside from cultural ties, Germany was also an attractive market. Despite political disunity—Germany did not become a single national state until 1870— the German language and culture had become widespread from the Rhine east to the Baltic states and south beyond the Danube. Much of this area was undergoing rapid industrialization and urbanization—as in the United States—which created both an urban working and middle class and considerable new wealth. The market for life insurance was developing rapidly.

American companies were remarkably swift to respond to this development, which opened up new markets for them outside the fiercely competitive arena of the United States. In 1868, the Germania, followed by several other American companies, engaged in what has been called a pioneering effort, which brought American principles of life insurance marketing to the Old World.[1] The success of these companies is all the more remarkable in light of the general cultural influence that Europe had upon America, the great flow of European capital into the United States through investments in railroads and other industries, and the high esteem in which American consumers held European manufactured goods.

Preliminary Moves

When Edward von der Heydt, a Germania board member, decided to resettle in Berlin in 1865, Hugo Wesendonck asked him to obtain information about establishing agencies in Prussia. Von der Heydt was a merchant and private banker, born in Elberfeld in 1828, the eldest son of Baron August von der Heydt, who was finance minister of King William of Prussia. In New York, where he was a partner in the firm of J. W. Schmidt and Company (at Broad Street and Exchange Place), Edward von der Heydt had been Consul of Prussia for many years. Through both his diplomatic and his familial connections, therefore, he was well placed to represent the Germania in its efforts to enter the Prussian market. While von der Heydt was scouting the situation in Prussia, Wesendonck proposed to gather additional legal opinions on the feasibility of the Germania's taking such a step. A year later, he informed the Committee on Agencies that he was in correspondence with the principal governments of Germany, and that he did not anticipate that these governments would obstruct the company's establishing agencies. Wesendonck had also received encouraging replies to his inquiries regarding the possibility of establishing agencies in other parts of Europe. The committee, therefore, voted to recommend that the board authorize the officers to set up agencies in principal European cities.[2]

By December of 1866, Wesendonck had taken the first steps toward setting up a branch of the company in Europe. He offered Hermann Rose, a board member then in Europe, the position of general attorney of the company for Prussia and the North German Confederacy, and to Hugo Rothschild the general agency in Paris. Wesendonck also developed a schedule of rates. Since the rates of the leading European life insurance companies were higher than the domestic rates of the Germania, Wesendonck proposed a schedule that was 5 percent higher than the American table but still competitive with the rates of European companies. He also proposed a similar increase in commissions.[3]

After much correspondence with Rose and other directors then residing in Europe, Wesendonck secured the board's approval of his plan for operation. In April, the board appointed Rose as the general attorney for Europe, according to the laws of the respective European states, and decided to ask three directors living in Europe—Edward von der Heydt, John H. Hardt, and Hermann Marcuse—to join Rose in forming a special board of directors for the European branch. The board further authorized the expenditures necessary for establishing this branch.[4]

With board approval, Wesendonck continued to negotiate with Hermann Rose, who was unwilling to accept appointment as manager of the European branch unless the company guaranteed him a minimum annual net income of five thousand Prussian thalers. Like Wesendonck, the Committee on Agencies and the Finance Committee thought this amount excessive in relation to the anticipated income from the European business; both committees recommended that the board defer its decision until Wesendonck could visit Berlin. After discussing the reports of both committees, the board of directors voted unanimously to "adopt the Report of the Committee on Agencies, to thank Mr. Rose for the great pains he had taken in the interest of the Company, and to authorize the officers to offer to Mr. Rose the General Agency of the contemplated European business on the basis of a liberal commission."[5] Rose responded with a counteroffer, received by the company in early October, that was referred to the Committee on Agencies. Before the committee could draft its recommendation for the board, however, Rose capitulated and agreed to assume the management of the branch on a commission basis.[6]

Along with negotiating the terms of employment with Hermann Rose, the company had to determine the degree of autonomous power to be granted to the European branch. In March 1868, the special board at Berlin proposed to the home office a set of rules and regulations for running the branch office. In addition to requesting that the company deposit bonds in Berlin in order to gain the public's confidence and thereby promote business in Europe, the special board asked for control over investing funds, issuing policies, and acknowledging claims. It also requested control over the general attorney in Berlin, including the power to execute binding contracts and to order payments within the limits of funds set by the board. Finally, the special board asked that President Wesendonck receive full power to negotiate binding terms and regulations with it.[7] In response, the board of directors passed two general resolutions on 8 April. First, it conferred upon the Berlin board oversight of the general attorney at Berlin, including the power to make regulations and engage in contracts that were not in conflict with the company's charter and bylaws. Second, the board granted Hugo Wesendonck broad authority to organize the European branch, including the negotiation of terms with general attorneys, agents, physicians, and other personnel, and to do anything he considered advisable, within the limits of the company's charter and bylaws, to ensure a profitable business in Europe. The board authorized a deposit of one hundred thousand dollars in U.S. registered bonds with a Berlin bank, but, adhering to existing bylaws, refused to grant authority to the special board at Berlin to invest company funds or issue policies or acknowledge claims.[8]

Shortly after the board made these decisions, Hugo Wesendonck traveled to Berlin to oversee the development of the European branch. He reported back "his satisfaction with the amount of business done and the class of risks taken in Germany," and he further noted that the Berlin office was very careful in its expenses.[9]

In a December report to the Committee on Agencies, Wesendonck again commented on the character of the risks, which he considered superior to those insured in the United States. He also expressed satisfaction with the men he had engaged as agents, although he admitted that to attract them he had offered extra inducements in the form of higher commissions which he admitted seemed excessive, but which were, nevertheless, justified. Wesendonck argued that a commission scale was essential if any business were to be done there, that commissions were safer and more advantageous to the company than guaranteed salaries or office expenses, and that the company could manage larger expenses because it charged higher rates of premiums in Europe for risks that were as good as if not better than the risks in America. After describing his efforts in establishing agencies in Germany, Switzerland, and France, Wesendonck proposed to the committee that he extend his stay in Europe for several months to establish agencies in Austria, Bavaria, Wurttemberg, Belgium, and Holland.[10]

While the Committee on Agencies approved of Wesendonck's intention to remain in Europe, it questioned the form of organization of the European business, particularly the setup of the Paris office as an agency of the Berlin branch. They felt that there was no necessity for such a connection and that instead of subordinating the agencies for large countries like France and Switzerland, where extensive business was expected, to the general agency in Berlin, they might be made general agencies transacting business directly with the company. Not only would this independence reduce expenses, the committee reasoned, but it would also be more acceptable to French applicants. The committee also considered the problems that might arise should hostilities break out between France and Prussia, in which case the Paris agency would suffer a serious interruption and would have to establish a direct connection with the home office, a process that would cause confusion and involve labor and expense. The committee therefore asked the board to suggest to Wesendonck that he discuss with the Berlin general agent the possibility of excluding the French and other agencies from the terms of the contract.[11]

Like the committee, the board was somewhat dissatisfied by developments with the European business. After an extended discussion, during which several motions were made but not voted upon, the board decided to continue its deliberation at a special meeting three days later.[12] At that meeting, the board discussed the resolution, recommended by the Committee on Agencies, to suggest to the president that he negotiate with the Berlin agent to exclude certain countries from his contract. The board passed this resolution, but limited the proposed exclusion to France and Switzerland. In a further move to gain control over developments in Europe, the board then asked Wesendonck to provide information regarding the working of the European business so that the board might decide on "the advisability of establishing additional agencies in those countries of Europe where no such agencies exist and to suspend further action on Agencies where high rates of commission make a profitable business doubtful."[13] When Wesendonck supplied this information several weeks later, the board discovered discrepancies between Wesendonck's estimates and those made by the officers at the home office. The board unanimously resolved to return both sets of estimates to Wesendonck and requested him to "explain their cause or to state objections to the calculations made here."[14]

Shortly after the meeting, the board received both a telegram from Wesendonck concerning estimated future earnings of the European business and a report on the Berlin office from Rose. These documents were referred to an ad hoc committee that had been appointed to examine all papers relating to the European business.[15]

The ad hoc committee did not submit its report to the board until the following July, after Wesendonck returned from Europe. Evidently his personal presentation allayed the board's fears, as the ad hoc committee made a favorable and unqualified evaluation of the state of the European branch. The European business, the committee declared, was established on a sound basis and promised to gain a considerable amount of business for the company. The reported expenses were not out of line with the scale of the anticipated business, and were justified by likely future returns. The committee also made several specific recommendations which the board endorsed unanimously. The board withdrew its objection to the commission paid to the directors on the special board because it had learned that the commission was limited to the income from the new business of each year rather than extending to the whole income. While expressing confidence in Mr. Rose's ability, conscientiousness, zeal, and energy, the board authorized Wesendonck to negotiate with Rose and his assistant, on the basis of Wesendonck's estimate of future business, for fixed salaries instead of commissions. As an expression of general approval of the European branch, the board resolved that its "business be continued as heretofore, subject to such instructions as the Officers of the Company may be called upon from time to time to give."[16]

The board also considered the problem of the Paris office. Although it had previously decided that the French business should be independent of the Berlin office, the board abandoned this position after discussions with Wesendonck.[17] Perhaps this decision was part of a trade-off in the protracted negotiations with the Berlin office, which had required the company's president to spend fourteen months in Germany.[18]

Wesendonck's confidence in the potential of the European business was reinforced by the progress report submitted in July 1870 by the special board in Berlin, indicating that the European business was expected to become large and advantageous to the company. According to the special board's data, the total net increase of insurance in force of the Germania's German business during the year 1869 was surpassed in only ten out of twenty German life insurance companies. Further-more, the average amount of the Germania's policies was greater than that of the German companies.[19]

Unfortunately, this encouraging news was followed almost imme-diately by reports that France and Prussia were at war.

Franco-Prussian War

The hostilities that erupted between Prussia and France in the summer of 1870 were, on the surface, a resumption of the Napoleonic wars of six decades before, when French armies marched east into the German states, Austria, Italy, and even Poland and Russia. The fall of Napo-leon removed France from primacy over Europe but did not diminish French hopes for a return to the days of empire. These dreams seemed to reach fruition in 1852, when a descendant of the Little Corsican led a coup d'état that again placed a Napoleon on an imperial throne in France. Napoleon III, however, lacked the skills, if not the pretensions, of his forebear, and had the misfortune to hold his throne at the moment when the collection of states known as Germany was on the verge of crystallizing into a single nation. In 1848, liberal nationalists like Hugo Wesendonck, Carl Schurz, and Richard Wagner had at-tempted to create a national German constitution that would bring the various principalities, kingdoms, and free cities into a loose federation. When this effort failed, through the refusal of the principal state, Prussia, to embrace a movement led by liberals and republicans, the reformers either fled abroad or struggled to protect themselves in defensive obscurity in Germany. The broad desire for a unified Ger-many continued to grow among most Germans, however, although they disagreed over how the unification should be accomplished. Some observers predicted that reform attempts such as that of 1848 would not work. Most agreed that one of the major Germanic states would have to take the lead, which meant either Prussia or Austria.

Chancellor Otto von Bismarck saw to it that the state was Prussia. In wars largely of his making he realized the dream of a lifetime when Prussian armies crushed first Austria (1866) then France (1871), allow-ing his lord, King William of Prussia, to resume the imperial title that many German nationalists viewed as a legacy of the glorious medieval past. Although the Franco-Prussian war was quick and decisive, it created problems that it took two world wars to resolve. As part of the peace agreement, France lost its national honor and Alsace-Lorraine, which it did not recover until after World War I. The militaristic spirit of Prussia overflowed into German government, administration, and nationalistic ideology during the succeeding decades, until it was shattered by Germany's defeat in 1945.[20]

All this was in the future, and the Germania would someday share in the bitter results. In the short term, however, the company's attention focused on more mundane concerns. The war immediately severed communications between agencies in France and their home office in Berlin. In Prussia, business fell sharply.

A pressing issue was the matter of war risks. On 26 July, the board of directors met in New York to consider an emergency request from the board in Berlin. It had been the practice in the European business to add a clause to its policies, when requested, that allowed for the inclusion of war risk upon payment of an extra premium of 5 percent per year or less. "Since however the present trouble had arisen between France and Prussia the General Attorney had apparently found this was not to be in all cases satisfactory and the following telegram had been received from him: 'Authorize suspending policies during war where war premium unpaid.'"[21] Wesendonck observed to the board that, since this was the practice of some German life insurance companies, he felt it expedient for the Germania to do the same, under proper restrictions. He also indicated that he had advised Hermann Rose, the general attorney of the European Branch, not to seek war risks but to accept them at his discretion at the established rate of 5 percent. The board further authorized a telegram directing Rose to "promise revival within three years on payment [of] back premiums without interest provided re-examination [was] satisfactory."[22] A few days later, the board of directors amplified its instructions. Upon the recommendation of the Committee on Insurance and after considering the practices of German companies, the board decided that the European office should advertise war policies not exceeding a thousand thalers, provided there were not more than ten in a military body of a thousand. The rate for these policies was to be the ordinary one plus an extra premium. The European board modified these instructions, however, by deciding not to solicit soldiers in the field.[23]

The European branch managed to hold its own for the duration of the war. In December, Wesendonck reported that business was "under present difficulties . . . progressing as much as might be expected." Shortly thereafter, the board in Berlin expressed concern over "the bad impression" made by the collapse of two American life insurance companies. By July 1871, after the end of the war, the European business had bounced back. Sales were increasing and the expense/income ratio decreasing. The Committee on Agencies congratulated the European managers on "their success under great difficulties."[24]

Return of Peace

The resumption of normalcy after the war brought a continuation of the Germania's steady penetration of the German market. In these efforts Hugo Wesendonck, as usual, played a leading role, spending most of 1872 and 1873 in Berlin. One of the problems he began to encounter—one that became more acute with time—was the frequent difference of opinion between the home office and the branch office over questions of authority and decision making. Basically, the home office wanted to retain as much control as it could, without causing the European business to suffer, while the Berlin office, arguing that it had special conditions to address in Germany and Europe, pressed for more and more latitude in all aspects of business.

In March 1872, Hermann Rose, the general attorney for the European branch, requested that President Wesendonck visit the Berlin office to discuss "various points which could not very well be settled by correspondence[—] . . . the whole system of conducting the business, internally and externally." The board of directors asked Wesendonck to visit Berlin to discuss these issues with the European staff because "the Company's European business has taken such dimensions as compared with the American business, that the utmost efforts to foster the European business should be made."[25]

Three months later, at a special meeting, the board approved the reorganization plan for the European branch, modeled on the organization of the home office that had been worked out by Wesendonck. According to the new agreement, Hermann Rose was appointed general director of the European branch, and he was charged with overseeing its affairs and with submitting to the president monthly reports on policies issued or lapsed, and quarterly reports on all business transacted by the branch, including income, expenses, payments, and claims.[26]

In the fall of 1873, Wesendonck and the Committee on Agencies discussed the advisability of asking Hermann Rose to visit the home office. Wesendonck thought this would help Rose become acquainted with the company's management, especially the actuarial and dividend departments. The president's ulterior motive became apparent in his statement that the European manager should be intimately acquainted with the workings of the home office in order to conduct the European business the same way. Wesendonck clearly hoped that through the direct, personal interaction of a visit the home office would impress its views upon the head of the European branch. The board of directors subsequently invited Rose to visit the home office and authorized the president to take up Rose's position in Berlin.[27]

From time to time, the home office sent staff to the European branch. These appointments included office personnel, field agents, and directors. In 1874, for example, an assistant to the actuary went to Berlin as administrative assistant. In 1879, Adolph Schniewind, the superintendent of agencies, who was confident he could effect a large amount of life insurance through solicitation in Germany, was assigned, at his own request, to work under the manager of the European office.[28] When, in 1880, the board of directors appointed Charles Sander as a member of the special board in Berlin, the European branch strongly objected to the home office's "lack of courtesy" in not consulting it about the appointment. "We consider it only proper," they went on, "that the Berlin Office should be consulted when new measures and regulations are formulated."[29]

Expansion in Europe

In its search for new business, the Berlin branch sought to establish agencies in other German states. The company encountered difficulties in doing so not only because there was no uniform insurance law in Germany, but also because the legal requirements for entry into these various states were not clear-cut.[30] Therefore, the branch office became involved in extended negotiations each time it sought to set up agencies in new territory. The Germania faced similar problems when establishing agencies in other European countries as well.

In mid-1870, for example, as part of his effort to set up an agency in Bavaria, Rose requested authorization from the home office to offer a deposit to the Bavarian government as an inducement to grant permission to do business there. The board, although recognizing the advantage of opening this new agency, sought to avoid the deposit and voted to leave the question of such a deposit until it was requested by the Bavarian state. They advised Rose to avoid any demand by the Bavarian government for the company to make a deposit, and particularly any demand to make a deposit in other than United States securities. Negotiations continued for almost a year. In April 1871, the Bavarian government requested a deposit of thirty thousand guilders. A month later, it agreed to reduce this amount to twenty-five thousand, and accept the deposit in U.S. government securities.[31]

Despite such difficulties, the European branch spread quickly throughout German areas. By the end of 1872, it had established agencies in southern Germany, particularly Bavaria, in the northern cities of Berlin, Hanover, and Mecklenburg, and in Westphalia and Saxony, the Rhenish provinces of Prussia, with the exception of Krefeld, and in the smaller states north of the Main.[32]

In mid-1873, on the suggestion of the European branch, the board voted to apply for a license to do business in Austria. Several months later, the Austrian minister of the interior gave permission to operate in Austria-Hungary but also demanded that the company maintain a representative in Austria with full power of attorney. The European directors were uncertain what to do because they understood this requirement to violate company policy, yet they were concerned that if they did not act quickly, another company might enter the territory first. They decided to grant their agent full power of attorney and at the same time to send the Austrian law to the home office for advice. The board of directors resolved the matter by authorizing the appointment of

the General Attorney of this Company for the kingdoms and countries represented in the Council of the Empire and to confer on him such authority and to give him such power of Attorney as may be required by the laws of the Empire of Austria or of the kingdoms and countries of the same represented in the

Council of the Empire and are not in conflict with the Charter and Bylaws (*statuten*) of this Company.[33]

Both President Wesendonck, then in Berlin, and the general agent in Vienna urged the home office to allow them to issue policies in Austrian paper currency. The Finance Committee unanimously recommended that the board reject this proposal unless they could find a safeguard against losses caused by currency fluctuations. At the suggestion of Hermann Rose, who attended the board meeting in New York, the board decided to allow the special board at Berlin to issue policies in paper currency with the proviso that, if, when a premium fell due, the price of silver had risen more than 10 percent, the amount over 10 percent be added to the insurance premium. At subsequent meetings, this was applied also to payments on policies when they became due.[34]

In the meantime, the European branch had developed a proposal of its own, that losses on exchange be covered by a special dividend fund. While the board of directors did not wish to push its plan against the judgment of the European branch, it also felt that the proposal from Berlin did not provide adequate protection for the company. The board therefore granted the special board permission to devise and adopt terms for insurance in Austria in Austrian paper currency through any means that protected the company from loss through any future rise above 10 percent in the premium on silver. A few weeks later, the European board decided to adopt the home office's initial proposal that both the policyholder and the company agree to pay the difference whenever the exchange rate between Austrian paper currency and silver exceeded 10 percent.[35]

The success of the Germania in Europe followed lines similar to the pattern in the United States, where the company made little headway outside German communities. Business in Austria-Hungary was never successful; taxes were so high that the European branch began to discuss closing down the agency by the end of its first year of operation. The Germania gained admission to the Swiss cantons in 1873, but was forced to pull out of St. Gallen by 1879.[36] The agency in Paris, which had been established simultaneously with the Berlin branch, always required some level of subsidy. The company experimented with different agency arrangements, but costs were always high and success limited. Finally, in 1878, the European branch decided to discontinue the rent subsidy "since there seemed little hope for success there because of the French people's animosity toward all Germans."[37]

The Field Force

During his trip to the European branch in 1872, Wesendonck visited various agencies. As a result, he concluded that it was necessary that general agents for the European branch, as in the United States, not engage in other employment that might distract them from their insurance work. His proposal to the special board met with mixed responses. Director Rose, who supported the general principle, thought it could not be adopted as a condition for employment because the insurance business was still so insignificant in the old provinces that it would cost the company too much to give the general agents a guaranteed income during the first few years. Rose added, however, that there were some territories, such as Mannheim, Stuttgart, Hamlen, Hanover, Lipstadt, and Schwein, where business was substantial enough to allow the company to require agents to give up their other business interests.[38]

By the end of 1872, the European branch was operating so successfully that it accounted for more than one-quarter of the total new business for the year. In his report at the end of the year, Wesendonck commended the branch officers: "The management of the European business in general has been found to be excellent. No more care could be applied in the acquisition of new business, in the selection of good risks and in making the Agents render quick and full returns, than the European managers do apply."[39] Over the decade, the contribution of the European branch to the Germania's income increased slowly; by 1880, it was providing some 28 percent. More important than the rate of growth, however, was the fact that the income came in predictably, year after year, for in the decade of the 1870s the Germania faced grave economic conditions in the United States that might have destroyed the company if it had not had the income from Europe.

[5]

Depression and Recovery

The first decade of the Germania's existence coincided with one of the most prosperous periods in the history of American life insurance. Industry sales in 1869 set an all-time high, and new companies arose to develop new markets or to compete for established ones. Even the national trauma of the Civil War did not halt the pace of expansion, although it channeled it in certain directions. During the next decade, however, economic forces beyond the control of any one company or even industry deeply shook the nation, including the life insurance sector. The days of seemingly unlimited growth passed under a cloud of uncertainty as the various life insurance companies, including some only recently founded, competed fiercely in a depressed market.

The pressures of competition weighed more heavily with each year during the 1870s, and called forth vigorous corporate efforts to prevent a decline in business and keep administrative and other costs under control. Both of these goals involved the Germania's agency system, which was simultaneously the major source of new business and a major center of expenditure, but even corporate offices did not escape cost-cutting measures. The Germania, like most companies during the 1870s, reorganized its agency system, and these efforts continued in later decades as well, even when the economic climate improved. The bad times of the 1870s and the attendant reforms of the agency and administrative systems thus encouraged the Germania to maintain close control over its finances, which was to serve the company well in future difficult periods.

The depression began in 1873, within days of the failure of Jay Cooke and Company, one of the nation's leading investment banking firms. The New York Stock Exchange closed for ten days, and the nation spiraled downward into what has been called "the longest cyclical contraction" in its history.[1] The life insurance sector was especially hard hit, since the rapid expansion of the industry during the 1860s had saturated the most lucrative markets and encouraged potentially unsound business practices.

Even during the prosperous late sixties, signs of possible weakness emerged at some life insurance companies, especially among the newer ones, which began to go bankrupt at a rising rate. In 1868 six companies failed, five of which had been in business for a year or less. In 1869 nine companies failed, none of which had been in business more than three years. New companies, which were at a competitive disadvantage with the established ones, were particularly prone to insure poor risks, to run a high expense-to-income ratio, to make unsecured investments with the premiums they received, and to make unreasonable promises to customers.[2] By 1870, the situation had become grave enough to elicit a warning from the New York State superintendent of insurance, William Barnes. "It is believed to be a fact, now causing quite general complaint," he declared, "that there are too many complicated schemes or plans of insuring, and conducting companies, as well as too many and too elaborate forms of contract or policy." Each new company, the superintendent continued, had been announcing various novel features in its business that would benefit the policyholder, producing so many plans, among the more than seventy companies doing business in the state, that if a potential policyholder were to investigate each seriously, he "would be likely to die before reaching a conclusion. . . ."[3]

While the significance of the small-company failures in 1868 and 1869 went unnoticed, the bankruptcy of the Great Western Mutual Life Insurance Company in 1870 did not. The Great Western, the first New York company to fail, was dissolved by the court in December as the result of action initiated by the New York Department of Insurance. The collapse of this company, along with the failures that followed, had a strong, negative impact on public confidence in the insurance industry, and "prospective buyers of life insurance . . . stayed away in droves." The officers of the Germania, too, noticed a "general reaction in Life Insurance businesses all over the U.S. which no effort at present can overcome."[4]

The sense of helplessness was well grounded in reality. According to

John A. McCall, later president of the New York Life, the decade of the 1870s was "the most trying period in the history of American life insurance."[5] In New York State, for example, there was a steady decline in the number of companies doing business, from a high of seventy-one in 1870 down to twenty-nine in 1881. On the national level, only 55 of the 129 companies doing business in 1870 survived into 1882. Business was so depressed that no life insurance companies were founded in any state between 1876 and 1883.[6]

The serious marketing problems the Germania had begun to encounter in 1867 intensified during the early 1870s, as domestic sales continued to decline and lapses to increase, so that the total amount of domestic insurance in force began to shrink. Hugo Wesendonck reported to the Committee on Agencies, at its first meeting of 1870, that business in the United States was becoming more difficult every year, owing to increased competition. The number of life insurance companies had doubled during the past three or four years, and the commissions the new companies paid were consuming their income.[7] More specifically, the president noted that the Germania had lost much of its business in the states west of the Alleghenies and east of the Mississippi. The new companies organized there were successfully appealing to westerners' resentment about the money that eastern-based insurance companies were annually taking from the West, only a small part of which ever returned in the form of policies due. The Germania, fortunately, was holding its own in New York City, California, the South, the Far West, and particularly in Europe. These areas, Wesendonck concluded, would have to sustain the company in the immediate future.[8]

Wesendonck's plan for preserving the company during the current hard times consisted of several parts. At its heart, the plan sought to attract business by increasing dividends to policyholders. Dividends would come, of course, from the surplus remaining after all policy claims were satisfied and the company had paid its administrative expenses. Since the company could do little in the short term to reduce the payout of policy claims, all efforts focused on cutting administrative costs, especially those of the extensive agency system. Wesendonck proposed to revise the system of agents' commissions, reorganize the field staff and the agents, and improve cash management, particularly the flow of premium money from agents to the home office.

Commissions

Since the commission rate of the Germania was lower than that of most other companies, Wesendonck thought it necessary to raise the rates to keep agents with the company during a period of intense competition and decreasing sales. While a few of the Germania's general agents received 25 percent on the first year's premium and 7.5 percent on renewals, the greatest number of its agents were paid only 10 percent on the first year's premium and 5 percent on renewals. Others were paid 15 and 5, 20 and 5, or 20 and 7.5 percent on the first year's premiums and renewals, respectively. Wesendonck moved to increase these commissions moderately, but not to exceed 25 percent on the first year's premium and 7.5 percent on renewals. He repeatedly argued against commissions greater than these despite his conviction that additional increases would undoubtedly improve sales.[9]

There were, of course, exceptional cases where unusually productive agents had personal leverage with the company. The general agent for several states and territories west of the Mississippi, Mr. Wurtzebach, for example, demanded an increase in his commission to 30 and 10 percent. Because he had been a faithful and efficient agent, Wesendonck recommended that the company agree to his demands. Similarly, when the co-agent in Colorado, Mr. Hoar, requested a commission of 50 and 3 percent as well as additional territory, the company compromised with a rate of 30 and 10.[10] Another case was the arrangement with Adolph Schniewind, the Germania's primary agent in New York City. Although the company had met great difficulty selling policies in the city during the early 1860s, Schniewind had managed to increase city business by 1870. His contract called for a commission of 1 percent of the amount insured and 3 percent of renewal premiums. The Germania was forced to raise these terms to keep Schniewind when other companies attempted to hire him away with offers of large guaranteed incomes.[11] By April 1871, Wesendonck had successfully negotiated a contract that fixed Schniewind's compensation at 1.25 percent of the amount insured on new business and 5 percent on the amount of renewals and guaranteed the agent an annual income of six thousand dollars.[12]

Occasionally, Wesendonck recommended monetary incentives as an encouragement for field agents. The company agreed, for example, to distribute in 1873 the sum of $1,200 among those general agents whose business in 1872 would show an increase in new policies as well as income.[13]

Reorganization

Along with increasing the size of commissions, Wesendonck moved to tighten up the agency system by consolidating existing agencies under a few full-time general agents. He particularly wanted to reduce the number of agents who devoted only part of their time to selling insurance or who, although full-time sellers of insurance, worked on behalf of several companies rather than solely for the Germania. In moving toward full-time agents who represented only the Germania, Wesendonck was following current practice in the industry. The concept of the full-time agent began, as noted earlier, during the 1840s, with the appearance of the earliest general agents, and evolved slowly over the next two decades, to emerge as the dominant mode of organization by the mid-1860s.[14]

Beginning in December 1870, Wesendonck made substantial progress in creating this new general-agency system. In July of 1871, he reported that he had established seven large general districts, with seats in St. Louis, Savannah, Detroit, New Orleans, Wheeling, Houston, and Louisville. Wesendonck was then negotiating to establish one general agency for New England and another for Tennessee, Arkansas, and Mississippi. Business in the remaining states of New York, Pennsylvania, Maryland, Virginia, North Carolina, South Carolina, and parts of Wisconsin, Illinois, Indiana, and Ohio was managed by local agents who were visited from time to time by inspectors.[15] In 1873, Wesendonck appointed Adolph Schniewind, the Germania's New York City agent, to a newly created position of superintendent of agencies to visit agents in other states. His contract called for an annual salary of three thousand dollars, a small commission for city business, and a per diem allowance of seven dollars and railroad fare while traveling. The following year his annual salary was raised to $4,200.[16]

Wesendonck continued to make adjustments in the general-agency set-up over the next few years. In some cases, changes were precipitated by the loss of the general agent. When, for example, the general agent for the Atlantic coast quit in 1874, he was not replaced; instead, the district was covered by local agents loosely monitored by Schniewind, from New York City. Local agents continued to receive support in soliciting from general agents or traveling agents. By the end of 1876,

Wesendonck was satisfied with the system that he had developed: "The company's agency system in the U.S. has been perfected during 1876. . . . The bulk of business is done through five or six large general agencies and in New York City. More local agents are existing in the Southern or New England states."[17] Wesendonck did, however, continue to redraw the district lines of general agencies from time to time. In addition, there is indirect evidence to suggest that, as part of the agency reorganization, Wesendonck even considered broadening the appeal of the company to groups other than German-Americans. The move was tentative, and never greatly emphasized in the surviving company records, but it suggests how pressed Wesendonck felt, given his statement in 1863 that "the Germania can . . . hardly expect that any considerable share of the business, other than German will ever be absorbed by it."[18] In the fall of 1871, Wesendonck hired the first non-German agent, to solicit for the company in New England. In 1875, Wesendonck engaged another American to solicit in Cincinnati, formerly a German stronghold, and entered into negotiations with yet another non-German for the position of traveling inspector for local agencies on the Atlantic coast. At the same committee meeting, however, Wesendonck also announced the appointment of three German agents for New York City.[19]

These few attempts to broaden the company's ethnic appeal never received a final, written evaluation by the Committee on Agencies. Probably the experiment was dropped when business improved during the 1880s. No doubt the strong performance of the European branch at this time tempered any thought Wesendonck had of making the company more American.

Cash Management

One area of operations that came under special scrutiny during the lean 1870s was accounting for income and expenditures. This matter had engaged the company's attention almost from the beginning, when the special committee, established by the board of directors to examine year-end accounts (see chapter 3), used the issue to challenge Wesendonck's administration of the Germania. In its report for 1861, the committee complained about the lack of proper internal record keeping. In the spring of 1862 the committee expressed concern about the difficulty of examining the company's year-end accounts and about determining their accuracy. In particular, the committee noted it could not vouch for income from premiums because there was no control over the number of policies issued, except the policy book and the honor of the officers. An examination of receivable premiums would require referring to the issue of the first policy of the company, a task that would become quite time-consuming in only a few years. In a related matter, the committee also complained of the lack of proper records about the issuance of stock. At the same time, however, the committee carefully avoided any personal accusations, commenting that because the company had such "excellent officers as at present," the lack of formal controls was of no consequence.[20] When the board requested the committee to recommend measures for internal control, the committee was unable to produce any substantial program, and the board took no action.[21]

The matter of record keeping was not dead, however, for the following year the special committee questioned the "correctness of the premiums received and accounted for by the Agents." Fortunately, the committee noted, a newly adopted system of receipts promised to resolve the matter.[22]

In the spring of 1864 the committee issued a report which criticized several internal procedures. It complained about a new practice of grouping expense items into fewer financial report categories than before. In particular the committee objected to the substantial amount of money put into the "other" category. This new practice, instituted to bring the company's reports into conformity with those required by the state superintendent of insurance (a fact that the committee explicitly recognized), was conducive "to the relaxation of proper checks over the expenditures."[23] In addition, the committee recommended that in its internal reporting the company keep each expense item separate and distinguish annual accounts of income from deferred premiums and accounts due from general agents. In addition, the committee proposed that the Auditing Committee meet monthly rather than quarterly, as had been the case, to examine the accounts of the preceding month.

Finally, the committee addressed the matter of charitable deductions. It criticized the practice of allowing such donations to be made at the discretion of the president. According to the expense book the president had contributed company funds in the amount of $2.00 in 1860, $14.50 in 1861, and $39.25 in 1862; in 1863 the amount had actually decreased, to $33.75. While acknowledging that these were very small amounts, the committee declared that "upon principle" it could not entirely approve of the president's having control over the funds, "but in view of the frequent calls upon the officers," the committee suggested the "appropriation of some small sum which may be devoted to such purposes annually."[24] As usual, in its report the committee praised the company's officers and avoided any hint of wrongdoing or impropriety.

Nevertheless, it was clear that the board had a delicate matter to resolve. It immediately delegated the matter to an ad hoc committee, which consulted with the officers, made its own deliberations, and issued a report that proposed a compromise solution. The officers agreed to keep separate accounts of the amounts due from general agents at the end of the preceding year, and of premiums due and in the process of transmission to the home office, but they objected to separating deferred premiums received from other premiums, for that would entail much effort on their part for small benefit. They also claimed that the company had adequate control over these accounts because every premium payable to the company appeared on its books, either as due or as received. In light of this explanation, the ad hoc committee made no recommendations to the board. The ad hoc committee did propose, however, that the officers follow the request of the special committee to classify those items grouped under "other expenses" in an expense book.[25] Evidently, the adoption of these new procedures was considered adequate; in any case the subsequent reports of the special committee focused on other issues, such as Wesendonck's negotiations for establishing the European branch, described in the previous chapter.

By the 1870s, concern had shifted from internal accounting procedures to the handling of funds by agents. With the slowing of business, some agents found themselves caught in a cash-flow bind, as they failed to reduce expenses to be in line with the lower level of income at their agency. The result was that some agents ran up large debts to the company in the form of premium payments not forwarded to the home office. At the end of 1872, for example, the general agent in Savannah had not accounted for such a large amount of premiums and policies that the home office became suspicious. Under pressure, the agent finally accounted for the greater part of these premiums and policies, and in settlement remitted a check for over thirteen thousand dollars on a Savannah bank, but the check was returned for lack of funds. Wesendonck went immediately to Savannah and completed a final accounting for an indebtedness of $14,770. Since the agent was unable to settle this debt, he assigned to the company a cotton claim. The officers were evidently satisfied with this method of repayment, since they allowed the agent to keep control over Savannah and its vicinity, but separated the rest of Georgia and the state of Alabama from the agency.[26]

Even the Germania's outstanding agents were sometimes unable to settle their accounts. In the fall of 1874, for example, Adolph Schnie-wind, the superintendent of agencies, was twenty-four hundred dollars in debt to the company. He cleared his overdue account by selling the company his claim for annual commissions on five years' renewal premiums for policies. A more serious situation developed in 1874 when Herman Kuhn, the general agent for Michigan, northern Ohio, and northern Indiana, absconded. The Germania was taken to task in the insurance press for neglecting to keep an eye on him. The amount in question was settled by his responsible bondsmen.[27]

In an effort to attain greater control over agency accounts, Adolph Schniewind, the superintendent of agencies, was sent on an inspection tour in October 1876 through the western states to examine the books and accounts of general agents. The officers were then considering scheduling two such tours a year. In addition to developing a system of regular auditing, the company was encouraging agents to send in their accounts during the "first ten days of each month for the preceding month, so that the accumulation of premiums in the hands of agents is avoided as much as possible."[28] The president was concerned about the effect of delayed remissions by agents, which were not considered income on the company's annual statements to state insurance departments until they were collected. "A large amount of unrealized assets . . . has often rightfully been censured, as indicative of loose management," Wesendonck informed the field force. "Being desirous of having the amount of unrealized assets of this company—which includes the item of 'Premiums due and in course of collection,'—appear in our next annual statement at the lowest possible figure, we wish our Agents to aid us." The president therefore requested that all agents send their reports and payments in timely fashion so that the home office would be able "to prepare a statement which will more than favorably compare with those of other companies."[29]

In his attempt to cut expenses, Wesendonck turned to another facet of insurance sales—the evaluation of the medical condition of insurance applicants. In 1875, he presented to the Committee on Insurance an analysis of all death claims from the beginning of the company to the end of 1874, showing the causes of death together with the most important items of the medical certificates at the time the holder applied for the policy. This information suggested to Wesendonck that the procedures of the medical examiners needed tightening up. The committee agreed to Wesendonck's proposal that he and the resident physician visit the various agencies to present these matters to the company's medical examiners and to instruct them on the leading points, which were important for the acceptance of future risks.[30]

The medical examiners' performance continued to be a matter of concern, however. In 1877, in order to get more complete reports, Wesendonck introduced a new medical examination form. Yet even this innovation did not uniformly improve the quality of medical examinations. In a circular addressed to the company's medical examiners, Wesendonck pointed out certain problems with the internal consistency of their reports. In some cases, he noted, replies did not correspond with the statements made in preceding questions. For instance: " 'Do these personal characteristics promise longevity?' has been answered 'Yes,' although the reply to question 3 stated that the applicant was very thin and pale, or disproportionately heavy. Also question 10, 'Does this family record promise longevity?' has been answered 'Yes,' although the reply to question 9 stated that parents and grandparents died young."[31]

Post-Depression Changes

The various changes in medical examinations, internal accounting and financial controls, and the agency system helped pull the Germania through a difficult period. By 1880 sales were improving, as the economy moved into another upward cycle, and by the end of 1881 the company had regained its pre-1873 level of policies.[32] Despite the favorable trend, however, Wesendonck was not satisfied with the general performance of the agents. The report on the first quarter of 1880 indicated that almost two-thirds of the increase in sales was generated in New York City, which suggested to Wesendonck that the agents in other areas were not sufficiently attentive to seeking new business. At a general conference of agents Wesendonck struck a new agreement with them intended to encourage the search for additional sales. In exchange for relinquishing their commission on renewal premiums, Wesendonck agreed to pay annual salaries. In addition, he raised the commission rate on the first year's premiums, out of which general agents were to pay commissions to their own local agents.[33]

The following year, Wesendonck proposed another revision of the standard agreement with general agents that he thought would both reduce company expenses and increase new business. The arrangement made at the conference of general agents in 1880 had put the company "in a most enviable position as to the collection of renewal premiums" since the annual salaries plus company-paid expenses amounted to "less than any fair renewal commissions." He further estimated that general agents used at least one-half of their commissions to pay the commissions of their local agents. Under these circumstances, their annual income was moderate, in many cases less than two thousand dollars and in every case less than three thousand dollars, while the company enjoyed the services of a cadre of experienced agents who represented its interest well and whose contracts bound them to work for the company full-time.[34]

Wesendonck now proposed to eliminate all but one traveling agent and, while eliminating that cost as well as the travel allowance paid to general agents, to increase the first year's commission paid to general agents to between 40 and 50 percent, depending on the type of policy. By such a change, Wesendonck argued, the company would decrease the expenses in case no substantial new business was done in the local agencies. The large first year's commission would allow the general agents to engage energetic local agents, thereby increasing the new business considerably. Even though a larger initial commission might increase the cost of new business, he declared, "the Company will be paid therefore by the exceedingly low renewal commissions."[35] The committee approved this proposal.

This system lasted only two years, however, for more changes came in 1883, as the face value of insurance issued by the Germania in the United States was again declining. Wesendonck attributed the decline to the poor performance of local agents and began thinking about additional ways to improve on the agency system that he had developed during the crisis of the 1870s. He observed that local agents had little incentive to sell because they had to divide their commissions with the general agent in their territory. Another problem was the tendency for local agents to rely on the general agents in acquiring new business, both through personal contacts and the publication and distribution of advertising and other publicity materials. The general-agent system itself came in for criticism. Wesendonck noted that because of the high costs of travel, general agents tended to concentrate their activities in their city or town of residence, and were not always providing the extensive support required by local agents. In any case, some of the areas covered by local agents had grown so much in population as to merit increased attention from the sales force. At the same time, the widespread improvement in communications all over the country (owing to the construction of new rail lines and the paving of roads in the more densely populated areas) was allowing local agents to travel over larger areas. Wesendonck therefore proposed a radical solution to the problem of declining sales: the company should "discontinue the General Agency System and have local agents who communicate directly with the company appointed in all places."[36]

This plan went into operation by the end of the year. In a report to the Committee on Agencies, which was by now a rubber stamp for Wesendonck's decisions, the president related that the general agents' districts had been reduced to limited centers and that many new agents had been appointed in those places where the general agents had previously been in charge. Support for these local agents was now provided by traveling agents instead of general agents.[37]

By the end of the quarter, Wesendonck noted improvement in American sales, which he took to bode well for the new system. Then, sales again worsened, in 1884 dropping 21 percent, compared to an 11 percent drop in 1883. Large as the Germania's agency system had grown, the company still depended heavily on a few key people. In his report for the second quarter of 1884, for example, Wesendonck attributed the decrease in business to the relocation to Europe of Adolph Schniewind, the superintendent of agencies and the principal agent in New York City, and the protracted sickness of the company's principal inspector and solicitor, Mr. William Cohn. At the end of the third quarter, Wesendonck cited the same factors to explain a drop in business for the entire nine months of the year.[38]

A second factor contributing to the steady drop in new policy issues was the loss of reinsurance business from the New York Life Insurance Company. Reinsurance was commonly used by companies to write policies that exceeded their stated limit for a single policy; the re-insuring company took responsibility for the difference between the value of the policy and the maximum allowed by the original insurer's regulations. The Germania and the New York Life had concluded such an arrangement in 1875, and under its terms the New York Life began writing policies. Several years later, their number began to decline, and then virtually ceased when the New York Life began taking risks up to seventy-five thousand dollars and so eliminated its need for a reinsurer.[39]

By the end of 1884, the Germania had discontinued all large general agencies and replaced them with special traveling agents. These special agents worked solely for the Germania, whose home office paid them their salaries and commissions directly. Some of the new agents were highly experienced, such as one from Cincinnati hired in 1887 to solicit for the Germania in New York City, who had been a successful worker for other companies. The special agents experienced a high turnover, however, and of eleven under contract at the beginning of 1885 only six remained at the end of the year.[40]

By 1888, Wesendonck had strengthened many local agencies by appointing associate managers or special agents. After dismantling the system of general agencies that looked after and shared the commissions of local agents, Wesendonck began to replace it by building up selected local agencies. Following the practice of other companies, these local agent-managers, who received extended powers and high commissions, were responsible for paying the salaries and traveling expenses of their solicitors. Therefore, instead of the home office's dividing the commissions between local and general agents, it now paid all commissions to the agent-managers who then paid their own staff according to their arrangements with them. These managers were appointed to geographical districts that were sometimes quite large. In the Northwest, for example, the agency of Doremus and Halteman, located in Helena, included the states of Montana, Washington, and Oregon as well as the territories of Idaho and Utah.[41]

The revamping of the agency system evidently contributed to an improvement in business, as the amount of new policies written in 1885 jumped 15 percent over the preceding year. The high point of the decade was 1888 when the amount of new policies issued through the home office more than doubled, from $3,075,000 to $6,419,000. Over half of this tremendous leap in sales was attributed to special efforts in St. Paul and Helena.[42]

The apparent success of the reorganization in improving sales encouraged Wesendonck to suggest yet another change, intended to give the company a better grip over the whole agency system. Wesendonck noted that the new system of local and special agents involved constant supervision of the company's managers, solicitors, and medical examiners, and that this resulted in a need for numerous changes in personnel, which sometimes required trips to remote places. Wesendonck therefore proposed creating a position responsible for overseeing all the agencies. The post should go to a salaried officer of the company, he thought, not to an inspector, because the latter shared the commissions of the field personnel and therefore had a personal interest in their activities. Since none of the officers could add this responsibility to their other duties, the president suggested that a board member be appointed as special director to assist with general management and especially to superintend the company's exterior service. The board agreed to this suggestion and immediately approved the president's candidate, his son, Max A. Wesendonck.[43]

Quality of Business

The Germania was a conservative company in its approach to issuing policies. Unlike some new companies, which wrote policies even on persons who were bad risks, the Germania tried to avoid such risks as much as possible, although it often had a hard time controlling agents in remote areas. However, during the tough times of the 1870s the company was concerned more with improving the volume of sales than with the yields or risks associated with the new policies. Even after business improved during the 1880s, the quality of new business did not receive a thorough analysis. Finally, during the early 1890s, Wesendonck turned to that issue.

The cost of acquiring new business, he discovered, was relatively high, owing primarily to the first-year commissions paid to agents. Agents wanted to write as many policies as possible, to gain the first-year commissions, but the company sought policies that would remain in force for a long time, to reduce the impact of the first-year commissions on the lifelong yield of the premiums to the company. This tension was common to the life insurance industry, and had been encountered ever since the agency system had arisen. The problem at the Germania had evidently become severe, for in his attempt to reduce the expense of acquiring new business, Wesendonck was prepared to tolerate a decrease in sales. Although the Germania had always tried to keep commissions as low as possible, the rate of first-year commissions had gradually and steadily increased as the company followed the industry in the battle for new business. During 1893, the officers of the Germania, risking a reduction in new business, negotiated new contracts with almost all of the company's managers lowering the scale of their first-year commissions.

The analysis of the Committee on Agencies on the staying quality of new business indicated that, except for New York City, it was very unsatisfactory. Only about 50 percent of new policies issued in 1891 were renewed at the end of the year. At the end of the second year, the committee observed, there were further heavy lapses, "and we have practically to do our business all over again every few years."[44] To some degree, the problem of lapsed policies was the result of an industry-wide practice of rebating, that is, the practice of returning part of the first-year commission to the insured as a way of attracting new business. Policies sold in this manner had much greater lapse rates than ordinary business, as consumers went from company to company to get the discount on the first year's premium. Following the lead of other companies, the Germania had introduced a high first-year commission in the 1880s to attract good local agent-managers. This had, unfortunately, also given the agent-managers incentive to force sales by offering applicants for new policies a rebate of nearly their whole first-year commission. Applicants would be insured by less than the premium for a temporary policy and "have no interest after a year to renew their policies. . . . They could get new insurance through . . . other companies for a merely nominal premium."[45]

The widespread use of rebates had attracted much attention in the late 1880s. Since an attempt by some companies to get an industry-wide agreement had failed, New York State passed an antirebate bill in 1889. Evidently the law did not immediately curb this practice, for in his report for 1891, the state superintendent of insurance attacked its continued use. Urging prudence, good management, and care, the superintendent advised companies to lower the rates of commissions to agents and to support the new antirebate laws, as means of eliminating the abuse.[46]

In 1892, Hugo Wesendonck wrote to the presidents of the Mutual Life, the New York Life, and the Equitable in an effort to get support for a mutual agreement to limit commissions as a way to end rebates. While all agreed that the rebate system should be abolished, most of them claimed that they had already done all they could to bring about abolishment, Wesendonck later told the Committee on Agencies.

Over the next eighteen months, the rebate problem became even more serious for the Germania. Wesendonck discovered that the rebate system was flourishing at the Utah agency, whose manager had taken applications in remote places, from unknown people, traveling with an unknown doctor. Since he suspected that many of the applicants were not insurable because of their health, Wesendonck prepared to travel with a physician to go over the whole field and have those risks reexamined. The Germania's officers, despairing of cooperation from other life companies and faced with a "ruinous" 50 percent lapse rate, unilaterally reduced commissions, declaring that more reductions might follow. Resolved not to issue policies under conditions that portended a quick lapse, they discouraged applicants by stipulating payment of the second year's premium along with the first.[47] Although Wesendonck and the resident physician had visited and inspected the company's agents and medical examiners during 1893, the committee remained dissatisfied with the company's mortality rates. Noting that occasionally deaths occurred a short time after policies were issued, the committee complained of learning only at that time that these were risks that should never have been solicited.[48]

In 1894, the Germania's sales entered another decline, from the severe national depression that began in 1893 and lasted through much of the decade. Precipitated by overexpansion in the industrial sector, combined with a sharp contraction in the money supply, the depression resulted in thousands of business and bank failures. An estimated 20 percent of the labor force was unemployed. As business began to fall off, the Germania decided to concentrate its attention on agencies in heavily populated areas.[49] Unable to stop the decline in new business until 1897, the company improved the policy-retention rate. The report on business for the first quarter of 1895 noted a marked decrease in the American business, but a more favorable lapse rate. Despite difficult economic conditions, policy retention was "offsetting to a great extent" the fall in new insurance. In 1897, the Committee on Agencies noted that the staying power of the American business was approaching that of the European branch, "whose record has always been favorable in this respect."[50]

6

New Offerings and Investments

The Germania's return to growth and prosperity derived not only from an improved national economy and a streamlining of the company's agency and administrative systems, but from changes in its policy offerings and in the way it invested its money. These changes followed the then-current practice of the American insurance industry, which underwent significant development during the last two decades of the nineteenth century. For much of the century, the appeal of life insurance had lain mainly with the middle class, which was the primary market for the Germania and other companies. By the later decades of the century, however, economic changes were adding new groups of people as potential buyers of insurance. The largest such group was the industrial labor force, the blue-collar workers in steel, manufacturing, mining, and other industries that were beginning to form the core of the American economy. The increasing number of such workers became evident by the 1870s, when a few American companies started to market insurance to them. Other innovations also appeared in the life insurance industry, such as the tontine policy. Connected with the matter of policies was the issue of how to invest the money that came in as premiums, an area that also witnessed significant changes both in the Germania and elsewhere. One of the most striking ways for an insurance company to invest was to purchase or have constructed an imposing commercial building to serve as the home office.

Industrial Insurance

In the fall of 1879 Hugo Wesendonck suggested that it was time for the Germania to branch out into a new area of insurance—so-called industrial insurance. Despite a general improvement in the economy, after nearly a decade of hard times, the company had been finding it increasingly difficult to compete for new business with its traditional products, and the development of a new line offered the opportunity to develop additional sources of income. This was no small decision for the Germania to take, however, for it amounted to creating a whole new division of the company.[1]

Industrial insurance, first offered in England in 1854, provided low-cost, low-value life insurance with weekly or monthly premium payments. It was sold and maintained in force through the efforts of a door-to-door sales staff. Industrial insurance was introduced in the United States in 1875 by the Prudential Friendly Society, which soon thereafter became the Prudential Insurance Company of America. This program was essentially a marketing plan to compete with cooperative, fraternal associations which provided insurance to the poorer working classes that had not yet been tapped by the American insurance industry.[2]

Impressed by the success of industrial insurance in England, the Germania's board authorized the officers to issue policies carrying weekly or monthly premiums, on terms to be determined by the Committee on Insurance. The committee authorized issuance of policies for weekly payment, the renting of office space for the new operation, and the hiring of a small staff. The pressure of competition in this new area of insurance caused the Germania to modify its payment policy for claims; henceforth the company would pay immediately upon receipt of proof of death, rather than after a sixty-day waiting period. Another change was made when the company's solicitors discovered that customers desired coverage for the entire family, not just the breadwinner. To make itself competitive with other insurance companies, the Germania followed their lead and agreed to insure children as well as adults. The new branch took up quarters at 32 East Fourth Street in Manhattan, under the direction of Dr. Victor Precht (presumably the same person referred to in the Annual Report of 1877 as inspector of agencies). At some time before 1886 the industrial branch acquired a new manager, K. Rohland.[3]

The Germania's trial in industrial insurance got off to a positive start. By mid-1880, the company had established branch agencies in Brook-

1. Hugo Wesendonck in 1849, shortly after his arrival in the United States, eleven years before he founded the Germania Life Insurance Company.

2. Hugo Wesendonck as president of the Germania in 1885.

3. Max A. Wesendonck, son of Hugo, as second vice president of the Germania in 1899.

5. Harry Arthur Hopf, noted management consultant to the life insurance industry. Hopf began his career as a secretary at the Germania in 1902. (Courtesy Ronald Greenwood)

4. Otto Wesendonck, brother of Hugo. A successful silk merchant, he served on the Germania's European board from 1868 to 1896. (Courtesy Nationalarchiv der Richard-Wagner-Stiftung/Richard-Wagner-Gedenkstätte Bayreuth)

6. Hubert Cillis, actuary of the Germania, was a founding member of the Actuarial Society of America in 1894. He later became the Germania's third president.

7. Cornelius Doremus, shortly after he became president of the Germania, in 1898, upon the retirement of Hugo Wesendonck.

8. Albert F. D'Oench, architect and member of the Germania's board of directors from 1894 to 1918, designed the company's Union Square headquarters.

9. John Fuhrer joined the Germania in 1874 and became actuary in 1898.

10. T. Louis Hansen became head
    of the Germania's Agency De-
    partment in 1910 and later a
    vice president of the company.

11. Carl T. Heye was secretary of
    the Germania during World
    War I and became the com-
    pany's fourth president.

12. Hermann Rose guided the Ber-
    lin office from 1866 to 1889.

13. Frederick Schwendler was vice president of the Germania from its founding until 1890.

14. Germania advertisement in the *Leitfaden für Deutsche Einwanderer nach den Vereinigten Staaten für Amerika*, a guide published in Germany for Germans emigrating to the United States.

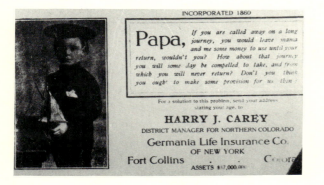

15. Advertisement by the agency in Fort Collins, Colorado, ca. 1900.

17. The Berlin headquarters of the European Branch, located at No. 12 Leipziger Platz from 1877 to 1902.

16. The Union Square home-office building, which opened for business on 1 May 1911.

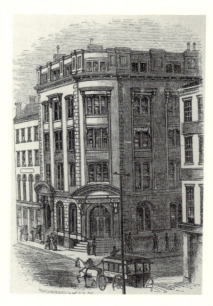

18. The first quarters of the Germania were in the ground floor of this building at 90 Broadway, corner of Wall Street, in lower Manhattan.

19. Image of Germania on a Germania Life stock certificate (detail).

20. Group portrait of agents at the Evansville, Indiana, agency, ca. 1922. The man seated in the center is probably agency manager Rudd.

21. Germania Life insurance policy form (detail) for use in Germany. Note the American eagle.

22. Germania Life tontine insurance policy (detail),
    issued in 1889 to a policyholder in Oshkosh,
    Wisconsin.

23. Dinner invitation to the field
    managers' meeting in 1901.

lyn, Boston, Fall River, New Haven, Hartford, Bridgeport, Philadelphia, Pittsburgh, Baltimore, Buffalo, Cleveland, and Cincinnati. With nearly $1,000,000 worth of industrial insurance in force, the Germania looked forward to a total of $1.5 million worth by the end of the year.[4]

There were, however, critical problems with the industrial branch. The ratio of lapses to new issues was very high. In the first three quarters of 1880, the company issued over fifteen thousand policies with a total face value of nearly $1.9 million. But after deducting the lapsed policies, valued at $920,000, only $955,000 worth of insurance remained in force. Wesendonck attributed the high lapse rate to the nature of the business itself. He told the Committee on Agencies that the working classes' circumstances changed so frequently for the worse, that they were often unable to pay even ten cents a week. Wesendonck also noted that sharp competition among insurers encouraged frequent changing from one company to another.

The most serious problem, which not only contributed to the high lapse rate but also was detrimental to the operations of the company as a whole, was the dishonesty prevalent among agents hired by the industrial branch. Wesendonck reported that a number of dishonest agents and physicians had burdened the company with fictitious policies. This was profitable to them because of the practice, common to other companies, of paying the agents' commissions in advance before the premiums were collected. Wesendonck introduced a new system for the collection of premiums and payment of commissions. He required the payment of four weeks' premiums in advance, out of which the agent received only the first. All future premiums were to be collected by a company-appointed collector rather than the agents. Since agents would not receive commissions until premiums were paid to the company, this procedure eliminated the opportunity for them to make money by reporting fictitious policies.[5]

This solution did not lack problems, however. The required advance payment of four premiums threatened to limit business, since many prospective buyers would be unable to make such a large lump-sum payment. Moreover, it caused a serious problem with the agency staff. Most of the agents, Wesendonck noted, would not work under the new system because they resented the curbs on their aggressive marketing efforts. Many agents left the company and tried to take their policyholders with them, which caused a drop in new business. Despite this, Wesendonck remained optimistic about the future of the industrial branch.[6]

Wesendonck's optimism seemed justified by the results of the last quarter in 1880, which showed an increase in the amount of insurance in force and paid for, as well as an increase in the paid-up proportion of insurance in force and a decline in the ratio of expenses to income. Three months later, Wesendonck described to the Committee on Agencies the great care and watchfulness that were being applied to every employee and agent in the effort to make the industrial branch safe and paying.[7]

These encouraging developments did not prevent Wesendonck from making a dispassionate appraisal of the industrial branch's efforts in certain areas of the country where it was not meeting success. To the Committee on Agencies, on 10 January 1882, he observed that the company was unable to control its industrial branch agents effectively in distant regions without incurring extra expenses. He then explained how during the previous autumn he had reorganized most of these agencies into collection offices, which did not write new policies. Without a marketing effort, lapses began rising and the total amount of insurance in effect was falling rapidly. Further, the company was reducing to a minimum "all doubtful business, such as insurance of Negroes and females, . . . that only the best class thereof has been accepted."[8]

Although Wesendonck tried to put the most positive construction on his reorganization, it was clear that the Germania had greatly reduced its commitment to the industrial branch. Instead of accepting a high level of bad risks as inevitable in that sort of market, and assuming that over time the benefits would outweigh the losses, Wesendonck had reverted to the formula that had worked so well during the past two decades. The Germania had always fared best when it sold to the market it knew best—the prosperous German-Americans and Germans in Europe who were so prominent a part of the middle classes. One may speculate that this market was the most congenial to Wesendonck and his associates, who had sprung from the upper middle class and had a special insight into its workings. It may be significant that by 1880 Wesendonck was no longer touring the American heartland as he had in the 1860s and 1870s, but had shifted his attention to Europe. It was in Europe that the largest German middle class existed, whereas in America German immigration was shifting, from the affluent to the aspirant, as peasants and workers moved from the German countryside and towns, looking for economic opportunity. The Germania's foray into industrial insurance was one tentative effort to reach these new immigrants, but it did not have the full weight of the company behind it.

After making his reorganization of the industrial branch, late in 1881 and early 1882, Wesendonck told the Committee on Agencies that the coming year would be critical for the branch. All agencies of the industrial branch had been withdrawn except those in the New York City area, Philadelphia, and Baltimore. The result was little new business and an unusually large number of lapses, but as a result of shrinking the industrial business, the branch broke even for the next year and a half.[9] In 1883 the branch was able to contribute a regular monthly return of one thousand dollars in cash to the company, an amount about equal to the branch's incoming reserve requirements. Nevertheless, a year later, the Committee on Agencies discussed the possibility of withdrawing from Philadelphia and Baltimore unless expenses could be reduced.[10]

The branch's performance improved in 1885, and the year-end report showed that it had even produced three thousand dollars above expenses and increases in the reserve. The following year the branch slipped a little, although it was still covered in its expenses and reserve requirements. In January 1887, however, the officers decided to discontinue offering industrial policies. The main reason given for the decision was that industrial insurance could only be successful if conducted on a large scale, which the Germania evidently felt unable to sustain.[11] This was another way of saying that the company preferred to have a relatively small number of affluent, dependable policyholders than a much larger number of poorer, more fickle ones.

Other New Offerings

Aside from the industrial branch, the Germania made several modifications in policy offerings during the last three decades of the nineteenth century, including a nonforfeiture clause, a tontine policy, an accommodation plan, and insurance for ocean travel.

In 1872 Wesendonck decided that the forfeiture practices of the Germania were discouraging many people from taking out policies. Forfeiture meant that if a policyholder allowed a life policy to lapse, either on purpose or for lack of funds to pay a premium, all the money paid in as premiums up to that time was forfeited to the company. In other words, the policyholder was not vested, and lost the total value of the premium contributions already made. This naturally made many people reluctant to start a life policy, since they risked losing their entire investment for failure to make timely payment of a single premium, even after twenty or thirty years of steady contributions. In fact, companies often made allowances for late payments, since they had no desire to alienate policyholders, but the principle of forfeiture nevertheless weighed heavily on marketing efforts.

Although some American companies had begun by the 1840s to allow a cash surrender value occasionally when a policy lapsed, the problem of policyholder losses from forfeiture was not addressed systematically by the life insurance industry until the 1860s. In 1861, the New York Life established the practice of providing a paid-up policy when the policyholder had made at least two payments on a ten-premium policy. The company did this by converting the value accumulated at the time of forfeiture into payment on a single-premium policy. During the same year, political efforts of the insurance reformer Elizur Wright resulted in a state law establishing a similar practice in Massachusetts. A few years later, in 1866, the Universal Life expanded protection for policyholders by agreeing to return the accumulated value to the policyholder upon surrender of the policy.[12]

When Hugo Wesendonck proposed that the Germania act to modify its forfeiture practices, in 1872, he was following the lead of most other American companies. No doubt he was right when he noted that the Germania's practices placed it at a competitive disadvantage, for most companies had more liberal provisions in their policies. Nevertheless, Wesendonck urged a cautious approach, lest the company be saddled with bad risks. He proposed that nonforfeiture come into effect only after the policy had been in force for two years, and that the agents and physicians prepare special reports to help the officers evaluate the risks involved. He also proposed that an extra premium of .5 to 1 percent, depending upon the payment period of the policy, be paid from the beginning of the agreement. In addition, this nonforfeiture option would not apply in cases of nonpayment of premiums or entry into military service. In these cases, as in the other life insurance policies issued by the Germania, the policies would revert to paid-up policies at a reduced face value. Finally, to protect those insured under the ordinary terms, nonforfeiture policies would be put into a separate dividend class. Wesendonck's proposal, recommended in its entirety by both the Committee on Insurance and the Committee on Agencies, went into effect upon its subsequent approval by the board.[13]

A year and a half later, noting that juries seemed inclined to find against life insurance companies even if the terms of the policy had been violated by the insured, Wesendonck proposed that the board clarify the company's position. At his urging, the board voted to specify in each policy that it became valid only upon payment of the first premium and that the full reserve would be returned in case of suicide resulting from mental derangement. In addition, the board expressed approval of the company's policies, in particular Article XI of the charter providing for forfeiture of all policies in the case of nonpayment of premiums or violation of any other condition of the policy and for retention of prior payments by the company.[14]

Related to the forfeiture issue was the matter of incontestability, that is, limitations on the company's right to question or contest payment of an insurance claim. Like forfeiture, this involved the company's ability to define the terms under which either the policyholder or the heirs would be able to recover the investment that had been made in the policy. Like forfeiture, incontestability only gradually became common in the industry. The first American company to introduce it was the Manhattan Life in 1861, and it did not become widespread until the Equitable added an incontestability clause to its policies in 1879.[15] As other companies followed this example, the Germania also found it necessary to do so. In 1883, the board of directors voted to make policies incontestable after three years for any cause whatsoever, except nonpayment of premiums, wrong age, or violation of the provisions concerning residence, travel, occupations, and employment. Five years later, the board authorized the officers to issue, when necessary, policies which were incontestable from the start. In 1892, the Germania liberalized its incontestability clause, making all policies incontestable as to travel, residence, occupation, suicide, and untrue statements in the application after one year from their date.[16]

In 1873, the Germania joined in a major development in the life insurance industry when the board voted to adopt a tontine plan. The tontine plan is named for its originator, Lorenzo Tonti, who devised it for Louis XIV of France as a way for the state to raise money. People were induced to make perpetual loans to the state, in return for which they received interest; as holders died, their interest payments reverted to surviving members. Thus the longest-surviving member received the interest due to the entire original group.

The tontine was introduced to the American insurance market by Metropolitan Life in 1866, followed by Equitable Life in 1867. It was essentially an endowment for ten, fifteen, or twenty years, during which time the insured paid premiums but received no dividends. If the policy lapsed for nonpayment, the insured received nothing. If the policy lapsed due to death, the beneficiary received the face value of the policy. Those who survived to the end of the endowment period shared the accumulated dividends and forfeited reserves of the entire original group. This version of the tontine was not well received, primarily because of the complete forfeiture of all reserves in lapse cases. In 1871, Equitable introduced a modified version of the tontine which included a surrender value. This very attractive version enhanced Equitable's position in the industry and soon became the best-selling plan for many life insurance companies.[17]

In the spring of 1873, the Germania home office decided to offer a tontine as an option on its whole life and endowment plans. Several months later, the European branch added the tontine to its offerings.[18] Unlike the plans of most life insurance companies, which offered the tontine for ten-, fifteen-, or twenty-year terms, the Germania based its tontine classes on the calendar year in which the annual premiums with annual compound interest at 10 percent would accumulate to the amount of the policy. Claiming to be the only company to do so, the Germania advertised this plan as one that was more equitable than other companies' plans. In the Germania plan, the tontine fund consisted of the dividends and interest accrued on members' policies and of the legal reserve of lapsed policies. In the event of a tontine member's death, the beneficiary received all premiums paid into the fund plus interest.[19]

The following year, 1874, Hermann Rose, the general director of the European branch, proposed a children's tontine which he thought would be no risk but would give the company a handsome commission and a gain in interest. Pleased with this proposal, the Committee on Insurance authorized the European board to organize the tontine. A few months later, the president reported back that the form of children's tontine which the Germania had adopted would not be well received by the German public. Therefore, the board agreed to add survivorship annuities. This modified plan would provide for nonparticipating life insurance policies on members of the children's tontine and for the return of all premiums paid should the child die, as well as policies on the lives of endowers so that payments on the tontine would continue in the event of their death.[20]

Several years later, in 1878, perhaps influenced by their experience in Germany, the Germania decided to establish tontine societies for children in the United States. Membership would cost one hundred dollars in full or eighteen payments of eight dollars each. After eighteen years, the company would pay to each survivor two hundred dollars plus a portion of the paid-up shares lapsed by death and of the installments forfeited by nonpayment. The advantage of this plan, according to Wesendonck, was "that the risk run by the Company in forming such societies would be the guarantee to pay compound interest at the rate of about four % p.a.; while the Company would gain the excess of interest realized by investing at a higher rate."[21]

During the 1880s, in response to popular criticism, several major companies began to market modified-tontine policies. In 1889, the Germania adopted a dividend-tontine policy with surrender value in case of nonpayment. Policyholders could, at the end of the tontine period, turn in their policies for the full amount of the legal reserve guaranteed in the policies. They also had a good chance to receive, at the end of the dividend-tontine period, a large dividend. The dividend tontine was an immediate success, and at the end of the year the Germania introduced it in Europe. By 1891, the dividend tontine was the bulk of the company's business, both in the United States and Europe.[22] (Aggressive marketing of tontines by the large companies, coupled with the speculative nature of many tontine policies, brought the policy into disrepute among reformers and led to a New York State law of 1906 which outlawed the dividend tontine. Without the dividend feature, the tontine was not salable.[23])

In its drive to increase new business, the Germania also experimented in 1875 with an accommodation plan, which was essentially an ordinary life policy with a modified premium schedule. The net rates for the accommodation plan were calculated so that during the first ten years they were exactly one-half of what they would be after ten years for the duration of life. Since the income from premiums during the first ten years would be reduced, there would be less money available for paying losses if mortality were excessive. To guard against this possibility, only men under forty years of age were accepted; certain risks were excluded altogether, and less than first-class risks were charged higher rates. Furthermore, during the first ten years, such a policy carried no surrender value or dividends. Since, despite its risk, this plan promised to attract new business, the Germania took it up with enthusiasm. The accommodation plan worked so well that within a few months after it was adopted, the board voted to expand coverage to include those between the ages of forty and fifty.[24] Three years later, the board made the accommodation plan even more appealing by forming classes of policies issued in a given calendar year and dividing the profits made on each class over a ten-year period, at the end of the period, among those with policies still in force. These profits were applied to a permanent reduction of the premiums.[25]

During the 1880s, the Germania instituted several types of endowment policies. In 1885, it approved a low-value, low-cost endowment with a monthly payment plan. The five hundred-dollar policy was incontestable and nonforfeitable after three years, but it paid no dividends. The same year, the Germania announced a new type of endowment called a bond policy, which could be taken out for one of several time periods in amounts from five hundred dollars to twenty thousand dollars. Like other endowments, these policies were incontestable and nonforfeitable after three years and had a cash surrender value. The bond endowment differed from the company's ordinary endowment policy in its method of dividend distribution. Dividends were to be paid every five years to living policyholders, and dividends on lapsed policies would accrue to those remaining in force. Several years after this plan was first offered, the board modified it by eliminating restrictions on age, travel, residence, and occupation after the policy was three years old. The bond plan quickly became the most popular of the Germania's endowment policies.[26]

In 1896, the Germania decided to offer a children's endowment policy that protected both the applicant and the insured child. If the applicant, usually the father, died during the endowment term, all premiums on the policy were automatically paid up. If the child died during the term, all premiums except that for the first year were returned to the applicant. The policy was also nonforfeitable after three years. All profits from these policies were distributed at the end of the endowment term to holders of policies then in force.[27]

The Germania instituted policy loans in 1890 as one way of responding to a shortage of its preferred type of investments. As a result of this investment difficulty, the Finance Committee authorized its officers to make loans at 6 percent on its policies in amounts not exceeding the regular cash surrender value. Loans were restricted to policies in effect for at least three years, required advance payment of the following year's premiums, and had semiannual interest payments.[28]

The Germania also liberalized its practice of insuring women during the 1890s. The company had always discouraged agents from taking applications on female lives. It made an exception for women married to men insured in the company, but charged an extra premium of 1 percent of the amount insured. In 1895, the company extended this exception to include wives of husbands insured by other life insurance companies. A year and a half later, the company decided to drop the extra premium charged on women's policies.[29]

As a result of consumer demand, the Germania raised the maximum amount it allowed on a single policy. In 1890, the board held a special meeting to discuss an application by a large manufacturer, whose employees were insured by the company. He was applying for a policy of fifty thousand dollars. The Germania's limit at that time of thirty thousand dollars would have forced the manufacturer to look elsewhere for the balance or perhaps even for the whole amount. The board, therefore, voted to raise the limit to fifty thousand dollars, provided that policies for that amount were approved in writing by all three officers and the actuary. The next year a similar situation arose when an applicant refused to take a policy for less than one hundred thousand dollars; the board then voted to raise the upper limit to that amount with the same conditions expressed the year before.[30]

In 1899, some of the Germania's representatives requested that the company offer gold-bond policies as did other companies, such as the Mutual and the Equitable. (These were policies that paid claims with gold bonds rather than cash.) After introducing this type of policy, the Germania conducted a major advertising campaign, with descriptive articles in the insurance press.[31]

Policy offerings became even more important in retaining field personnel after new insurance laws limiting commissions were passed as a result of the Armstrong Committee hearings (see chapter 8). Once rates were controlled, in the public eye the critical difference among insurance companies was the attractiveness of their respective policies. In 1909, the Committee on Insurance reported to the board: "Agents now drift to the Companies known to offer the greatest benefits to the insured at the lowest net cost, and it becomes more and more difficult for a Company with less liberal policies to secure new business and retain business already on its books."[32] As a means of remaining competitive enough to retain its sales staff, the committee decided to "adopt the lower rates of premiums and the higher guaranteed surrender values of the Mutual Benefit," which was the life insurance company with the most attractive terms.[33] Some years later, this step was hailed as "an important milestone in the Company's career[:] . . . its adoption of attractive new policies, embodying all competitive new features."[34]

Investment Practices

From industrial insurance, tontines, endowments, and other policies, the Germania in the 1880s and 1890s received a constantly growing pool of premium money that had to be invested prudently if the company were to meet its future obligations. During its first five years, the company had invested mainly in U.S. government securities and in mortgages, as noted in chapter 2. In 1868, the Finance Committee began to invest in local government bonds, as the board of directors had recommended some time earlier. In July the committee authorized purchase of up to fifty thousand dollars' worth of 6 percent construction bonds of the County of New York for a new courthouse (the so-called Tweed courthouse, which still stands in Manhattan today and whose construction lined the pockets of many local contractors and politicians). A week later, however, the Finance Committee substituted purchase of Brooklyn Water Loan Bonds, and a year later, the committee authorized the purchase of $125,000 worth of New York and Brooklyn city bonds. The committee still looked positively on U.S. government securities, and in 1869 authorized the officers to buy them if they saw favorable opportunity.[35]

In addition, the company continued to invest in mortgages as long as they were profitable. During the economic hard times of the 1870s, however, the Germania and many other investors were sometimes unable to find attractive mortgages, for the decline in new construction and monetary deflation forced mortgage interest rates continually down. In 1873, for example, the officers reported to the Finance Committee that they had received many applications for bond and mortgage loans but in the existing state of financial affairs they would not recommend granting them. The soundness of this conservative approach to investment became evident in 1876 when the company was forced to foreclose on a number of properties. In order to dispose of some of these properties, the officers had to grant new buyers loans for part of the purchase money. In February 1877, the Finance Committee acknowledged the difficulty of finding good applications for mortgage loans despite declining interest rates and opted for additional investment in U.S. government securities. A year later, the committee authorized another major purchase of U.S. securities because it saw no prospect of good mortgages.[36]

With mortgage rates dropping, holders of outstanding mortgages began to request interest-rate reductions. During the summer of 1877, the Finance Committee received a number of applications for the reduction of interest on outstanding mortgages. At that time, the committee declined to reduce the interest. Additional applications for interest reduction continued to come in, with intimations that the applicants would pay off their mortgages if their requests were denied. The company's officers estimated that at least $275,000 of mortgages had been paid off because the Finance Committee had refused to renegotiate a lower interest rate. In October, the committee recognized that it had little choice but to begin to grant interest reductions.[37] This practice continued through 1880.

In the fall of 1880, the Finance Committee began to discuss investment options other than mortgages. A board member proposed the purchase of New York Central and Hudson River Railroad stock, but no decision was made. Discussions on this topic continued until February 1881, when the committee authorized the purchase of one hundred thousand dollars' worth of New York, Lake Erie and Western Railroad Company bonds, pending legal opinion. Although no action was taken, seven months later, in July, the committee reauthorized the purchase of these bonds (again no action was taken).[38] As a result, the Germania's investment portfolio in 1880 still resembled that of twenty years earlier: a mix of mortgages and government securities. The major difference between the situation in 1880 as opposed to 1860 was the much higher proportion of mortgages to securities, about three to one.

The first diversification of the portfolio occurred in 1882, when the Finance Committee reopened discussions about investing in railroad securities, although the officers questioned whether New York law allowed such investments. These discussions grew out of attempts by the committee during the previous year to find investment opportunities that were more promising than the still-depressed government securities and mortgage markets. In April 1883, Wesendonck lobbied the Albany legislature on the company's behalf for a change in the state insurance law regarding investments.[39] Several weeks later, he reported that passage of a new state law meant the company could begin investing in railroad bonds. The Finance Committee chose five bond issues and began purchasing. By 1897, 16 percent of all invested assets and 87 percent of all investments in stocks and bonds were in railroad securities.[40]

Home-Office Building

In March 1869 the Germania moved from its original headquarters, at 90 Broadway, into larger rented space at 293 and 295 Broadway. The economic depression of the 1870s that reduced the Germania's opportunities for investments in mortgages also opened the way for the company to consider buying its own office building at a good price. With real-estate values depressed, it was an appropriate time to move the company out of its old quarters and into offices that more suitably expressed the hard-won corporate success of the past two decades. In February 1872, even before the depression hit, Wesendonck had called a meeting of the Finance Committee to discuss bidding at an auction of a nearby office building. The committee's lack of support caused the effort to die, and instead the committee rented larger quarters at 287 Broadway, at Reade Street.[41]

Wesendonck persisted, however, and in 1876 again proposed that the company buy its own offices. He observed to the Finance Committee that the depressed value of real estate offered an opportunity "to acquire a desirable property . . . on terms which would even offset a possible loss on the lease of the present offices."[42] Concerned that such an opportunity might require immediate action, he asked the board to authorize the Finance Committee to act according to its best judgment, if necessary, and the board formally agreed.[43]

Early in 1882, the company began to look for an office building both for its own use and as an investment. After considering several sites, the company learned that the building on the corner of Cedar and Nassau streets owned by the bankrupt Continental Life was to be auctioned off. With rent rolls of $43,000 and expenses of $13,000, the building produced a net profit of $30,000. Although the Finance Committee was willing to go as high as $510,000, it was able to make a successful bid at $462,500. Two years later, in the spring of 1884, the Germania moved into its own office building at 20 Nassau Street.[44]

Although Wesendonck had stressed the investment side of the new building, he might also have been considering the need for additional space for the growing company. By 1875, the Germania home office on 287 Broadway housed a staff of eighteen to twenty people, organized in two departments, the Actuarial Department and the Cashier and Mortgage Department. By 1896 the number of staff members would rise to about forty-five, including managers, and the staff was still organized in two departments. At the Nassau Street building, the main-floor office consisted of one large room, about fifty by one hundred feet, subdivided into offices for the president, vice president, and medical examiner, with a cashier's office partitioned off with wire. An iron spiral staircase gave access to the second floor, where the Actuarial Department occupied three rooms of about fifteen by twenty feet each. Sometime around 1900, the actuarial space was enlarged into one large office about fifty by seventy-five feet, connected with the main office on the first floor by a new wooden staircase.[45]

In 1886, the company took up the idea of purchasing a building as headquarters for its agency in St. Paul, Minnesota. In December, Wesendonck sent the company's mortgage specialist, Cornelius Doremus, on a trip to inspect possible building sites in the city. After several consultations on various possibilities, Doremus purchased a lot on the corner of Fourth and Minnesota for some seventy-five thousand dollars upon which the company erected an eight-story building at a cost of about seven hundred thousand dollars.[46] In an address he gave fifteen years later, when he was president of the Germania, Doremus explained that the new building was intended to make the company popular in the Northwest, provide an agency headquarters, and be an investment for the company funds. The plan succeeded admirably in its first two goals, but with regard to the third, he noted with considerable understatement, "had not yet proved to be the success as an investment which was hoped for."[47] The building was completed in time to enter the real-estate market during a major economic downturn, the panic of 1893. By 1896, the situation was disastrous. Several spaces, including the most desirable office, were vacant, and many tenants were in arrears.[48] Even with the return of national prosperity, the company found it necessary to offer low rents to attract tenants to the building, which was not fully rented out until 1899. By 1901, however, the building's promise was great enough to warrant adding two additional stories, rented in advance for ten years. The one hundred thousand-dollar cost of the additional floors and of a major renovation of the existing structure was wholly written off, to ensure that "for all time a fair rate of interest on that particular investment [would] be realized."[49]

Given the poor timing of the St. Paul building's entry into the market, it was perhaps fortunate that the Finance Committee had earlier refused a suggestion by Wesendonck to construct an office building in Buffalo. In 1888 he had tried hard to persuade the committee of the investment's soundness, only to be met with the reply that the building would involve laying out too much money because of the large size of the lot, and that the committee did not want to add to the company's real-estate holdings at that time. When Wesendonck proposed purchase of a building lot in Milwaukee, the committee again refused.[50]

Despite the rebuffs he suffered at the hands of the Finance Committee, as the 1890s began, Wesendonck must have felt sanguine about the Germania's fiscal health and its prospects. Business was growing, the company was profitable, and management had steered safely through the depressed 1870s. Equally important, the Germania had sent up a new shoot in Europe. Indeed, the German operation of the

European branch became an immediate success and contributed significantly to the company's cash flow during the tough 1870s. The European managers were not content to be a sideshow, however, and pushed aggressively for more business and more control over their operation. Increasingly during the 1880s and the 1890s, Wesendonck and his colleagues in New York found themselves dealing with pressing matters on the other side of the Atlantic.

7

Consolidation in Europe

While the home office struggled with economic hard times during the 1870s and then with reorganizing the agency system, introducing new kinds of policies, and realigning its investment portfolio, the European branch enjoyed steady and impressive growth. The branch had its greatest success in Germany, where it seemed destined to become a permanent fixture, barring perhaps a war between Germany and the United States—an unlikely event, it must have seemed. One sign of the branch's rapidly growing European roots was the desire of the Berlin agency to purchase its own office building. Another was the urge to change the home office's operating practices in certain aspects of insurance to stay abreast of European competitors. To meet competition during the early 1880s, for example, the European branch began to insure women at a premium surcharge below that usually imposed in the United States.[1]

The Germania's consolidation within Europe occurred when other American insurance companies were also enjoying remarkable success in foreign markets. By the 1880s, companies such as New York Life, the Equitable, and Mutual Life of New York, which had followed the Germania to Europe, were doing an increasing portion of their total business abroad. In 1870, for example, American life insurance firms had about $2 billion worth of policies in effect, only $1.921 million of which (.10 percent) was from non-Canadian foreign sales. In 1875, during the middle of the depression in the United States, the total amount of insurance in force actually fell, to $1.922 billion, while the amount from non-Canadian foreign policies rose to $6.272 million, or .33 percent of the total. Insurance written in the United States continued to fall through 1880, while non-Canadian foreign policies in force rose, to .60 percent of the total amount of insurance in force. By 1885, when total American-written insurance had risen to $2.3 billion worth, non-Canadian foreign policies had grown to $192.985 million worth, or 8.39 percent of the total amount of insurance in force. By 1890 the proportion reached 11.01 percent of the $4.049 billion worth of insurance in effect through U.S. companies, and in 1895 it rose to its all-time peak of 11.15 percent.[2]

Although the Germania experienced a similar pattern of business during this period, its European business was a significantly higher proportion of the total than for other American companies. As noted in table 3, in 1870 the European branch was responsible for about 6 percent of the company's total business, a proportion that rose to over 28 percent in 1880, over 34 percent in 1885, more than 42 percent in 1890, and peaked at 48.16 in 1896. The European branch saw its total amount of insurance in force increase year by year, in contrast with the domestic American part of the company, which saw significant declines in insurance in force between 1870 and 1880. By 1900 the European branch was virtually as large as the domestic part of the company, and historical rates of growth in the two markets suggested it would soon surpass the American.

TABLE 3

Germania Life Insurance Company Growth in Life Insurance in Force from 1870 to 1910

Year	Total Face Amount Life Insurance in Force	Face Amount Life Insurance in U.S.	Face Amount Life Insurance in Europe	European Insurance as a Percentage of Total
1870	$32,053,962	$30,132,473	$ 1,921,489	5.99
1875	34,421,675	28,150,121	6,271,554	18.22
1880	33,885,522	24,388,226	9,497,296	28.03
1885	39,979,985	26,147,307	13,832,678	34.60
1890	57,322,243	32,751,464	24,570,779	42.86
1895	69,025,662	36,369,093	32,656,569	47.31
1900	82,542,059	43,394,150	39,147,909	47.43
1905	110,979,307	63,386,191	47,593,116	42.88
1910	127,503,533	69,462,127	58,041,406	45.52

Source: Exhibit of Policies, 1860–1914, The Guardian Life Insurance Company archives

For much of this period, the European business was directed by Hermann Rose, who worked amicably with President Wesendonck, even when the two did not agree. In 1889 Hermann Rose retired as general director and became general attorney. His third cousin, Heinrich Rose, a subdirector since 1878, was, at his cousin's request and by unanimous consent, appointed general director of the European branch.[3] He would hold that position for the remaining years before World War I, a period when changes in the German insurance market and pressures from the imperial government worked to push the European branch along different paths than its home office.

When Hugo Wesendonck retired in 1897, a powerful unifying force in the company disappeared, and the European operation increasingly went its own way. Thus the period of consolidation of the European operation, during the closing decades of the century, witnessed growing friction between the parent firm in America and its powerful offspring in Germany.

Branch-Office Building

In 1875, in discussions about purchasing its own office building in Berlin, the European branch stressed the positive impact that it would have on sales: "The public would not fear that the Company would leave the German market, as some other firms have done recently. Also, the acquisition of property would give the public more reason to have confidence in the Company." The European branch used a similar justification for preferring to purchase the building with cash in full, rather than with a noncancelable mortgage. Full purchase would "make a good impression," the office noted, although a mortgage "would not hurt" the company's reputation.[4]

The home office temporarily declined to authorize any real-estate purchase because the New York State superintendent of insurance expressed doubts about the legality of such an investment. The Finance Committee therefore pursued with its legal counsel the possibility of a special legislative act allowing the company to buy a building in Europe for its own use. Within a few months, it secured state legislation allowing corporations to purchase real estate in foreign countries for office purposes.[5]

While these negotiations were taking place and success seemed likely, the board authorized the European branch, with the consent of the Prussian government, to make this purchase. Several weeks later, Hermann Rose requested special power from the board authorizing him to complete the purchase of a property on Leipziger Strasse and Leipziger Platz. The building chosen by the European branch was one consistent with its intention of using real estate to enhance the market position of the Germania. The building housed the English and Turkish embassies, and, after purchase, space was rented to the court marshall's office for the Superior Court Ministry.[6]

In 1902, the Germania sold its building in Berlin at a substantial profit. Shortly afterward, the board of directors in New York authorized the European board to acquire another office building in Berlin.[7] Within three months, the Berlin office bought a bank building on Behren Strasse opposite the prestigious Deutsche Bank for less than half of the selling price of the old building. The following year, the board of directors consented to the purchase proposed by the European board of an office building in Vienna.[8]

Points of Conflict

Occasionally, the European branch requested authority to modify company practice in order to offer to its policyholders the same benefits offered by competing German companies. One such innovation was the making of loans on policies. Although the home office refused to allow policy loans through 1877, the European branch pursued the question and began to link it with the then-high rate of lapses. In October, the European branch asserted that it was necessary to allow borrowing on policies in order to encourage policyholders to revitalize their lapsed policies.[9] Convinced by this argument, the board of directors agreed to allow third-party loans. The company would pay a 1 percent commission to banks that loaned to policyholders who wanted to use their policies as collateral.[10] After several years of arranging loans on the company's policies through banks, the European branch requested authority from the home office in 1883 to make these loans directly. In this way the company would not only receive the interest paid on the loans but would also save the 1 percent commission it paid the lending banks. The board agreed to authorize such loans for an amount not exceeding 90 percent of the cash-surrender value. At the urging of the officers of the European branch, the board later increased the amount of loans to the entire cash-surrender value.[11]

During the early 1870s, the home office and the European branch often contended over the issue of policyholder dividends: their size and their method of distribution. On both sides of the Atlantic, the company emphasized dividends as a means of attracting new business, especially from customers who conceived of life insurance as a form of investment. In planning strategies for coping with the economic problems of the 1870s, officers of the company usually took into account anticipated changes in the company's dividend rates. In 1870, for example, Wesendonck argued against "forcing the business" before an increased dividend anticipated for the year 1872, which he thought would make an increase of business easier.[12]

Since paying its first dividend in 1865, the Germania had used a percentage method for calculating the amount; that is, all policyholders received a share of the surplus based on a uniform percentage of the premiums that they had paid. In 1870, the company changed the method of calculating its policyholder dividends to the contribution plan. During the 1860s, many life insurance companies, beginning with Mutual of New York, started to adopt the contribution plan, in which the dividend of each policyholder was calculated at a rate proportional to his contribution to the company's surplus.[13] This method took into account the type and face value of the policy, premiums paid, and the company's experience with the various policies during the dividend period.

At its meeting on 12 January 1870, the board of directors discussed the merits of the contribution plan. Wesendonck declared that the proposed change in the method of calculating dividends had a "great importance" and deserved thorough deliberation. He then embarked on what the minutes call "an exhaustive exposition and comparison" of the two systems.[14] In the ensuing discussion, the board considered several factors, including a recommendation made by Elizur Wright (1804–1885), one of the great names in the history of American life insurance. For forty years, first as Massachusetts commissioner for insurance and later as consulting actuary, Wright attacked what he saw as abuses of trust and inefficiencies of administration on the part of life insurance companies, making many friends and enemies in the process. Wright's comments, which the board had in written form, suggested that the traditional percentage plan was arbitrary and unjust to policyholders, and did not fit with his generally progressive views on policyholder rights and company responsibilities.

The special board in Berlin had submitted a formal protest, seconded by telegrams and letters from Hermann Rose and individual directors. The special board predicted that the new plan would be "fatal" to the European business and would expose the company to public attacks for "swindling." It would provoke investigations impugning the honesty of the company, the board thought, and might even jeopardize the European licenses.[15] Wesendonck disagreed. While allowing that the change might cause a temporary check on business, he argued that a proper explanation of the system would resolve any problems. In a conciliatory gesture, he offered to postpone introducing the change until the 1872 dividend.[16] The board, on its part, observing that the contribution plan had been successfully adopted by the most prominent life insurance companies, and acting despite serious objections by the European Board in Berlin, voted unanimously to adopt the new plan.[17]

In addition to the disagreement over the method of distributing dividends, there were also conflicts over the amount of the annual dividend. In 1872, the directors of the European branch became extremely concerned when they were informed that the dividend for 1873 would be very low. In a special report to the board of directors, the Berlin office requested an increase in dividends for German policyholders. Fearful of an outcry on account of the smallness of the dividend, the European directors predicted that the effect would be ruinous. Indeed, they thought that the gains in reducing mortality among policyholders in Germany justified an *increase* in dividends on German policies.[18]

The request of the European branch was considered at length first by the Committee on Agencies and then by the board of directors. Both groups appreciated the concerns of the European directors but agreed that the company could not raise the dividends. "It cannot be doubted," the board resolved, "that the smallness of the Company's dividend in 1873 will create great dissatisfaction in Germany as well as in the United States among those who may not appreciate the highly conservative ground taken by the Company." The board declared that it would not be lawful to divide the company's surplus unequally between American and German policyholders, without totally separating the German branch from the general business, and that such a separation would be neither wise nor convenient, "and would produce, owing to the large expenses in Germany, a result fatal to the German business."[19]

Dissatisfied with this decision, the European branch asked for further clarifications. In the meantime, it decided to inform the general agents of the matter and to have them inform the policyholders. In an effort to avoid the predicted disaster, they also decided that the annual report should contain as little as possible about the dividend.[20]

At the end of the year, perhaps as a result of this conflict, the board of directors voted to divide the field into three dividend classes, northern United States, southern United States, and Europe. The classes were distinguished according to variations in mortality rates across geographical regions, as well as differences in local taxes and license fees. When announcing the three-class system, the board observed that sanitary conditions differed among the northern and southern states and Europe. These very substantial differences might well continue into the future, the board noted, and should be taken into account in the company's contribution plan. The same was true of the various license fees and taxes that the company paid in the United States and abroad. The only exception the board saw was the New York City tax on the capital of the company.[21]

Implementation of the three-class dividend system resolved the last major point of contention between the home office and Berlin, and for the next decade and a half the two sides of the Atlantic apparently worked in harmony. This is a reasonable inference based on the lack of any significant controversies in the surviving documentation from the period. Yet the fundamental tension between the two operations remained, to reemerge again in the 1890s, as the European share of the Germania's total business grew. In 1891 it exceeded 40 percent, in 1900, 46 percent. Wesendonck observed to the board that the increasing European business was requiring more frequent trips to Berlin. In 1894, he requested blanket authority to visit Berlin whenever he thought it necessary.[22]

Foreign Regulation

One of the issues that required the home office's urgent attention during this period was the growing weight of legal requirements and regulations that European governments were placing on all insurance companies. German insurance companies did not welcome foreign competition, and began asking the German state governments to take action. The first move came in 1891, at a time when the wave of American business in Germany was moving to its crest. German and Austrian insurance companies began to attack American companies through the press. The government of Prussia, which was by far the largest German state, started to impose restrictions on foreign companies, beginning with requirements that they hold investments in German government bonds, followed by regulations on tontine policies in 1892. A year later, the Prussian government revoked the licenses of both Mutual of New York and New York Life.[23]

These events received national attention when President Grover Cleveland linked them and other restrictions on American life insurance companies with similar curbs on American food exporters. The late nineteenth century saw a sharp rise in the world supply of foodstuffs and growing competition among major agricultural product-exporting nations. American products began to encounter both price competition and greater tariff barriers, as Germany and some other European nations tried to protect their own farmers. Americans such as President Cleveland saw the antitrade measures and the moves against American insurance companies as part of a wider attack on American exporters. In his state of the union message of 1895, the president warned that the continuation of "unfair discrimination" and "vexatious hindrances to the enjoyment of our share of the legitimate advantages" of proper trade relations "would meet retaliation."[24]

In the literature and speeches of its day, this controversy appeared as a contest of free trade against unfair protection (although the United States had been protectionist for most of its history up to then).[25] It is possible that another element was also at work which prompted the German state governments to take action against American insurance companies. During the late nineteenth century, Germany, like England and the United States, was becoming a major industrial power. Like them, it was experiencing rapid changes in society and in the nature of productive work. The growth of an urban industrial working class stimulated the rise of political parties such as the Social Democrats who favored a socialist outlook. Unique among the three nations, Germany chose to co-opt the burgeoning labor movement by offering reforms, including state-supported unemployment and life insurance. It was the hope of Chancellor Bismarck and others on the right, as well as many moderates, that this safety net for workers would foster social stability and forestall the rise of both liberal and radical political parties.[26] Although the state-supported insurance program had a life of its own, separate from the kinds of insurance purchased by the prosperous burgers with whom the Germania dealt, its existence may have sensitized the state bureaucrats to the whole issue of insurance. In their minds it may have seemed connected with matters of social stability, in a way that would have seemed odd to American or English legislators or administrators, accounting for the increasingly stringent regulation, first by Prussia, and later by the Berlin central government.

In all this, the identity of a firm as foreign, as non-German, was crucial, which may explain why the Germania suffered so little at the hands of the German regulators. A writer in the 7 December 1895 issue of *The Weekly Underwriter* explained the Germania's apparent immunity from the new regulatory stance. The company was able to place itself in compliance with the new tontine regulations by having its books remodeled by German experts, without actually changing the substance of the tontine offerings. But the most revealing comment of all was the allegation that the Prussian government did not consider the Germania a foreign company. "The idea in Berlin is that the company started in New York as a German organization, and still continues nominally to do business in the United States, but that its chief business is done from the office in Berlin."[27] The view received credence from the existence of the Germania's special board in Berlin, composed of well-known Germans.

From 1898, as the Prussian government escalated its demands for larger security deposits from foreign insurance companies, the Germania's home office gradually conferred greater autonomy on the Berlin office. In the fall of that year, the board authorized more discretion to the European board in purchasing securities and making the required deposits.[28] In 1901, a new insurance law made regulation and supervision a function of the German Empire rather than of the individual states as it had been. In addition, the law required the deposit of securities equal to the entire reserve.[29] In order to comply with these requirements, the home office sent the necessary funds to the Berlin office for investment in German securities. Here the company encountered a serious problem, for it calculated its rates on the assumption of a 3.5 percent annual return on new-business investments, whereas the German securities it now had to purchase returned only 3 percent.[30]

The European board, keenly aware of this, thought it could resolve the problem by investing in bonds and mortgages on real estate in German cities (which evidently offered a higher return than securities). The following year the board of directors amended the company's bylaws to allow the Berlin office to make such investments.[31] By 1906 the special directors in Berlin had invested some thirty million marks in Germany. In 1907 the board of directors authorized Berlin to make mortgage loans in Vienna and several Swiss cities.[32]

Attempts to Expand

Throughout the 1880s and 1890s, the European branch continually sought to expand its geographic territory. In 1885, it attempted unsuccessfully to establish agencies in Scandinavia.[33] In 1886, the European board decided to reestablish an agency in Austria with headquarters in Vienna, and to seek admission to Switzerland.[34] In order to do so, the Germania was required to deposit with each government securities of its country. Three years later, the board authorized the European branch to extend into Hungary.[35] In 1897, the European board suggested that the Germania extend its business into the South African Republic, where three major American companies—the Equitable, Mutual of New York, and New York Life—were already well established. Action was deferred until the company could gather further information about the salubrity of the climate, the death rate, the business and social conditions, and the efficiency of the medical profession in South Africa. At two subsequent meetings, the company finally concluded that conditions were not favorable for such a venture.[36]

Although the reasons proffered were reasonable, they may have masked a reluctance on the company's part to commit itself at a time when it was undergoing a major change; on 27 January 1897, Hugo Wesendonck announced to the board of directors that he would step down as president at the end of the year.[37]

Hugo Wesendonck Retires

By the time of his retirement in 1897, Hugo Wesendonck had become the Germania's patriarch. His full white beard and deep, resonant voice, complemented by impeccable dress, lent him an air of indisputable gravity and authority. One employee, looking back to Wesendonck's last two years, described him as "benign and venerable," a man viewed "with respect (I might say awe) and admiration. . . . One instinctively felt himself in the presence of a person of distinction, a squire as it were—a courtly gentleman of culture and nobility."[38]

Although Wesendonck's retirement moved him out of the daily business of the company, he was not forgotten. In December 1899, on the fiftieth anniversary of his arrival in the United States, the home office staff gave him a floral tribute, which he answered with a personal letter. Each clerk received an engraved copy of this letter written in Spencerian penmanship:

New York, December 1899

To the Assistants of "The Germania Life Insurance Co."

Gentlemen:
    Thanks, many thanks, for the beautiful flowers which you sent me on the 5th inst.—the 50th anniversary of my arrival in this country.
    May you be happy at all times, now and hereafter, and be convinced that we all appreciate the conscientious labor of even the youngest of you.

Yours sincerely,
[signed] H. Wesendonck

Hugo Wesendonck died on 19 December 1900. The Germania's officers and home office staff attended the funeral service at Liederkranz Hall on Fifty-Eighth Street in Manhattan and the interment at Greenwood Cemetery in Brooklyn. The weather was very cold, and since the ride to the cemetery was a long one in those days before the automobile, each clerk received a package of three sandwiches and a small flask.[39]

Wesendonck was not the first of the company's founders to leave the scene, but he was the most important. Even in the rather scanty historical sources that survive, his mark is strong and frequent, whether in sales, investment, or management. If he did not always have his way with this committee or that, it may be because he refused to run against the collegiality that marked the company's first four decades. By working within consensus, he was able to avoid or ameliorate the personality conflicts that emerged after his retirement. He also preserved thereby the sense that the company was an enterprise of the whole German-American community, which may have defused whatever criticism of Wesendonck existed both within and without the company. He possessed unassailable personal integrity; whatever disagreements his colleagues had with him could have been argued out only on the merits of the cases, not on grounds of self-aggrandizement or desire for power. It was a management style well suited to a small company that aimed at an affluent, educated, and extremely respectable clientele.

[8]

New Leadership, New Challenges

Hugo Wesendonck's retirement did not seem to entail any major change in the Germania's operations, for his successor, Cornelius Doremus, was another founding member of the company. An 1860 graduate of the New York Free Academy (later City College of New York), Doremus began working with the Germania, from its founding, as an office boy. He quickly rose to important positions and eventually became secretary, responsible for much of the company's internal organization. In addition, he became involved in financial affairs, and was credited by a later company president, Carl Heye, with the major share of the Germania's fine investment performance during the 1890s.[1]

The accession of Doremus was one part of the management change that occurred as members of the founding generation began to leave the scene. Frederick Schwendler, whom Carl Heye called the financial genius of the company, died on 7 June 1890. Schwendler was "a man of high principles and congenial manner, and, although leading a retired life, was well known in German American circles," according to his obituary in the *New York Tribune*. He was born in Frankfurt and came to the United States during the 1850s. After some "mercantile pursuits," the obituary continues, "in 1860 he founded with Hugo Wesendonck the Germania Life Insurance Company, and had been its vice president ever since, attending to the financial affairs of the company with rare success."[2]

The void in leadership created by the departure of Schwendler and Wesendonck gave Cornelius Doremus both a great deal of latitude in running the company and a host of problems associated with the lack of a generally acknowledged central figure like Wesendonck. Shortly after he assumed office, friction among the officers flared into the open in a way that had been unthinkable during the Wesendonck years. In addition, the Berlin office continued to press for more control over its affairs, which Doremus resisted with great difficulty. During his tenure, the Germania and the other life insurance companies were held up to public scrutiny by the Armstrong Committee, and before this exposé unfolded, the Germania had to fend off a hostile takeover bid. In addition, Doremus himself faced a direct challenge from dissident members of the board. The Doremus years began with a period of siege for the company, although the situation improved markedly after 1905.

Takeover Attempt

In 1901, rumors of several years' standing came to a head, rumors that a group of investors was attempting to gain control of four small New York life insurance companies, including the Germania, by purchasing a majority of their stock. According to *The Chronicle*, "Figures that would be considered exorbitant, in the average daily business proposition, have been freely offered, under various guises, and as freely declined."[3] Who the principals in this attempt were is not known, but it is possible to speculate on the identity of the stockholders they were wooing. When the company was founded, the two Wesendonck brothers secured the largest single block of shares, although evidently not a majority interest. Other officers of the company also bought stock, and their shares along with the Wesendoncks' might have been enough to make any takeover bid hopeless. But during the 1890s some of these original stockholders had died, and the stock had passed to their heirs, who would not have had the same personal attachment to the company. They were the most likely targets of a takeover bid, since their blocks of stock were probably substantial.

Once the officers and directors lost voting control over the stock, the company was vulnerable. Its appeal as a takeover target is not hard to see, for as a conservatively managed corporation its real value was probably far higher than its stock dividends would suggest. The original stock capitalization had been only two hundred thousand dollars, a figure dwarfed by the growth of the company's business and investments since 1860. The stock was thus grossly undervalued as an expression of the company's profitability, and would have yielded much higher returns under less conservative management by adding to capitalization through transferring profits into the capital account. Once the new managers had gotten control of the company, they could benefit from this and perhaps other methods of increasing the company's return to them. Similar practices had been applied to other insurance companies, not only by takeover groups but by the original managers themselves.

In casting about for a strategy of defending "the management under which [the Germania] had been so very successful" during the four decades of its history, President Doremus hit upon the idea of extending voting rights to policyholders.[4] Through such a partial mutualization, the management would increase the number of voters beyond the ability of any takeover group to control. Since the policyholders would tend to vote by proxy, not in person, the officers would through the proxies exercise an effective control over the vote. Moreover, stockholders, being self-conscious investors and often persons of acumen in business affairs, were much more difficult to control than the mass of policyholders, most of whom had no business experience at all. These elements working in favor of control by a small group of managers made mutualization appealing to other insurance companies around the turn of the century. Thus the Germania, under the impetus of the takeover bid, moved toward mutualization at the same time as many other American insurance companies.

The board of directors, on its part, had in previous years considered bringing policyholders more closely into the direction of the company. During the 1870s, the Germania had begun to encounter difficulties in filling seats on the board. In 1879, with several seats vacant, Wesendonck suggested that the board consider asking the state legislature to authorize a reduction of the number of directors, or to sanction the selection of some of them from among the policyholders. The board established a committee with power to decide with the officers on necessary changes and to initiate appropriate action.[5]

A year and a half later, in June 1881, the legislature passed a law authorizing the reduction of the number of directors of life insurance companies. The board immediately authorized the officers to begin the required action for reducing the number of directors from thirty to twenty, the reduction to be made as natural vacancies occurred.[6] For the next few years, vacancies went unfilled, until only twenty members remained on the board in 1890. The board again considered legally reducing its size. At a special meeting held for that purpose in April 1890, the board voted to amend the bylaws to reduce its size from thirty to twenty seats.[7] As it considered this reduction, the board also discussed increasing the pool of those eligible for election as directors by including not only stockholders but also policyholders. In 1883 the board voted to ask the New York State legislature for permission to change the company's charter to allow the election as directors of policyholders whose lives were insured by the Germania for not less than five thousand dollars. Evidently, no action was taken, since the board passed the same resolution several years later.[8]

No such lack of decisiveness encumbered the board in 1901, as it faced a possible takeover. Doremus proposed that policyholders receive one vote for each hundred dollars of reserve attributable to their policies. He claimed this was the first time that the participation of policyholders in an insurance company's direction had been arranged according to their degree of contribution to the company. He also revived the earlier suggestion of permitting policyholders to sit on the board; the only requirement would be to have a Germania life policy in force with at least five hundred dollars of reserve funds attributable to it.[9] Doremus predicted that these two changes would reduce the control of stockholders over the board and prevent a takeover. In fact, during the next few years, on the average about thirteen thousand of the Germania's approximately sixty-three thousand policyholders voted by proxy in elections to the board.

The board immediately approved both amendments to the charter. Rumors of an attempted takeover persisted for about another year, before petering out, and prompted Doremus to issue a formal statement. "I wish to assure the public," he announced, "that all efforts to buy the control of the Germania Life have been and will continue to be futile." The company, he said, having received and refused many offers, remained in the hands of a management which traced its "line of succession" to the organizers of the company in 1860. Accordingly, present and future policyholders could "rely in all confidence" on the continuation of the practices and personnel that had "brought the company to its present position of unsurpassed financial strength."[10] This statement seems to have ended the matter.

Internal Strife

By the spring of 1902 the takeover threat had disappeared, and the Germania management suffered a breakdown that had begun to appear several years earlier. In fairness to Doremus it should be noted that Wesendonck himself had commented during the early 1890s about problems in the working relationships among the officers of the company. Wesendonck once explained to the Committee on Agencies that heads of departments were in the habit of acting without consulting the other officers. Attempts to solve the problem through the introduction of regular officers' meetings had failed, he noted. Wesendonck therefore proposed, and the board agreed to, the establishment of an advisory committee, chaired by a board member, which would meet monthly to consider appointments and all other matters relating to agency managers, physicians, and any other business brought by the officers or chair.[11] The new committee may have resolved the problem, although Wesendonck's personal authority must also have helped. After the president's retirement, the tendencies toward fragmentation reappeared.

The complete breakdown of working relations threatened the company's integrity. The officers, lacking any formal provision for handling such an impasse, asked advice from the Nominating Committee that had been instituted to smooth the process of electing directors to the board. After several informal meetings, the committee declared that the dissensions among the officers were potentially detrimental to the company and had to be resolved in some way. The committee thereupon asked the board of directors to appoint a committee "not only to inquire into the details of the management by the Officers, but to control their actions as far as seems desirable, and to act as counsellors and umpire when friction is threatened."[12] This committee was to relieve the board from having to deal with the internal conflict and to allow problems to be resolved privately.

Several weeks later, the board met to consider the proposal to create a new executive committee or to enlarge the powers of the existing Nominating Committee. Opting for the latter, the board voted to add to the duties of the Nominating Committee the "general supervision over the administration of the Company's business, and . . . [the] power to summon the Officers of the Company for such information regarding the affairs of the Company as it may require."[13] In particular, the committee was empowered to approve all employment decisions, to adjudicate differences between officers, to handle the proxies of policyholders, to require the president to call meetings of the board of directors, and to make referrals to the various committees.

Although the committee and the board had avoided direct accusations in considering the antagonism between officers, by the end of the year a challenge to the presidency of Cornelius Doremus had solidified. At the annual meeting for the election of officers held in December 1902, the Nominating Committee, adhering to its usual custom, recommended the reelection of all officers. For the first time in the history of the Germania, there was opposition to the nomination for president. The opposing minority was led by Carl Schurz, then in his seventies, a Forty-Eighter of Wesendonck's generation, former U.S. Secretary of the Interior, former U.S. minister to Spain, and more recently editor of the *New York Evening Post* and chief editorial writer of *Harper's* magazine. He was perhaps the major public figure in the German-American community. Allied with Schurz in the minority on the board of directors was William Schramm, a director since 1894, and related to Hugo Wesendonck by marriage.

At the December board meeting Schurz presented the minority report, which he prefaced with the note that he had become a member of the board (in 1892) at the request of his friend Hugo Wesendonck, who had thought that Schurz's name would add weight to the board of directors. Schurz went on to say that he bore no ill feeling toward Doremus, whom he had seldom met outside of company business. However, as a result of the various matters the Nominating Committee had considered over the past year, he, Schurz, and his friend Mr. William Schramm felt compelled to make the report denouncing Doremus.[14]

Although Schurz did not elaborate on the reasons that had led him and Schramm to take this weighty action, there is little doubt the issue was Doremus's personal integrity. In a letter of 8 June 1902, to Hermann Rose, Max Wesendonck accused Doremus of violating the by-laws by taking a share of real-estate commissions on sales in Germany. Wesendonck said that Doremus's actions made him sorry for the company, but that he could not retire in protest since he needed the money. In a letter of the same date to another director, Thomas Achelis, Wesendonck declared that Doremus had been "disloyal" to him. Doremus had forced his own family to receive his mistress and had taken his son to a house of ill repute in Butte (Frederic S. Doremus was manager of the Helena, Montana, agency). The matter had become serious, Wesendonck went on, and Schurz and Schramm were threatening to quit at the end of the year, which would create a bad impression of the company in Germany.

The charges suggest that Doremus was using his newly acquired office for his own purposes, much as was being done at other life insurance companies of the time. In comparison to the activities of executives of the large firms, Doremus's offenses seem minor, but they involved matters of personal honor in the German-American community and were also capable of being used by anyone who wanted to take control of the Germania.

In a letter of 12 December to Schurz, director Albrecht Pagenstecher wrote that the Nominating Committee had arranged a reconciliation between Doremus and Wesendonck. Meanwhile, Schramm had written to another director, Alfred Roelker, that it was necessary to make the Doremus affair public, something that Roelker wanted to avoid, since it would force Doremus to resign. By now, Schurz and Schramm had so closely identified themselves with the move against Doremus that a collision was inevitable in the December meeting of the board.[15]

At the meeting, Schurz moved that the board elect the other officers but refer the question of the presidency back to the Nominating Committee. This motion was opposed by the chair of that committee on the ground that the committee had already considered these matters very thoroughly during the year. In addition, he noted that the special board in Berlin had also recommended the reelection of Doremus. In the first roll-call vote recorded in the board's minutes, Schurz's motion lost, eight to four. Doremus was then elected president, eight to three, with three abstentions. At the end of the meeting, both Schramm and Schurz resigned.[16]

Within the company, the controversy over Doremus soon abated. Over the next few years, however, several of his business practices were criticized by the examiners for the state insurance department. Some criticisms involved relatively minor issues, such as payments Doremus received for the use of his personal car on company business, but some criticisms were more substantial. In the examination for 1909, state auditors called attention to Doremus's practice of changing the rate of interest on some mortgages. In responding to the report, Doremus admitted that he did sometimes change the rate of interest on mortgages when he found it "proper" and in the company's interest to do so. While he had never reported these "minor" matters to the Finance Committee, "he would gladly do so from now on." [17]

In 1915 Doremus was succeeded as president by Hubert Cillis, who had joined the Germania in 1869, at age twenty-one, as an actuary. Cillis had been active in the emerging profession of actuary science, being a founding member in 1889 of the Actuarial Society of America. He was also active in public affairs: he was a trustee of the German Society and president, from 1917 to 1919, of the Mayor's Citizens Advisory Committee, which during World War I dealt with questions raised by the presence in the United States of German aliens. As one of his first moves, President Cillis addressed the internal dissensions that had characterized most of the Doremus years. He began to hold weekly officers' meetings in addition to those of the Advisory Committee that had been established during the final years of Wesendonck's tenure to improve relations among the officers. By the end of 1915, Cillis was able to report to the board that improvements in the management situation warranted abolition of the Advisory Committee, and the board assented. [18]

The Armstrong Committee

On 26 September 1905, at New York City Hall, State Senator William W. Armstrong convened an official inquiry into alleged ethical and legal wrongdoing by many large life insurance companies. The allegations included nepotism, enormous salaries for officers, and collusion with major corporations in financial dealings. These charges received considerable airing in the press, and began a major reform effort in American life insurance practice. A manifestation of the general reform movement that so characterized the age of Teddy Roosevelt and the muckrakers, the investigation addressed serious abuses among the larger companies in an industry that had grown into a major economic force. In 1880, American life insurance companies had collected $53 million in premiums; by 1900 this sum had soared to $338 million. Assets grew from $479 million in 1880 to $1.842 billion twenty years later.[19] The management of such vast wealth subjected officers and directors to enormous temptations, as well as to visions of corporate power and grandeur that were not always in harmony with the public-service aspect of the insurance business.

State intervention in the insurance industry dates to the mid-nineteenth century, when Elizur Wright became Massachusetts super-intendent of insurance. Slowly other states followed the Bay State's lead in creating an office of insurance superintendent. By 1890, state regulation was quite fully developed, although the regulators were often friends of the industry and reluctant to act contrary to its declared interests. For rather complicated political reasons, in New York the regulatory agency found itself suddenly in a much stronger position in 1905, as the press picked up the scent of scandal in the life insurance industry. From 26 September to 30 December of that year, the Armstrong Committee called to its hearing room scores of prominent insurance executives—including those of the very largest companies—whom it cross-examined at length and in public about practices in the industry. The hearings received national press coverage for months, helping to generate deep support everywhere for a general reform of the life insurance companies.

The Germania's turn to offer testimony came on 20 and 21 December, when President Doremus and the actuary John Fuhrer appeared before the committee. The interrogation was conducted mostly by Chief Counsel Charles Evans Hughes, a brilliant young lawyer who would later become governor of New York. By the time Doremus and Fuhrer testified, the great investigation was nearly concluded, and Hughes had become quite an expert on the life insurance industry.

Hughes directed the inquiry along lines designed to illuminate several possible areas of misconduct or impropriety: 1) excessive concentration of authority in the hands of a few officers; 2) attempts to influence the state legislature and other lawmaking bodies; 3) manipulation of assets; 4) "forcing" of business through monetary incentives to agents; 5) misrepresentation of the size of dividends anticipated on policies; 6) computation of dividends in ways that denied full benefit to policyholders; and 7) participation in syndicated financial dealings that redounded to the benefit of privileged insiders. Hughes's technique was to follow a line of questioning only as long as it might lead to a possible clue to or instance of wrongdoing.

Hughes began by asking about the Germania's partial mutualization, as enacted in 1901, and the degree to which policyholders actually voted in elections to the board of directors. (Of the Equitable's half a million policyholders only about twenty-five thousand actually voted or tendered proxies at elections.[20]) When he learned from Doremus that some thirteen thousand of the approximately sixty-three thousand policyholders voted by proxy in such elections, Hughes moved on to the issue of improper political influence. As a preliminary to the actual testimony, on 4 November the committee had sent the company a letter asking for an enumeration of all contributions to political campaigns for the previous ten years. (The New York Life Insurance Company contributed more than forty-eight thousand dollars to the Republican party campaign fund of 1904.[21]) In a letter signed by Doremus and dated 5 December, the company responded by declaring that it had never contributed to political campaign funds. However, it had recently made two small contributions—of $250 and $500 each—to pay a share of the costs associated with lobbying in Albany for the passage of two bills relating to mortgage law and the mortgage tax. The company could provide few details regarding the lobbying effort, which was directed by various real-estate and insurance interests in the city.

Hughes questioned Doremus closely about the two contributions but could produce no evident misconduct on the part of the company. He therefore moved on to an examination of assets and investments. Here he seems to have been trying to determine if the company's investment policies worked to the unfair benefit of any individuals inside or outside the company. His close questioning of Doremus (who occasionally referred the committee to Fuhrer, sitting beside him, for details) revealed only that Doremus preferred a very conservative investment philosophy that placed most of the assets in real-estate mortgages and bonds. As this line of questioning seemed unlikely to yield any startling evidence, Hughes moved on to comparing the Germania's business in the United States and in Germany. Was the German business profitable? "It has been in every respect," Doremus replied, "better than any business in this country; costs less and stays better."[22]

Hughes then asked how much rebating occurred in Germany. When Doremus replied that he did not think it was known at all there,

Hughes was incredulous and asked why rebating had come about in the United States. Doremus attributed it to companies' desire to get ahead of their competitors. Hughes pursued the argument, asking why a company couldn't stop rebating if it wanted to. Doremus replied that he didn't see how it could, noting that agents had to compete with agents from the larger companies who had larger commissions.

After a discussion of agents' commission rates (about 35 percent in Germany and 65 percent in New York), Hughes asked if there were any more differences between business in Germany and business in the United States. Doremus noted that business in Germany was much more stable because the Germans tended not to drop their policies. He thought that a matter of national temperament, not of any lack of competition. Also, Doremus noted, in Germany mortality was better than in the United States, although an evening-out was becoming evident.

"Now do you really think," asked Hughes, "that the mortality is in itself better over there than it is here, or is it because the crowding to get business in this country results in a poorer selection of risks?" "No," Doremus said, "but we get better medical service in Germany than we do here in making examinations."[23]

After a recess, Hughes returned to the question of the two donations the Germania had made for lobbying purposes, to clear up some omissions and errors in the earlier testimony. As soon as Hughes hinted at any impropriety Doremus assured him that the Germania did not do business that way. When Hughes asked what steps the Germania had taken to be kept posted on matters of legislation with reference to insurance companies, Doremus replied that the Germania kept itself informed exclusively by reading the daily reports in the newspapers. (At the hearings the president of New York Life had admitted that his company had paid a lobbyist more than $1 million over the previous ten years to further its interests in Albany.[24])

Hughes then moved to another topic—the cash balances in the company's bank account, which had fluctuated in ways that Hughes found hard to understand. Doremus described, evidently to Hughes's satisfaction, how the sudden drop after September 1905 was due to the working of the newly passed state Mortgage Tax Law, not to any desire to manipulate company funds.

Then Hughes discussed the company's loading premium for expenses. "I notice that your expenses in 1904 were 114.31 percent of your loadings. What is the explanation of that?" Hughes asked. "That it costs much more to get business to-day than it is worth, almost," Doremus replied.[25] The imbalance had existed during the past several years, Doremus stated upon inquiry.

Asked what had been done to correct that state of affairs, Doremus said the company had pared down items that had seemed excessive. This involved mainly the trimming of territory managers' allowances for traveling expenses. Asked about salaries, Doremus responded that the president earned $18,000 a year, the vice president $12,500, the second vice president $10,000, the actuary $6,000, and the secretary $5,000. These salaries had increased only slightly during recent years. (For comparison, the president of Washington Life, a smaller company than the Germania, which had recently undergone reorganization in the face of possible bankruptcy, paid its president $20,000;[26] the president of the Mutual of New York, one of the giants, received an annual salary of $150,000.[27])

The economies Doremus enumerated seemed minor in relation to the expenses incurred, as Hughes suggested in his question: "Isn't it the fact that you cannot get your expenses down within your loadings without changing the commissions paid to agents?" To which Doremus replied, "I fear that is the case. . . ."[28] To the question whether the company had tried to reduce commissions, Doremus answered that it would have resulted in the company's losing business because a good agent could get more than the Germania's commission scale almost anywhere else. Hughes concluded that the Germania had to offset the loss on its loadings through gains in mortality to keep its surplus intact. Doremus agreed but added that gains on interest also helped offset the losses.

Hughes was referring to the fact that most life companies suffered a lower rate of mortality among their policyholders than would be expected according to their actuarial calculations. As Doremus went on to note: "The expectation table is based, not upon selected lives, but upon lives at large. Our experience is based upon the lives selected by examinations."[29] As a result, each year, the Germania made a gain on the expected mortality cost; in 1904, as Hughes noted to provide an example, actual mortality was only 73.73 percent of expected mortality, producing a gain of $251,602. An additional $185,466 in gains came from lapsed and surrendered policies, and $231,392 from interest on surplus. From these gains the company had to deduct $146,978 lost on the loadings, leaving a total realized gain of $521,057. Thus, although the Germania was exceeding its loadings, it was still making a solid increase in its surplus. The bleak picture of competitive pressures painted earlier in the testimony did not prevent this relatively small company from prospering.

At the end of the first day's testimony, Hughes brought up the matter of the dividends estimates concocted by agents as a means of helping sales. The idea was to show prospective customers how much additional value, through dividends, their policies would have, in advance of the end of the year. Since these were only estimates, they had little necessary relation to the actual value of dividends declared, and agents often would err on the side of the bigger dividends. Both Doremus and Fuhrer steadfastly maintained that the estimate books, as they were called, were put together by the agents without the knowledge or approval of the company. When Hughes asked if Doremus had one in his possession, Doremus said he had not and that the books had never been authorized. Hughes insisted that Doremus obtain one of the estimate books for him to examine and that Doremus prepare a statement of the Germania's actual results on its annual dividend policies.

At the very end of the session Doremus formally declared that neither the company nor any of its officers had participated in any syndicate where the Germania had acquired securities floated by the syndicate. At four in the afternoon the two witnesses were excused.

The second day of testimony was quite short, and involved only John Fuhrer, who brought with him one of the agents' estimate books along with a statement of the company's dividend distribution for 1905. A comparison of the two revealed that the estimated dividends were considerably higher than the actual. Hughes must have been expecting such a difference—based on the testimony of other life insurance companies, whose agents indulged in similar schemes—for he did not press the matter, and the session came to an end.

The final result of the Armstrong Committee was a report, whose findings were the basis for a series of laws passed by the previously pro-insurance-industry Albany legislature. The regulations limited the amount of new insurance a company could write in a year, curbing the

growth of the largest companies; required companies to divest themselves of securities issued by industrial corporations, banks, and
trusts, thus breaking their financial tie with these entities; legislated a
maximum allowable level to the annual surplus, so as to reduce the
amount of "free" cash floating around; placed controls on lobbying
efforts; and limited the activities of agents, for example, by making
rebates illegal.[30]

The Germania did not receive any specific criticism. One modern
observer of the life insurance industry has commented that the commission regarded all life companies, large and small, as having committed serious abuses, and that the lack of specific criticisms directed at
a given company should not necessarily be taken as proof of inno-
cence.[31] In the eyes of the Germania and its agents, however, the
testimony clearly benefited the company. Indeed, the company published a complete transcript of the testimony by Doremus and Fuhrer,
for use as a sales piece, and on the very first page the following
statement appears: "It is deemed unnecessary to print here any of the
numerous and favorable newspapers' comments, preferring to let the
testimony speak for itself."[32]

The Field

In addition to internal dissension and a takeover bid, the company also
experienced falling sales and a shake-up of the field network. By the
time Wesendonck retired, in 1897, the national economy was strength-
ening, after the depression of the early 1890s, and the Germania was
enjoying good times. In 1900, however, the company had a setback, as
the sales of new policies dropped 14.6 percent and the amount of new
insurance issued dropped 11.6 percent. Rather than changing the field
structure developed by Wesendonck in the 1880s, based on managers
who were responsible for appointing and paying local agents in their
own districts, President Doremus concentrated first on raising the
morale of field personnel and second on modifications of individual
contracts to create additional incentives. In an effort to infuse more life
into the domestic agencies Doremus held a home office convention for
the Germania's managers and agents in 1901. This event was attended
by twenty-five managers and agents, who came, with their wives,
from as great a distance as San Francisco.[33] At the banquet, Doremus

spoke about the company's financial history, stressing its policy of subordinating "all other considerations, even that of popularity" to the safety of the assured.[34] He then asked, "Is there any reason why we in our own country should not do an amount of new business proportioned to the company's desserts? Can we not do much more than we are now doing?" Urging the field staff to greater exertion, Doremus continued:

I say most emphatically, yes. I say there is every reason why we should, and why we must, do an amount of business in this country to exceed that done by any other of the companies which are not run at high pressure. I know that it can be done, and I know that it can be done by the field force which we now have.[35]

When reporting to the Finance Committee on the success of this convention, Doremus described it as "the best investment that had been made of the Company's funds for a long time past."[36]

Over the next few years, Doremus encouraged the establishment of local agencies by allowing special compensation to area managers. In 1902, for example, he supplemented the standard commission of the manager headquartered at Raleigh, North Carolina, with a monthly allowance of $150 during the first eight months of his contract as partial reimbursement for the expense of establishing local agencies. New business quickly improved, and continued growing until 1904 when it again slackened; in 1907, the total amount of insurance in force began to decline as both the number of policies and the amount of new issues sold dropped by over 50 percent.[37]

Doremus responded to this crisis with personnel changes and limited geographic reorganization. In February 1908, for example, he terminated the contract of the manager who had long been in charge of the Ohio state agency, and divided the territory between two new managers. Another territory, which included Minnesota, North and South Dakota, Montana, and Idaho, was broken up into several smaller districts.[38] Doremus also began to withdraw from areas that were extremely unprofitable, such as Massachusetts in 1908 and Connecticut in 1910. On the other hand, the territory of the company's outstanding agent, Frederic S. Doremus, the son of the president (and formerly head of the Butte, Montana, agency), was expanded to include not only the five boroughs of New York City but also Long Island (he received the title of general manager of the Metropolitan Department).[39]

As a result of the New York Armstrong Committee investigation in 1905, the state legislature revised the general insurance law. Among other reforms, it limited salaries, commissions, and advances to agents. Consequently, in 1907, the Germania renegotiated most of its managerial contracts to include an annual salary plus a commission of $2.50 per $1,000 of insurance placed. By 1909, evidently to satisfy the state insurance department, this additional allowance was almost entirely discontinued.[40]

In 1910, Cornelius Doremus instituted a new practice to inspire agents to make special efforts to bring in business. In celebration of his fiftieth year with the Germania, he designated "Doremus Month" as a sales drive period. The field staff responded to this announcement with a then-record production of more than $3 million of new business "in his honor."[41] The designation of months for sales drives in honor of particular officers became a regular practice.

Despite these efforts, dissatisfaction remained among the field staff concerning the support they were receiving from the home office. These difficulties carried over from the presidency of Doremus to that of his successor, Cillis. In 1914, for example, at a meeting in Cincinnati, the agents and field managers had complained to Doremus about several matters, including perceived inequities in agency contracts with the company.[42] This discontent spurred the New York office to take several measures, whose effects became visible later. One was the more rational use of the company's financial leverage to help local agents by making large deposits in local banks. In January 1915, the district manager in Georgia asked the Finance Committee to make time deposits in local banks, which would help the agency to obtain a considerable amount of new insurance. Remarks made by President Cillis to the Finance Committee on 27 January 1915 suggest that some states were complaining that out-of-state insurance companies were taking cash out of the local economy through premium payments without a corresponding inflow of cash through payment of death benefits. This was an old complaint, noted earlier by Wesendonck regarding the states in the Midwest and West, and was related to the whole issue of regional economic friction. The Germania Life Insurance Company, like the majority of American insurance companies, was headquartered in the East, and shared in the suspicion directed at the eastern establishment. It is noteworthy that the issue was brought to the Germania's attention by an agent in Georgia, for that state was one of the most economically undeveloped in the nation and would have suffered the most from any withdrawal of cash from the local economy. At first Cillis was skeptical about the need to use the company's money in the manner suggested by the agent, but gradually he changed his mind. It seems to have carried considerable weight with him that other leading insurance companies were making such bank deposits, and the Finance Committee, in evident agreement, authorized the practice. By the end of 1916 and for the next several years, the company often made deposits in local banks to aid its sales force.[43]

Another device was elaborated which had been introduced several years earlier by Doremus. The company declared March 1916 Hansen Month, in honor of the twentieth anniversary of the superintendent of agencies, T. Louis Hansen. For the occasion, Cillis asked the fieldmen for a concerted effort to make March a record-breaking month with a production of 3.5 million dollars' worth of insurance. The field force responded with nearly that level of sales, making March 1916 the best month in the company's history. The company continued to use this effective device in succeeding years; October 1916 was Cillis Month, April 1917 (Max) Wesendonck Month.[44]

By 1916 talk arose about the need for a convocation of the field managers. The previous meeting, the one at Cincinnati where the agents and managers had raised their complaints, suggested that perhaps the New York office should send as its representative an officer who was especially well regarded by the fieldmen. In the summer, the Kansas City manager, N. E. Berry, wrote to Vice President Carl Heye to suggest that the company's agents and field managers meet at the upcoming convention of the National Underwriters' Association. Berry and the other agents all agreed that Heye was the most appropriate officer the company could send to such a meeting: ". . . You have the same things under consideration and are interested perhaps more than any other Home Office official." Berry also commented on the bond of unity between the fieldmen and the New York office that would result from such a meeting. The choice of Heye proved excellent and the meeting went extremely well. "It would have done you good to see what high type men they were," wrote Heye to Cillis afterward, "and I was especially pleased to find that their feeling toward the Home Office had greatly improved since the last meeting which we had at Cincinnati."[45]

In January 1916, the Germania introduced *Service*, an internal publication to improve cooperation between the home office and the fieldmen and to motivate agents. *Service* provided information and advice to field staff and also highlighted the achievements of outstanding agents. Yet another aid to the field agents came through the adoption of new policy-related features that made the Germania's policies more competitive. In 1915, the board amended the company's charter to allow the sale of health and disability insurance. A year later, the Committee on Insurance, in response to requests from agents in the field, recommended the adoption of a double indemnity benefit, which provided double the policy face value in cases where death was caused by accident while the insured was traveling on public transportation and occurred within sixty days of the accident. The committee urged its adoption because it would make the Germania's policies compare well with those of other companies and because it would show a progressive mentality that would inspire the agents.[46] This recommendation was immediately passed by the board. Two months later, following the example of one of the major companies, the double indemnity benefit was extended to all accidents and the time limit was increased to ninety days.[47]

In 1915, the Germania introduced a health service for its policyholders of more than three years' standing. The company provided without charge an annual full medical examination followed by recommendations for any problems discovered. This service was well received by the company's policyholders; by September 1916, nearly 3,500 had applied for the service. A year and a half later, the Germania became the first life insurance company to offer this service to new policyholders.[48]

Owing perhaps to policy and sales innovations and efforts to improve relations with the field force, 1916 was the "banner year of the Company as regards new issues, the business written in the United States in 1916 exceeding the best previous year by about seven millions, and being equal to the best previous year of the American and European Branches combined."[49]

Growth and Investments

Between 1898 and 1913, the assets of the Germania doubled, from $24.326 million to $48.981 million. From 1913 to 1921, they rose again to $60.287 million, even though the company had meanwhile changed its name and begun divesting itself of the European operation. In 1921 assets fell sharply to $39.783 million, as the company revalued downward the worth of its holdings in European currencies that had suffered inflation since the end of the war. Doremus gave preference in investing first to mortgages, and second to stocks and bonds. Except for the years 1902–1904, the company kept over half of its assets in mortgages, reaching a high of 62 percent in 1907. Conversely, the proportion of assets invested in stocks and bonds reached as high as 34 percent in 1903 but fell to less than 25 percent from 1906 on. By 1913, because of demand, loans to policyholders had also become a more important form of investment. Until 1903, policy loans accounted for only about 5 percent of the company's assets. This proportion began to grow slowly over the next few years and reached a high of 12 percent in 1913.

As assets rose, so did the need to manage them. Doremus continued the centralized manner of investment-making that Wesendonck and Schwendler had begun. Decisions on mortgages were made personally by the president, who selected the most desirable applications for approval by the Finance Committee. In 1898, Doremus informed the committee that an unusually high number of mortgages were being paid off because borrowers could secure loans with lower rates of interest elsewhere.[50] This situation continued, as other companies, particularly Mutual Life, New York Life and the Equitable, were approaching the Germania's mortgagees with offers of lower interest rates. The following year, noting that the company was losing its best mortgages, the Finance Committee decided to lower its interest rate on loans from 5 to 4.5 percent, and a further reduction to 4 percent when necessary. Doremus immediately began to reduce interest rates on existing mortgages, and continued to do so for the next two years.[51]

During periods of high interest rates, Doremus attempted to secure long-term investments in domestic securities. These investments, however, were monitored by the Prussian authorities, who occasionally forced the company to dispose of certain securities. In 1898, for example, the Prussian government objected to the company's investments in several American railroad companies. Since the railroads in question were in receivership or otherwise on shaky financial footings, the Prussians thought them unsuitable for investment by an insurance company. The Germania's Finance Committee, fearing a loss if it sold, responded that in the United States judiciously chosen railroad bonds were considered the best kind of investment in negotiable securities, and that the company needed such liquid assets to meet sudden cash drains. The committee also claimed that its losses on the bonds had been light.[52] Unconvinced, the Prussian government demanded sale of all railroad and transit company securities and the Germania complied.

A good summary of the company's investments and investment philosophy appears in the testimony that Doremus and Fuhrer gave before the Armstrong Committee in December 1905. Doremus described the Germania's investments as conservative securities and bonds and mortgages on real estate. In all, the company held about $35 million in assets, including $18 million to $19 million in real-estate mortgages and bonds, about $10 million in securities of all kinds, and slightly more than $3 million in real estate. The real-estate bonds and mortgages were very stable investments, Doremus observed, but had involved a small loss to the company, whereas the company had always gained with its negotiable securities. Why, then, asked Hughes, did the company invest so great a proportion of its assets in real-estate bonds and mortgages? Doremus replied it was because of the stability. Hughes asked if the company invested in stocks, and Doremus said that it did not because the German government would not allow it. A little later Hughes asked Doremus what real estate the company owned and Doremus said it owned more than he would like, but that the total holding of real estate was $3,111,069.37 worth. Upon request, Doremus enumerated the holdings: the home-office building in New York (book value, $507,731; cost, $462,500; market value, $1.35 million); a building in St. Paul, Minnesota (cost, more than $800,000; book value, $700,000); in Berlin, a building that cost $291,947; in Vienna, one that cost $180,799.87; and finally, foreclosed real estate, mostly in New York City, which had amounted to $1,337,481 at the end of 1901 but which had been reduced to $861,744 by the end of 1904.[53]

The most visible investment of the company during the Doremus years was its new home-office building. The decision to leave the old building in favor of another was made when it became clear that the current building was not competitive with surrounding structures and would soon become unrentable. The company began having problems finding tenants for the building in 1908, when for the first time since the Germania owned the building, the banking floor lay vacant. New skyscrapers such as the Singer Building were drawing the most desirable tenants away, not only from the Germania's building but from others in the neighborhood.[54]

On 24 June 1908, President Doremus suggested that the Germania and one of its neighbors, the Fourth National Bank, enter into a joint venture to build a modern office building on their combined sites. After some discussion, the Finance Committee came to no decision. Only a few months later the committee definitely killed the plan by voting to sell the home-office building to the bank, and then, in a subsequent meeting, offered its own plan.[55]

The committee began by observing that the company would soon be celebrating its fiftieth anniversary, and that there was no more fitting way to mark this milestone than to buy land, erect a building, and open the company's new offices in it on 17 July 1910, fifty years from the date of the issue of the first policy. A subcommittee appointed to search for a site examined about thirty, and eventually settled on one at Fourth Avenue and Seventeenth Street. The Finance Committee decided that the new building would have to be at least sixteen stories high, lest it be dwarfed by the surrounding structures. The original sixteen-story design was later altered to include a mansard roof with an additional four stories.[56]

In July 1909, the company agreed to buy 50, 52, and 54 Union Square for $535,000; in May 1911 it bought 105 East Seventeenth Street, to protect air and light for the new headquarters, at a price of $65,650. The new building was designed by the architect Albert F. D'Oench, of D'Oench and Yost, who sat on the Germania's board of directors and was a member, along with Doremus, Casimir Tag, and Albert Roelker, of the site-search subcommittee. A committee composed of Doremus, Henry A. Caesar, and Casimir Tag was appointed in December 1909 to oversee details of design and construction, with D'Oench as adviser. Work then began on demolishing the existing structures on the site, which was completed by June 1910. On 15 April 1910 the New York Department of Buildings had approved the architect's plans and issued a construction permit. The builder was Charles T. Wills, and the agents were Stephen H. Tyng Jr. and Company. According to reports of the Finance Committee, as of 31 March 1913, the cost of the new building amounted to $1,453,230.02, in addition to the amount spent to purchase the site. When the building opened for business, some of its floors—1, 2, 5, 6, 9–17, 19, and the basement—were rented out to other companies.[57]

On 6 May 1911, the Germania held open house for about two hundred guests at its new office building, described in the press as a masterpiece of artistic design and modern construction. The writer praised the main staircase as "one of the handsomest in New York City," remarked on the "excellent taste" of the executive-office furnishings and the "businesslike appearance" of the workrooms, and concluded that all these benefits flowed from the "well-ordered and masterful mind which has guided the affairs of this sterling old company for more than a half century." The substantial but unostentatious fabric of the structure was a fitting monument to commemorate more than half a century of "honorable dealing with the public."[58]

The new home-office building was the most visible product of the Doremus years, yet it was not necessarily the most important to the company's continued success. The company, after all, was not a pile of brick and steel, but an ordered array of individual employees, managers, and agents. The task of selling insurance, managing the investment portfolio, and paying claims was governed by certain rules of actuarial practice, by state regulations, and by principles of successful investment; but a large additional area—general management of the sales force and the home-office staff—had never received close attention from the Germania's managers, except under the pressure to cut costs. Yet during the presidencies of Doremus and Cillis, American business entered the modern era of management, and in this development the Germania played a small but interesting role.

New Ideas in Management

In its formative years, the life insurance industry, like the American economy in general, ran largely on the basis of received knowledge and common sense. Insurance agents learned their trade on the job, as did the staff at the home office, both in small companies like the Germania and in the very largest. Yet the enormous growth in the size of most life insurance companies was causing problems that outpaced the conventional wisdom and intuitive approach under which agents and staff worked; in addition, competition encouraged companies to find more efficient ways of doing business. The greater needs were felt in two areas—more effective sales, and a more rational administration of the processing of policies, record keeping, and claims resolutions— where new ideas began to take hold among the larger companies by the turn of the century.

Although the need for change was perhaps strongest at the large life insurance companies, whose home-office employees might number in the thousands, smaller companies too found it necessary to adjust to growing staffs and increasingly complex administrative and accounting procedures. This was true at the Germania, where between 1915 and 1920 the home-office staff increased fourfold, from about 60 or 65 to 250, with a concomitant rise in the complexity of the whole operation.[1] It is therefore not surprising that at about this time one of the Germania's employees, Harry A. Hopf, attempted changes in the office to make it more efficient; nor is it surprising that the conservative management of the company resisted these efforts at rapid change and opted instead for a more careful approach in keeping with the Germania's tradition. The move to modernize seems not to have penetrated beyond the middle managers. For Harry Hopf, however, the experiences at the Germania were both the beginning of a distinguished career as an international expert in office efficiency and a case study of the insurance industry.

Scientific Marketing

By the turn of the century, the increasing size of most life insurance companies, the growing complexity of their offerings, and the pressures of competition were causing a change in the nature of the sales force. Companies began paying greater attention to the skill and commitment of their agents, as the idea of the insurance agent as a trained professional came to the fore. Whereas Hugo Wesendonck had sold his first policies to friends and associates in the New York German-American community, and the Germania's first agents probably did likewise in other cities, with time the growth in the number of policyholders made such sales less common than sales to persons who were known to the agent simply through the business relationship of buying and selling life insurance. This placed growing importance on the agent's command of information and the techniques of successful selling. The large life insurance companies began seeking out well-educated young men (and occasionally women) and offering them profitable careers if they could master the increasingly sophisticated techniques of sales and were willing to make a long-term commitment to the company (since from the company's perspective it made little sense to invest heavily in agents who would soon leave). The new sales techniques were dubbed "scientific" since they relied on formal, explicit, ostensibly objective criteria and concepts.

In 1902, Equitable Life began recruiting college graduates as agents and preparing them through a formal training course. At the same time, several educational institutions, such as Wharton and Yale, initiated insurance-marketing courses within their own programs. Two decades later, in 1919, the Carnegie School of Practical Life Insurance Salesmanship was founded as an affiliate of the Carnegie Institute of Technology to offer professional training. In 1927, the industry established general professional standards with the incorporation of the American College of Life Underwriters, which granted the title of Chartered Life Underwriter to those who passed qualifying examinations.[2]

The Guardian sought to give its agents a more systematic training in sales, but not until after other companies had led the way. An article in the *Eastern Underwriter* of 19 March 1920 spoke of the company as one of those that had taken an enthusiastic interest in scientific salesmanship and had affiliated itself with the Carnegie School of Practical Life Insurance Salesmanship. The Guardian announced in 1920 that it had established a training school for its agents. Three years later, the company expanded this program to include a graduate course for those who completed the first program. The company also sent home-office personnel to courses held at other institutions. In 1922, for example, the company awarded five "Columbia Scholarships" to a course taught by a Mutual Life actuary.[3]

The move toward sales professionalization occurred at the same time as a growing trend toward home-office control over the field force. The impetus for this came from the very large life insurance companies, such as New York Life and the Mutual of New York, whose vast sales forces required an increasing degree of central control if the company was to operate in a coherent way. The large amounts of money invested by these companies also called for enlarged staffs of financial specialists and actuaries, grouped into constantly growing departments. The effort to give agents more formal sales training fit well into the centralized approach, since it promised to lend a uniformity of operation that was quantifiable, predictable, and thus manageable. In 1910 the Germania, too, began to reorganize management of the field structure by establishing an Agency Department in the New York office. Several years later, like other modernizing insurance companies, the Germania further centralized its field-management structure by placing the department under the direction of an officer. In 1918, T. Louis Hansen, then supervisor of agencies, was promoted to the new position of vice president and agency manager.[4]

The Agency Department continued and expanded several practices initiated to give cohesiveness to the field operation. In 1917, the company had held its first convention of field agents that was independent of the meetings of the National Underwriters' Association. This annual event, for those agents who had qualified through the production of a required minimum amount of new business for the convention year, served several purposes. It reinforced company loyalty, rewarded achievement, and promoted communication between the Agency Department and the field. Occasionally, smaller regional meetings were held for all field staff. In 1924, for example, an area conference was held in Philadelphia for staff in Pennsylvania, Maryland, and New Jersey.[5]

Scientific Management

The effort to improve the training and performance of the sales force had a counterpart in an attempt to increase the efficiency of the home-office staff, for it would be pointless to improve sales if the company were unable to keep up with ensuing paperwork, claims, and movement of resources. A new approach to these problems was emerging under the name of scientific management. Although the earliest writings that advocated such views came from newly industrializing Great Britain in the early 1800s, the major innovators in the field were Americans, including Henry Metcalfe (1847–1917), who spoke of the science of administration; Henry R. Towne (1844–1924), who emphasized the need for careful observation in managing and administering any enterprise, exhorting managers in various companies to exchange information among themselves; and Frederick W. Taylor (1856–1915), the most influential of the new breed, who declared that the principles of scientific management involved a drastic change in mental attitude on the part of both workers and managers, whom he urged to produce "the largest possible surplus" and substitute "exact scientific knowledge for opinions or the old rule of thumb or individual knowledge."[6]

The new techniques came to the life insurance industry shortly after the turn of the century, with the publication of *Insurance Office Organization, Management and Accounts,* by the Englishmen T. E. Young and Richard Masters in 1904. This and other works of its type that began to appear preached the importance of substituting rational, efficient methods for traditional ones, and for replacing the idiosyncrasies of both workers and managers with standardized procedures proven to be efficient. An important part of the system was to rethink how things were done, based on careful observation and analysis, rather than merely to tinker and patch up what was inefficient.

One disciple of the new techniques was Harry Arthur Hopf (1882–1949), who was born in England and emigrated to the United States when he was sixteen and in 1902 became employed at the New York office of the Germania. Hopf's early contributions to the emerging field of scientific management centered around improvements in worker and office efficiency, an area only beginning to be developed in the life insurance industry of his day. Like most of his scientific management peers, he concentrated his attention on the specific work situation—in the case of other innovators this was often in an industrial setting, in Hopf's it was an office—but gradually his work led him to broader issues. By the 1930s he had become much more interested in the importance of long-term corporate planning. Instead of "scientific management" he preferred to describe his field of expertise as "optimology," which he defined as "that state of development of a business enterprise which tends to perpetuate an equilibrium among the factors of size, cost, and human capacity and thus to promote in the highest degree regular realization of the business objectives. . . ."[7] Although modern management techniques had enabled American businesses to deploy hitherto unheard of numbers of workers and amounts of money in vast enterprises, Hopf argued that the very scale of operations was engendering new inefficiencies which, in the end, would become self-defeating unless brought under control. For any given enterprise, Hopf concluded, there was an ideal, or optimal, size, beyond which inefficiencies set in. The secret of good management, accordingly, was to identify the optimal size and adhere to it as closely as possible, through rational planning and management.

Planning and management required organization, an area where Hopf had many critical observations from his experience of thirty years as a consultant. Too often, he thought, business organizations arose from "personality and power rather than logic and strength of proper structural relationships."[8] Lacking rational principles of organization, a business would eventually reach a plateau of efficiency, beyond which it could not move, and might even decline.

Perhaps Hopf's greatest contribution to modern management was his insight that numerical data could be analyzed to improve the operation of a business—a view that did not fully develop until the advent of the computer in the business world. Using mathematical models, Hopf analyzed life insurance companies as a whole as well as their managements and concluded that from 1906 to 1930, the net cost of company operation to policyholders decreased with the size of the company, until a certain size was attained, after which net cost rose. He concluded that the point when net cost began to rise with increasing size was the point just beyond the optimal size of the company.

Hopf's statistical-mathematical approach led him to pose some intriguing questions, such as whether there existed a limit to the capacity of management to contribute to operating results. Since he could not obtain sufficient psychological data concerning the executives of the ten life insurance companies under study, he chose "objective" characteristics such as age, education, and promotional progression, which he then sought to correlate with company income and expenses. He used a great mass of data in his analysis, which covered a twenty-five-year period starting in 1906. From his study, Hopf made numerous observations and developed theories about management efficiency in the life insurance business, among them that "beyond a certain point, age and length of experience constitute limiting factors in the influence of managerial capacity upon company accomplishment"; in other words, "after a certain average age has been reached and a given average length of experience attained, the managerial personnel loses in effectiveness, and may even exert an adverse influence over company progress."[9]

Throughout Hopf's later writings runs the thread of managerial versus entrepreneurial organization and motivation. Hopf well understood that he was witnessing a transformation: the great American business barons were leaving the scene to be replaced by hired managers, who would never have the same attitude about the company as the founders. In this regard, Hopf's years of work with insurance companies—beginning with the Germania in 1902—gave him an impressive background for understanding the managerial mentality and mode of operation, since by then most if not all life insurance companies were run by hired personnel.

At the Germania, the young Hopf made his first suggestions about improving efficiency in 1907 as a staff foreign-language stenographer. This effort met stolid resistance from the chief clerk, whom Hopf described as a Prussian type, but the next year Hopf was promoted to secretary to one of the vice presidents, either Hubert Cillis or Max Wesendonck, a position that gave him more opportunity to press his ideas.

In 1908 he suggested that the Germania publish a house newspaper. He argued that worker productivity was a factor of communications, an area where the Germania had much to learn. The agents in the field, he claimed, rarely heard from the company except for complaints, and were prevented from doing their best by a general lack of information about what they were supposed to do and what the company would do for them. The lack of communication prevented development of a healthy competition among agents and of an esprit de corps.[10]

In the past, Hugo Wesendonck and Cornelius Doremus had tinkered with the agency system, or revised its lines of command and personnel, but this was the first time, it appears, that anyone tried to approach the problem systematically. Hopf's suggestion came to nothing in the short term, but eight years later the company began the newsletter *Service*, first a monthly and after 1921 a weekly, which tried to do exactly what Hopf had urged in 1908. The publication was the company's vehicle for educating its field force, and carried articles on topics such as selling techniques, insurance, taxes and estate planning, and health and death statistics. Furthermore, through its biographical articles, *Service* personalized both the home-office and field staff and, like the annual conventions, provided recognition for successful performance.[11]

Despite his initial setback with the newsletter, Hopf persisted. He arranged to visit the offices of two competitors, the Travelers and Penn Mutual Life, which he claimed held many lessons for the Germania. The Germania should place its agents under the inspection of the Retail Credit Company of Atlanta, he recommended, following Traveler's practice of checking closely the creditworthiness of prospective policyholders. Also on the model of Travelers, he urged the Germania to furnish all agents and officers with an up-to-date list of approved medical examiners, and to use an office-map system for locating the examiners quickly.[12] The fate of these suggestions is unknown.

Meanwhile, Hopf received a new forum for his ideas when he became head of the Medical Department. This department was charged with maintaining accurate files on the medical history of Germania policyholders, especially impairments reported when the policies were written. The department's corps of medical examiners, assisted by staff who did the paperwork and the filing, used the files to make the final decisions on health matters. The filing, however, was causing problems. In 1900 the department's Index Section had committed only 69 filing errors, but in 1905, 240 errors, and in 1910, 436. Each error meant a lost or misplaced file, or information delivered too late to be useful.[13] Clearly, the filing system was not keeping pace with the general rise in company business, and something had to be done; it was a perfect situation for the new methods of scientific management and administration, which preached the virtue of rethinking problems rather than applying traditional solutions.

Hopf's solution was to analyze the work of the Medical Department as a series of steps, all aimed at the goal of company prosperity: finding potential low-risk policyholders through the sales agents, selecting the most attractive prospects from among candidates, processing the policies, and keeping track of all health-related claims. This was a process not unlike the industrial systems created by Taylor and his followers. Like the factory, the secret to success in the medical department was to apply an "unwavering routine," which would supplant personal idiosyncrasy with measurable procedures. In the case of the Index Section, the routine was crystallized in a system of file cards, scrupulously maintained and updated, which provided accurate and immediate access to all important information in the files.[14] (Many of Hopf's mature ideas, developed in the 1920s and 1930s, anticipated the use of computers to perform administrative and record-keeping tasks.) Hopf reorganized the Index Section in 1910, with the services of nearly sixty different workers, over an eight-month span, at a cost of $4,615.[15]

Success with the files spurred Hopf to approach President Doremus directly about beginning a formal survey of every department in the company, as a general examination of the arrangement of the office work and workforce. The president, whom Hopf later accused of lacking vision and being prejudiced and indifferent to matters that did not come under his direct personal observation, expressed no interest in this great task, leaving Hopf to carry out an analysis of his own organizational status and that of his department.

Hopf described himself in this analysis as an executive in charge of the Medical Department, supervising the work of four groups of clerks, conducting conferences with other heads and with visiting agents, writing up reports, and acting as head of the Applications Department and secretary to the vice president. In his view, he also had the responsibility for "improving" staff procedures and training, but this seems to have been a self-appointed function that received little if any approval or encouragement from his peers or superiors. Although after much effort Hopf managed to have the Medical and Policy departments combined into the Department of Issue, in his view an improvement in efficiency, he did this largely on his own initiative.

Hopf's reorganization at the Germania became the topic of his first public address, delivered in 1912 at the Medical Section meeting of the American Life Convention, San Antonio, Texas. In this paper, he formally articulated the principles that he had worked out in practice at the Germania, including the importance of relating each task and procedure in a company department to the ultimate well-being of the company.[16]

Whatever reception his reforms received at the Germania, Hopf's ideas began to attract attention from other companies. Within months of giving his San Antonio address, Hopf signed a one-year contract with the Rand Company to direct a consulting service for life insurance companies. At the time, he was one of the few life insurance managers engaged in consulting work, a point he stressed in negotiating his contract with Rand. He argued with evident success that if Rand did not sign him, someone else would, since the new management and administrative systems were just beginning to attract wide attention in the industry.

The contract with Rand seems to have gone well, producing praise for Hopf from the president of the Pan American Life Insurance Company, who claimed that the reorganization in processing policies was both educative to staff and more efficient in the use of time. In particular, Hopf had encouraged staff to relate ends to means, rather than to treat specific problems as unrelated to the broader goals of the company. Despite this success, Rand did not renew his contract at the end of 1913, and Hopf found himself as isolated as ever at the Germania, whose management he censured as unprogressive. Shortly thereafter, he left the company to take up a position at the Phoenix Mutual Life, and his association with the Germania ended.[17]

Before he left for the Phoenix Mutual, Hopf became involved in a curious incident that surely added to his frustration with the Germania. During 1913, the Germania, at whose urging is unknown, formally began offering monetary awards to home-office employees who suggested ways of improving administrative efficiency.[18] In a memorandum of 16 October, addressed to Hopf, one Marie A. Rennenberg, of the Department of Issue, suggested that the company could save considerable time and expense through a change in the method of registering certain policies in the Policies Issued Book. Hopf, in his own memorandum, approved the change and raised two

related issues: that the Policies Issued Book be abolished as unnecessary and that all employee suggestions related to a department's administration be approved by the head of the department, not by the
secretary of the company, as had evidently been the procedure established at the Germania. These two points met immediate resistance.
According to an unsigned and unattributed copy of a memorandum of
31 October, probably addressed to secretary Carl Heye, the Actuarial
Department and John Fuhrer were as firm as ever in their opinion that
the Policies Issued Book should continue to be used. The writer also
criticized Hopf's second point, regarding approval by department
head only, noting that the matter had been discussed thoroughly at a
home-office organizational meeting. The writer went on to cite the
need for an impartial committee or person to decide the merits of
employee suggestions, and raised the example of the Metropolitan
Life, whose suggestions were addressed to the secretary and passed
on, and which granted prizes by a committee of the officers.

While Hopf's memorandum was being discussed by Fuhrer and
others, the secretary approved Miss Rennenberg's suggestion and
directed the cashier to pay her a two-dollar prize. When Hopf learned
of this, after the event, he was upset at the way the matter had been
handled; he felt the granting of awards should be left in the hands of
the department heads. Then Hopf declared that Miss Rennenberg's
suggestion was actually his, submitted to test the working of the
employee-suggestion plan, and he urged that the matter be brought to
Heye's attention. In what seems to be a later typed addition to the
memorandum that provided this information to Heye, it is stated that
Miss Rennenberg claimed the suggestion to be her own. The ultimate
resolution of this whole affair is unknown, but it must have helped
Hopf determine to leave for friendlier surroundings.

At the Germania, Hopf had experienced mixed success in his drive
for improved efficiency. His reorganization of the Medical Department
was significant enough to put Hopf's name into the first book ever
devoted to the study of office management, *The American Office* (1913),
which described him as the "insurance office specialist connected with
the Germania Life Insurance Company," who had "made an empirical
study of large-scale filing and indexing operations."[19] Success like this
was impossible elsewhere in the company, however, because the
managers resisted the new approach.

In this regard the Germania was not unique among life insurance companies. Throughout his career, which spanned four decades, Hopf constantly chided the life insurance industry for its adherence to old ways. As late as 1935, he claimed that no American life insurance company had "consciously tried to achieve and adhere to the optimum, as the highest expression of service to policyholders."[20] But perhaps the Germania was not so conservative after all, if it is considered that during the rather brief span of seven years Hopf successfully implemented a reorganization of a major department and planted the seed for publication of the company newspaper.

Limits of Change

Amid the effort to change there remained certain elements of continuity, especially at the highest level of management, where men like Doremus and Cillis embodied the old ideas and values, untouched by scientific management techniques. Here, where the idiosyncrasies of personal judgment held primacy, the most important management decisions were made, as in the case of an ongoing financial crisis in the Berlin office that became evident in 1913.

During the presidency of Doremus, the European branch had operated more or less independently of the home office, despite visits by various company officers. Gradually, Doremus and his colleagues became concerned over a continuing decline in the branch's annual surplus, and advised the Berlin office to attend more carefully to policyholder mortality, administrative-expense rates, and investment interest rates. In previous years, as Hugo Wesendonck and others had been quick to note, the German business had outperformed the American and contributed disproportionately to the Germania's profits. After the turn of the century this began to change, and by 1912 was reversed. Death rates in Germany were now actually higher among the company's policyholders than in the United States. Another problem for the Berlin office was a drop in yield of German stocks and securities as compared with American, which probably derived from the stronger American economy.[21]

The Berlin office did not confront the situation until 1913, in the face of a serious financial crisis. For several years, the home office had been unable to get complete information on mortgage loans made in Berlin.

In July 1913, Heinrich Rose, the general director at Berlin, notified the home office that a depreciation in the market value of the company's securities and an unusual demand for loans by policyholders, prevented him from paying the reserve deposit required by the Austrian government without a sizable temporary bank loan. Although Rose anticipated repaying the loan out of current income by the end of the year, he also requested that the home office send funds to insure timely repayment.[22]

The home office notified Rose they could not make such a remittance without sacrificing some of its securities, which it hoped would be unnecessary. A few days later, the home office informed Rose that in any case it could make no remittance before 15 August. Rose then advised the home office that he had negotiated a bank loan on condition that the entire amount of 1,600,000 marks be repaid by the end of August, and asked that it carry out his promise.[23] The board of directors was very displeased with Rose's unilateral commitment. "Where is the head office of the Company? Here or in Berlin?" asked one member, and another suggested that Rose be severely censured. After much discussion the board voted to make "the great sacrifice" of sending Rose a million marks, although it thought that if need be Rose could manage without. To make this remittance, the home office had to borrow $450,000, and Doremus found it "an exceptional, and not a particularly pleasant condition for a Life Insurance Company, which should be a lender, to be a borrower of money."[24]

Doremus attributed the problems in Europe to lax management in Berlin and a supervisory failure by the home office. He could think of no solution, except to send a deputy across the Atlantic to reorganize affairs there, "but we have no one capable of this work who could possibly be spared."[25] If this was true, it was a telling comment on the thin ranks of the Germania's senior management at that time, for the European branch had possessed a special importance for the company during the previous forty years and ought surely to have received all the attention it needed from New York. Perhaps the falling profits of the German operation were a factor in the reluctance to commit resources for a reorganization. The decade after 1900 saw a slight drop in the amount of life insurance written by American companies abroad, but a very great increase in the amount written in the United States. By 1910 non-Canadian foreign insurance had declined to only 6.26 percent of all insurance written by American companies, compared with 9.21 percent in 1900.[26] With business so good in the States, Doremus may have felt that Berlin could get along on its own.

Whatever its real thoughts on the matter of the loan to Berlin, the Finance Committee preferred to attribute the problem to "the simultaneous occurrence of several unusual contingencies," when it wrote Rose later in 1913 in response to a request for the creation of a special contingency fund to be under Rose's control. The committee suggested instead, in a letter written to Doremus, that this was unnecessary since the Berlin branch had all necessary support from New York in handling finances.[27] Not much more than a year later, the advent of the First World War severed relations between the two parts of the company and effectively ended the support of the committee, board, and president.

Although the problems in the European operation and the departure of Hopf in 1914 suggest that the Germania was not particularly receptive to new ideas and that, in the end, the old ways usually won out, in fact there was no going back, even if men like Cillis and Doremus had wanted to. The real issue was not whether change would occur, but how it would occur and at what pace. The changes that Cillis made, at Hansen's urging, to rejuvenate the agency system, are one indication that the company retained its ability to adapt to new conditions. Beyond such upper-management concerns, however, lay the fundamental changes in American life and business that were driving all major enterprises toward a more rational, efficient use of people and resources, and would lead, decades later, to the popularity of the computer. Hopf had correctly identified control over information as a crucial element in achieving improved efficiency, and his innovations during 1910–1913 may have helped the Department of Issue avoid drowning in paper, as its file cabinets of records increased from 19 in 1911 to 102 in 1936.[28] And it was a lack of information that had exacerbated the problems between the home office and the European operation. But Hopf did not have the patience or the personality to work within the Germania system as then constituted, and the full impact of his work, which is difficult to assess, was lost to the company.

[10]

War and the End of the Germania

In August 1914, forty-four years of European peace ended when war broke out between the German Empire and its allies on the one side, and Great Britain, France, Russia, and theirs, on the other. For a brief time, this war seemed deceptively similar to the Franco-Prussian War of 1870, which had been short and decisive. Accordingly, in 1914 the officers of the Germania assumed that hostilities would not last long and that their decrease in business would be made up quickly after peace had been restored. They anticipated no problems with foreign investments, since over 60 percent were conservative first-mortgage loans on Berlin property, with the remainder in securities of the highest class, which, although depreciated in value, were expected to recover rapidly after the war. Nor did the officers anticipate an unusual demand for policy loans, since most policies at that time had no loan-on-demand clause, and in addition it seemed likely the clause, where it existed, would be legally suspended because of the war. Always, the officers spoke of the return to normalcy, of the temporary interruption that would not last long.[1]

Many other people shared these views. During the first months of the war, the American press reported optimistically on how the insurance industry was faring. So favorable and upbeat was the coverage that the Germania circulated one of the articles to its field force to help it answer questions from policyholders. Entitled "War Does Not Bother United States Insurance Companies," the article stressed that mortality risks were under control through extra-premium war clauses and that assets were safe.[2]

The optimism soon faded. A rapidly growing demand for loans on European policies led the Association of German Life Insurance Companies to advocate imposition of a rigid limitation on all loans made on policies. The Germania was compelled to remit large sums to the Berlin office to cover depreciation of its German investments.[3] Frequent interruptions in mail service between the Berlin and New York offices made it increasingly difficult for the two parts of the company to work together. In 1916 the home office detached the Madrid office from Berlin's jurisdiction and began dealing with it directly. In 1917 the operation in Switzerland also came under the direct supervision of the New York office, not only to improve communications but also to comply with the American Trading with the Enemy Act, for by then Germany and the United States were at war.[4]

Fortunately, for the United States, the war remained a foreign event for several years. American manufacturers and shippers quickly learned to benefit from Europe's escalating need both for munitions and for civilian-related items that were no longer being made at home. Great Britain, which had the most powerful fleet, successfully closed off most of the ocean to German merchant vessels. Soon after the war began, British warships began to stop and search neutral vessels for contraband, which raised diplomatic and legal issues. The British felt compelled to stop the foreign munitions trade with Germany through any means available, yet were reluctant to alienate the American government, which controlled access to Britain's largest foreign suppliers. As much as possible, the British tried to place the onus on the Germans, whom they accused of prosecuting an immoral, unjust, and atrocity-marred offensive war.

The German navy unintentionally contributed to this image by allowing its submarines to attack ships without warning, something that struck hard at Victorian beliefs in fair play and chivalry. Once surprise attacks were condoned by the navy, it was only a matter of time before an "incident" would occur. It finally came to pass early in 1915 with the torpedoing of the *Lusitania* off Ireland. Had Americans regarded both the British and the Germans in a similar light, they might have blamed both powers for the disaster: the Germans for acting rashly, the British for exposing so many people to waters that the Germans declared were in the war zone. But American opinion had coalesced on the British side of the balance, and the British version of events prevailed.

President Woodrow Wilson had little difficulty persuading Congress to approve a formal declaration of war on 6 April 1917. The

Germania's New York office soon lost direct touch with affairs in Germany, and the company became suddenly smaller. But the real impact of the war was yet to come, for the anti-German prejudices fanned during the early years of the war were having their effect on the whole German-American community. The process started soon after war began, during the closing years of Doremus's tenure and the beginning year of the new president, Hubert Cillis.

The German-American community was vulnerable to charges of un-Americanism because it retained a strong self-identity and vigorous ethnic-community institutions that kept it somewhat separate from the general populace. America was dotted with German lodges, alliances, clubs, and publications; parks contained statues of famous Germans, such as Goethe and Schiller. In 1917 there were still 522 German-language newspapers and journals publishing in the United States. The unification of Germany in 1871 and the glorification of the restored empire by Germans and German-Americans alike fortified the sense of ethnicity and created a feeling of special relationship between the immigrants and the home country. The four decades after unification saw pan-Germanism flourish as never before, and with it ideas about Germanic superiority that offended or unnerved many onlookers. It was during this period that the image of Germans as stolid, gentle farmers was replaced by one of disciplined workers and soldiers. The German immigrants who continued to enter the United States until the war began, in 1914, carried this image with them and helped reinforce the new stereotypes.[5]

The reaction of Americans to the new Germanism varied, revealing an ambivalent feeling. Theodore Roosevelt of New York, the state with the most German-Americans, criticized German clannishness in 1894 and accused immigrants who retained their ethnic identification of being suspect Americans. There were also several political areas of contention between the native-born and the German-American, such as prohibition, women's suffrage, and immigration policy, that generated additional hard feeling. On the other hand, particularly as immigration from eastern and southern Europe increased toward the turn of the century, Germans came to be considered the preferable immigrant group. In 1911, the Dillingham Commission, constituted by the House and the Senate in 1907 to investigate immigration, considered Germans to be racially superior and therefore highly desirable immigrants.

Similarly, the *American Journal of Sociology* published an article in 1916 that ranked ethnic groups on ten personal traits and, like the Dillingham Commission, rated the Germans second only to native-born Americans.[6]

The entrance of the United States into the war threw into high relief the issue of German ethnic consciousness and national identification. From the beginning of the war in 1914, many German-Americans had been rather active in support of Germany and therefore constituted a political pressure group for an American policy of neutrality. With the American declaration of war, these segments of the German community did an about-face and began to engage in public ceremonies such as flag presentations to demonstrate their loyalty to the American government. At the same time, shortly after declaring war, the federal government created the Committee on Public Information to mobilize support for the war. Headed by George Creel, a progressive journalist, the committee published massive amounts of propaganda, much of which contributed to a national wave of hysteria against German-Americans. A campaign to eradicate all presence of German culture swept the country, resulting in acts such as state prohibition of the teaching of German in public and private schools, the removal of German books from libraries, bans on the use of the German language in public, and even the denial of concert halls to German artists. The names of towns, streets, schools, and businesses were changed as a demonstration of patriotism.[7]

The public crusade against Germanness put the Germania on the defensive. Although the officers insisted that the company no longer depended upon the German community for its business, the Germania was indeed a German-American company. Its officers were German-born, and the board of directors was still predominantly German. Of twenty members, four were German immigrants, five to eight were of German extraction, and six resided in Germany and constituted the special European board in Berlin. One board vacancy was filled three weeks after the United States entered the war by Carl Heye, a German immigrant who became the company's next president. Many of its managers and agents were of German extraction, and the company still kept an eye toward doing business in the German-American community. In December 1915, for example, to assist the new manager in Chicago in his efforts to generate business, the Finance Committee approved time deposits in five local banks with German clientele.[8] A year later the committee voted to make a substantial loan to the YMCA in Evansville, Indiana, for the reason that "Evansville was a very progressive town of about 100,000 inhabitants, about half of whom were either Germans or of German descent, and that the consummation of the aforesaid loan would be of material help to Mr. Rudd [the local Germania manager] to firmly establish a prosperous agency for the Company there."[9] Finally, the Germania maintained a European branch, located in Berlin, that, until disrupted by the war, generated as much as 47 percent of the company's annual business. The war between the United States and Germany, then, undermined the very foundations of the Germania.

On 6 April 1917, the day the United States declared war on Germany, President Cillis sent a circular letter to the field staff affirming the company's Americanness.

In our annual statement attention was called to the fact that Germania is an American institution, true to American ideals and traditions. In amplifying such statement today I wish to say that every officer of the Company is an American citizen, and as far as we know all our managers, with but two or three exceptions, were born in this country.[10]

Some weeks later, Vice President Heye informed agents that the company was no longer automatically publishing its annual statements in German.[11]

As further protection against possible attacks of un-Americanism, the company took steps to make itself visible in support of the war effort. Several days after the war declaration, Cillis proposed that the company initiate a campaign to encourage policyholders to join in the National Economic Mobilization (the term used to describe the government's program of war-related economic activity). In discussing this with the Germania's Nominating Committee, Cillis declared that life insurance was an important factor in the economic life of the family and of the nation. If life insurance could aid mobilization by encouraging every policyholder to join in it, every life insurance company should feel duty-bound to help in such an effort. The obligation was especially great, Cillis noted pointedly, if a company was "in the position of The Germania," for then the help was "also dictated by its own business advantage." Cillis stressed the enlightened self-interest aspect later in his discussions with the committee. "In the extraordinary position of the Germania," he observed, "it is reasonable to suppose that the above expenditure would be more than compensated for because of the strong moral support it would give to the Company's agents, of the disarming of competition."[12] The costs alluded to were ten thousand dollars for the printing and mailing of bulletins to policy-holders regarding health, insurance, and family income management.

As Cillis predicted, the program had immediate publicity benefits when it was put into operation. The bulletin entitled "Be a Soldier of the Soil: Vegetable Gardens," for example, won the Germania praise from the National Emergency Food Garden Commission. Several leading newspapers carried articles on the program in early May. Garden committees, school libraries, and corporations asked the Germania for copies, and International Harvester requested permission to reprint the bulletin in its gardening handbook.[13]

The Germania also made a point of investing in war loans. The first Liberty Loan Act was authorized two weeks after the United States entered the war; although initially subscriptions lagged, the Germania purchased five hundred thousand dollars on the first day, thus becoming the first insurance company to do so.[14]

In the fall, when considering a subscription to the second Liberty Loan, the Finance Committee discussed decentralizing its purchases as a way to aid the field staff, in much the same way that making local time deposits had done just a few years earlier. The company had been requested, according to Cillis, to place a portion of the subscription through the local banks in the different cities where it was represented, and he felt it would be in the interest of the company's agencies to do so, even though it would involve somewhat more work than if a single subscription were made in New York. The decision to apportion the subscription was well received by the field force, for at a subsequent meeting, the secretary reported that the managers were pleased with the proposed apportionment, and held it of considerable value to their respective agencies. The Germania's agents derived valuable publicity from their local Liberty Loan bond subscriptions. The *Omaha Daily News*, for example, featured a front-page photograph of B. R. Plotts, the company's local manager, delivering twenty thousand dollars to the Federal Reserve Bank there.[15]

The Germania continued the practice of local distribution with its subscriptions to the third and fourth Liberty Loan drives. It determined the amounts of subscription not only by its investment needs but also by comparison with the subscriptions of other life insurance companies.[16] Because the loan drives were unsatisfactory, pressure was put upon insurance companies, as major investors of capital, to increase their participation, and the Germania was very responsive to these appeals. In October, Governor Benjamin Strong of the Federal Reserve Bank asked the Germania to increase its subscription to the fourth loan. The previous Wednesday the Finance Committee had agreed that the company should not pledge more than six hundred thousand dollars toward the new loan, since it was expecting a heavy cash payout for claims arising from the terrible influenza epidemic then sweeping the nation. Despite this weighty consideration, Cillis told the Finance Committee, the urgent appeal of Governor Strong had persuaded the Germania's officers to pledge another three hundred thousand dollars through anticipation of its income for the coming year.[17]

A New Name

When efforts such as those described above failed to protect the company fully against accusations or insinuations of un-Americanism, it became necessary to take additional steps, the most obvious one being to change the company's name. The first overt step toward a name change came in September 1917 at the company's first general convention of its agents and field managers.[18] At the meeting for managers, approximately three-fourths of those speaking favored a change. Some managers complained of trouble securing and keeping agents. The manager from Shreveport, Louisiana, for example, reported that a promising agent had recently left his agency because of the company name. Others reported that it was becoming more difficult to sell policies. Even the Germans in Davenport, reported the manager in Iowa, refused to buy insurance because of the name. Two managers stated that they did not use the Germania name in their advertising. One of the New York City managers, who himself had a German surname, thought that a name change would lower his production, but supported the change because of the comments made by his colleagues. He further proposed that the company replace its German directors and anything else which suggested Germany.[19]

The opinions expressed by managers were carefully noted and became part of an ongoing discussion at the home office. Both Carl Heye, vice president, and T. Louis Hansen, superintendent of agencies, before going to New Orleans, had concluded that the time had come to consider a change in the name. They were encouraged by the agreement of the field force.[20]

During the few weeks after the convention, the company's officers and board of directors discussed the pros and cons of a name change. On the one hand, a change of name risked upsetting present policyholders, particularly those who were German or German-American; involved considerable expense and time; and would have a negative impact on the European business. On the other hand, a name change would significantly aid the sales force in doing business; inspire loyalty and efficiency in the field force; and generate good will from the New York State Insurance Department, which would help the company get through the difficulties of the financial and mortuary losses expected in Europe. It would also enhance the company's status with other life insurance companies, which had always considered the Germania as an outsider and would be more likely to cooperate with it on reinsurance and other mutual interests if the name were changed. The impact on the European business was more or less disregarded because the increasing bitterness Germany felt against the United States made it doubtful the company would be able to do business there in any sizable volume for at least ten years, if ever.[21]

Timing was important. The company had not yet actually suffered a reduction in new business, but such a reduction was likely to occur soon. It would look better if the company changed its name while business was still good, rather than after it had declined. Equally important, the United States was not actually engaged in active fighting in Europe. A name change would seem more patriotic before casualties occurred than after, as a confidential memorandum noted with graphic imagery.

When the American forces have suffered losses in Europe, however, when transports have been sunk, when the first ships arrive with the caskets of fallen soldiers; when the transports return to the United States with mutilated and maimed men, blind soldiers led by their mates and paralyzed and other wrecks of humanity carried on stretchers, a change of name at that time would be commented upon—not as an act of patriotism, but of compulsion, and would probably be too late to have much beneficial effect.[22]

In late October 1917, the board met to consider changing the name of the Germania. At that meeting, T. Louis Hansen, superintendent of agencies, presented an impassioned plea on behalf of the Agency Department and the field force for a name change. Unless the name were changed, he predicted, the company would be ruined.

Should it be decided not to act favorably on the overwhelming request on the part of the fieldmen that a name be adopted which does not raise the question of German origin or affiliation, I do not believe it possible for any human agency to save the Organization from eventual discouragement and disruption under the present circumstances, since such adverse action would be viewed by the men in the light of a disinclination on the part of the Company to remedy a desperate situation, and even though wrongly, that sentiment for something German has greater weight at the Home Office than the needs of the Company, its policyholders and fieldmen.

Furthermore, Hansen pointed out, more delay might deplete the company's field force. "Good life insurance men" were in greater demand than salesmen in other lines, and other companies were constantly approaching Germania fieldmen with "flattering" offers. No one, Hansen concluded, could foresee for how long they would resist the temptation to give up the struggle.[23]

A month later, the board held a special meeting to vote on the proposed name change. In the meantime, Cillis had explored with the New York State Department of Insurance the possibility of changing the name of the company to either the Union or the Guardian.[24] After considering material on name changes by other German-American institutions, the board unanimously resolved, on 5 December 1917, that the name of the Germania Life Insurance Company be changed to The Guardian Life Insurance Company of America. The change was to take effect as soon as the legal requirements were fulfilled.[25]

The company lost no time in announcing the board's decision. On the same day, Cillis sent an announcement to the company's managers describing the decision as a positive and necessary response to the needs of the field force. News articles covering the name change appeared in the New York City press the following day. The public hostility toward Germanness surfaced in the press coverage. In an article entitled "Germania Life Company to Bear American Name," the *New York Herald* reported: "Desiring to prove that their company is thoroughly American, the officers of the Germania Life Insurance Company, of this city, determined at a special meeting yesterday to apply for an order authorizing the organization to be known as the Guardian Life Insurance Company. It will take about ten weeks to obliterate the Hun title."[26]

The change in name took effect on 1 March 1918. The company celebrated its new name by designating March "Guardian Life Month," and launching an honorary sales drive. This extremely successful effort produced over $4.8 million in new business, the largest monthly production in the company's history.[27]

Withdrawal from Europe

In 1917, the future of the European business became part of the deliberations on Americanizing the company through a name change. The detrimental effect of such a change on the European business caused the officers and board members to assess carefully the postwar prospects in Europe. General agreement emerged on two points: The first, mentioned by the board in previous deliberations, was that there seemed little chance the European business would revive within the decade if at all; the second, that linking the discontinuation of the European business with the name change would help the field force overcome the company's image as a foreign entity.[28]

There were precedents for the company's abandoning operations in a foreign country, with the possibility, however faint, of someday returning. One example was Canada. The Germania entered the market there during the 1860s, but withdrew in 1868, along with most of the other American insurance companies doing business there, when the government in Ottawa passed a law requiring foreign insurance companies to deposit fifty thousand dollars with the Minister of Finance, and then subsequently to bring the deposit up to one hundred thousand dollars. Hugo Wesendonck visited Montreal in 1875 and became convinced that the company should reenter the market. The Finance Committee agreed, but no action followed. When Wesendonck repeated his suggestion, in 1887, the board approved and the company opened an office in Toronto.[29]

A second example, and one fresh in everyone's mind, was Mexico. In 1902 the company sent Max Wesendonck to Mexico to open business there. The first few years went well, despite the company's practice of issuing policies payable only in American gold coin, not

Mexican silver as the other companies did. (Eventually the company's agents persuaded the home office to begin issuing policies payable in Mexican money.)[30] In 1912 the Germania reviewed its business in Mexico, after the government in Mexico City demanded that foreign insurance companies immediately purchase and deposit with them Mexican securities equal to the amount of premiums received less expenses. The Finance Committee recommended that the company accede to this demand to protect its valuable business there.[31] The company agreed to the deposits, but, before it had made them all, began having second thoughts. What gave it pause was the increasingly shaky position of the government in Mexico City, in the face of serious social and political unrest. In measuring the severity of the problem, the Germania followed the lead of New York Life, which also did a substantial Mexican business. In 1913 the Germania began negotiating for an extension in making additional deposits with the government, as a way of slowing the increase in its financial exposure, but when these attempts failed the company allowed its Mexican license to expire, on 1 December 1913.[32] Although the evidence is not clear, it seems that the company had its license reinstated early in 1914, for in a Finance Committee meeting of 8 March 1916, it was stated that the company had done a slight amount of business in Mexico during the past three years. At the same meeting, however, it was resolved to terminate the contract of the agent in Mexico, as of 1 July 1916.[33]

The European business was far more important to the company than the Mexican, but the principle was the same: the company, headquartered in New York City, was in essence an American entity, which had to be defended and protected even by the most extreme measures if necessary. This was the final conclusion in a long chain of logic that had been working itself out in the company since the war began. Every discussion or decision by the board, the officers, and the various committees served to advance the argument another step, as the company decided first that it would mute its Germanness, later that it would suppress its Germanness, and finally that it would pull out of Germany and Austria altogether. The next step would be to withdraw from all foreign countries, as a symbolic and substantive move to demonstrate the company's utter Americanness. The Canadian and Mexican episodes provided both the model for such withdrawal and the unspoken possibility of an eventual return.

On 5 December 1917, the board of directors unanimously voted to stop the writing of any new business outside the United States. As Cillis later explained to the European branch, the board regretted the need to do this but saw no alternative. He added that the board considered its action final.[34]

Despite these strenuous efforts, the company still found itself on the defensive, even years later. When Cillis retired from the presidency and was succeeded by German-born Carl Heye in 1921, for example, one trade journal used the occasion to remark on the continued presence of Germans in the company.

The Germania Life Insurance Company of New York and Berlin, which, during the war, found it expedient to change its name to the Guardian Life Insurance Company of *America*, has had a shake up in its official staff. Hubert Cillis has resigned the presidency, which has been handed over to Carl Heye, and T. Louis Hansen has been made first vice president. The other officers with strikingly American names are John Fuhrer, vice president and actuary; Fred A. Goecke, secretary; Rudolph C. Neuendorfer, secretary and Charles Kruse, cashier. Nearly all of these eminent American gentlemen were born in Germany, or some other part of Europe.[35]

In addition to problems with its image, the company also had to contend with actions by the American government. On 6 October 1917, two months before the board voted to stop writing insurance abroad, Congress passed the Trading with the Enemy Act, which gave the president authority to control enemy property and to appoint an official for this purpose. Two weeks later, President Wilson appointed A. Mitchell Palmer as the Alien Property Custodian. While the original legislation set strict conditions for the sale of alien-owned property, Palmer's testimony resulted in broader legislation giving him general power of sale over all seized property. A subsequent executive order further expanded his power to control completely all seized property.[36]

As required by the new law, and on advice of counsel, the Guardian submitted to the Alien Property Custodian a list of its enemy alien stockholders. These amounted to 1,548 shares, or 38.7 percent of the total capital stock. The custodian first demanded their stock certificates, and subsequently asked that replacement certificates be issued in his name.[37]

In April 1918, the custodian, "in view of the comparatively large holdings of the Company's capital stock by alien enemies, had expressed the wish to be represented on the Board by nine gentlemen of his own selection."[38] The board requested an opinion from the company's counsel, who advised it to comply with the request.

> It was never intended that minority stockholders or their representatives should control the action of the majority of the stockholders in the selection of directors or otherwise, and, in our opinion, the Alien Property Custodian, solely as the representative of minority stockholders and standing in their shoes, has no authority in law to dictate who shall be directors of the Company. . . . As we advised you orally, it would be to the best interests of all concerned that you appoint, or elect, to fill the vacancies in your Board, if you so desire, such parties as the Alien Property Custodian recommends to you to fill such vacancies in the manner provided by law.[39]

Advised by counsel to comply voluntarily and too vulnerable to object, the board proceeded to act on the custodian's request. In May, therefore, the board declared vacant the six seats that constituted the special European board at Berlin, all held by German citizens whose stock had been seized. The additional three vacancies were obtained by resignations. At the special board meeting in August, the nominees of the custodian were elected to the board and appointed to the committees as he had designated.[40]

After the war was over, in the spring of 1919, the custodian put up for auction the 1,548 shares of seized Guardian stock. To prevent "disruptive elements" from gaining control of the board of directors, Cillis put together a consortium that successfully bid on the entire block of stock.[41] Memories of the takeover bid during Doremus's tenure were still fresh.

Armistice and Epidemic

On 11 November 1918, a new German provisional government agreed to a cease fire with the Allies. The Kaiser had abdicated and fled, as food riots and other disturbances spread throughout the country. The navy was struggling with mutinous sailors, the army had just suffered a decisive defeat on the western front, and leading military men saw no hope of victory and feared invasion. Amidst all the turmoil of the war's last days and the uncertain beginnings of peace and normalcy, came a kind of modern-day plague, influenza. Unlike the seasonal outbreaks common in most years, this influenza epidemic carried a special potency, which killed anyone too young or too weak to resist. No part of Europe or the Americas escaped, and in all, an estimated 21 million people died worldwide.

The epidemic had an effect on the life insurance companies that almost overshadowed the end of the war. An article in the *Chicago Evening Post* of 30 December 1918 declared that the epidemic's "tremendous and extraordinary death loss" had raised mortality rates "from 50 to 250 per cent." Policyholders should expect their policy dividends to be small next year, the article continued, and in fact the Guardian and other life companies reduced the dividends they expected to pay in 1919. The magnitude of the situation is evident from Cillis's remark that while the war losses might be "ignored entirely at this time [12 December 1918], it is quite different with the influenza epidemic, nothing similar to which has been experienced in the entire history of life insurance." Cillis went on to say that the American deaths from the epidemic would probably exceed "the entire number of casualties among the American troops engaged in the war." Even the next year, when the epidemic had abated, the Guardian's dividend rose only slightly. Cillis in that year recommended "conservatism regarding this subject," partly because he thought the epidemic might recur.[42]

Liquidating the European Business

While the company adjusted to peacetime conditions and coped with the influenza epidemic, it also began addressing the issue of its European operation. The New York office had received little information about the business in Germany once the United States had entered hostilities. Peace meant the resumption of communications. In 1919, the home office finally received information on the European business for the first three quarters of 1918. The branch in Berlin had been able to conduct its business during the war without interference from either the German or Austrian governments, and losses by death were well below the rate of the previous year. Even more impressive, the European board had been able to finance itself during the war years without transfer payments from the home office.[43]

On 7 July, President Cillis wrote to the Berlin office for the first time since 1916. In the letter, he informed Berlin about several important developments in 1917 and 1918, which included the change in the company name, the government seizure of German-owned stock under the Trading with the Enemy Act and the automatic removal of Germans from the board of directors, and the board's decision to restrict the company's future business to the United States.[44] A few weeks later, Carl Heye, vice president and secretary, went to Berlin at the request of the European board to confer on important business matters. When he returned in October, Heye advocated the creation of a special advisory committee consisting of four former European board members and an additional person with a finance subcommittee to oversee the business as the board had before.[45]

Before this committee could be put in place, the former special European board at Berlin "urgently" requested reconsideration of the decision of the board to cease the writing of new business in Europe. The Nominating Committee informed the special board that the board of directors had decided to discontinue business in Europe in order to help the company's agency force overcome the continuing prejudice against the company in the United States because of its European connections. In addition, the board felt that conditions in Europe would not be favorable for profitable business for years to come. The committee explained that economic, social, political, and hygienic conditions in Europe as a result of the war made it unwise for the Guardian to continue its business there.[46]

Having decided to discontinue issuing new policies in Europe, the Guardian began to consider the possible sale of the existing business a few months after the war ended. During the summer of 1919, the Guardian requested an opinion on the matter. The superintendent of insurance in New York stated that he would not consider reinsurance by a German company that had not been admitted in New York. He did, however, favor the sale provided that American policyholders were relieved of all contingent liability, that the sale did not involve payments greater than investments held by the company in Europe, and that at least 90 percent of its European policyholders signed consent releases.[47]

Disposition of the European business was not officially discussed again until the fall of 1921, when the Finance Committee considered several alternatives, including purchase of outstanding policies and sale of the business to a foreign company or syndicate. The committee quickly rejected the buy-back approach, since other American companies that had tried it were encountering unreasonable terms. Sale to a foreign buyer or buyers looked better, although conditions varied greatly among the various countries involved. It was an attractive option in Czechoslovakia and Yugoslavia, where new laws made the sale relatively easy. In Austria and the other succession states to the now dissolved Austro-Hungarian Empire, the exchange of government securities held by the company made it possible that the Guardian, as its sale price, would receive a considerable amount of valuable securities. In Germany, however, the legal and political situation, as well as economic uncertainties, prevented the company from making a sale even though it urgently wished to.[48]

The need to liquidate the European business as quickly as possible was underscored by the difficulties of conducting business there. Because of economic instability following the war, the European board repeatedly requested increases in salaries as well as special benefits for its staff. In 1919, for example, it asked the board of directors in New York to reconsider the salary it had voted for Rudolph Goose, who replaced Heinrich Rose as general director when he died in 1918. The board made a limited concession, but strongly defended its decision against a major salary increase.[49] The following year, the company agreed to make a severance payment to Goose upon liquidation of the European business. But the bickering over his compensation continued to annoy the New York office because, according to the president, the European directors sought as high a compensation as possible for Goose without appreciating the company's view that the amount should be based on conditions existing in Germany. Furthermore, the president continued, this was making an unfavorable impression on the company's officers, who felt the home office should take a firm attitude in the matter.[50]

The staff in the Berlin office also made requests of the New York office. In March 1920, the president reported that the Berlin staff had twice asked him urgently to ship a box of foodstuffs to relieve the distress caused by the prevailing high prices, as the New York Life Insurance Company had done. In response, the home office cabled a remittance to the Berlin office with instructions to use the money for the relief of all employees, especially the lower salaried ones. A similar request for relief was received from the office in Vienna. As a result of agreements negotiated between the Association of Insurance Employees and German insurance companies, the Guardian was required to pay additional amounts to employees who were not officers as high-cost-of-living allowances. The company also continued to send occasional sums for special relief. In addition, the company created a pension fund for the Berlin staff, as proposed by the older employees, to safeguard their future, which was threatened by the liquidation of the European business.[51]

In addition to the difficulties of supporting the European staff, the Guardian also had problems handling business in the chaotic economic conditions of postwar Europe in a manner that would strengthen or at least not undermine its business at home. In particular, the Guardian was pressed to modify its dividend policy and its accounting procedures for determining valuation on its foreign securities. Although it did not do so at first, finally the company had to rethink its formula for distributing dividends to reflect these economic conditions. In 1919, as a result of losses caused by the influenza epidemic, the Guardian had decided to use only half of the available surplus for the year 1918 for policy dividends. As the company recovered, it gradually increased the proportion of the surplus allocated for this purpose. In 1921, the Finance Committee, concluding that it was neither necessary nor proper any longer to treat the domestic and European departments equally regarding dividends, asked the board to distinguish between them when deciding upon dividends for 1921.[52] The board then voted that there be no dividends on business in the former Austro-Hungarian Empire, 50 percent of the standard contribution for the business in Germany, and 80 percent for the remainder of the European business. The following year, the board eliminated dividends on policies in Germany as well as in the former Austro-Hungarian Empire, but raised the rate for the rest of Europe to 90 percent of the standard contribution.[53]

Rapid inflation in postwar Europe produced fluctuations in the value of the company's foreign securities. It was obvious that the company would eventually have to devalue these securities in its annual report, and that a large drop in the value of the company's assets could injure the domestic operation. The Guardian therefore sought to make the devaluation when it would do the least harm.

Discussions began as early as February 1921 and concluded in November, when the failure to devalue threatened to create excessive paper profits. Other payments from Europe, including receipt of a large amount of interest from Austrian securities that had been temporarily suspended during 1920, would force the company to show an increase in the surplus in excess of dividend requirements, which would result in a high liability for federal income taxes.[54] Therefore, the president advocated lowering the rates of currency conversion. The adoption of new conversion rates reduced the value of both the assets and liabilities of the European branch by almost 90 percent.[55]

Since the write-down might adversely affect morale among the fieldmen, the New York office sent T. Louis Hansen to discuss the matter with the regional managers. Hansen reported finding a lot of optimism, but, of course, some pessimism at the deflation program, which the managers accepted as a wise move. All agreed that the real impact of the program would depend on how it was received by the insurance press.[56]

As negotiations for liquidation dragged, Carl Heye, the company's new president, went to Berlin in the summer of 1922. His goal was to dispose of the European operations as expeditiously as possible, beginning with the operation in the former Austro-Hungarian Empire, which was the least desirable, and moving on to the more desirable operations in Germany, Belgium, Spain, Holland, and Switzerland.[57] By autumn Heye had negotiated contracts approved by the board of directors to sell the business in Austria to the Phoenix Life Insurance Company of Vienna, and that in Czechoslovakia to the Slovanska Life Insurance Company located in Prague. At the same meeting, the board authorized the officers to dispose of the remaining business in the other succession states. At the request of the Czechoslovakian government, the contract for business in that country was later transferred from the Slovanska to the Elbe, a company that did most of its business with the German population of the new nation.[58]

Negotiations with the Phoenix for the sale of the remaining business continued, although there was some apprehension that policyholders in Belgium, Holland, and Spain would object to having their business handled by an Austrian company.[59] During the summer of 1923, Vice President Hansen went to Berlin to finalize the transfer of the German business.[60] By October, despite numerous legal and governmental difficulties, Hansen had successfully completed negotiations with the Phoenix for the business in Germany, Austria, and Hungary, and all the territories ceded by them to other countries in postwar treaties, except for the Czechoslovakian business which was transferred to the Elbe, and the business in Romania which was transferred to the Steaua Romaniei Insurance Company of Bucharest. To protect the Guardian from future liabilities, most of the business taken over by the Phoenix was reinsured by the Munich Reinsurance Company, while the Phoenix itself reinsured the business taken over by the Steaua Romaniei.[61]

Shortly after the Guardian had sold its European business, the Berlin office discovered that in transferring the German business to the Phoenix, it had overlooked the so-called German foreign policies written by the German general agencies on the lives of persons living outside of Germany. An accounting conducted some months later revealed that this oversight included 209 policies, half in Switzerland.[62] The German foreign business was then included in ongoing discussions with the Phoenix for the transfer of the remaining European business. In 1927 President Heye went to Berlin to complete this transaction.[63]

Although the board of directors approved the terms negotiated by Heye, the German authorities delayed implementation of the contract over the issue of liability for revalorization.[64] The postwar inflation in Germany had virtually wiped out debts contracted before the war. The average prewar Germania policy, for example, had been issued for eight thousand marks; by 1923, these policies were therefore worth much less than the four hundred thousand marks postage it took to file a claim.[65] In 1924, the German government enacted revalorization legislation to protect creditors at least partially against loss from inflation in those cases where the basis of the debt retained its value. The scope of this law, which required the reinstatement of mortgages in gold at 25 percent of their face value, extended to all contracts backed by a reserve consisting of all or part of such obligations, including insurance. Life insurance companies were then required to contribute both the revalorized gold assets and additional amounts from other assets to a fund for the revalorization of their policies.[66]

The German government established the revalorization liability on an individual-company basis. After extended negotiations, the German Insurance Department determined in 1930 that the Guardian should contribute $670,000, a sum the company considered "a serious encroachment" upon the rights of the company's other policyholders. The Guardian then asked the New York State Insurance Department what it thought was an appropriate contribution to the revalorization fund.[67] The department supported the company's view that the German authorities were requesting an excessive amount. Such a contribution would "dangerously impair" the company's financial position, the superintendent observed, to the prejudice of all its non-German policyholders, and would undermine public confidence. The superintendent suggested that the company's contribution to the German revalorization fund not exceed $150,000.[68]

In 1931, ostensibly as a result of the position of the New York Insurance Department, the German authorities reduced the amount requested from the Guardian for revalorization to $265,000. Since this amount was still above the figure suggested by the state superintendent, the Guardian sought a legal opinion. Pointing out that the German authorities had substantially reduced the amount assessed, the company's legal counsel advised payment. "If you did not accept this settlement and make the contribution," counsel warned, ". . . protection to the interests of the American insured would be entirely defeated, because you would thereby be precipitated into a prolonged and expensive litigation in Germany, and the result of that litigation might well be quite disastrous to you."[69] This contribution was then approved by both the board of directors and the State Insurance Department, and the formal entitlement plan was later announced in the German press.[70]

With the revalorization issue settled, President Heye returned to Berlin to finalize the contract with the Phoenix for the remainder of the European business. Although Heye negotiated a tentative agreement, the Phoenix failed to follow through. The Guardian therefore concluded that the Phoenix did not wish to proceed with the transaction while the conditions in Europe were uncertain.[71] Nor did the Guardian pursue liquidation with any other company. These policies remained on the company books until 1952 when the last of them were finally bought back from their purchasers.

Mutualization

Mutualization, a topic of discussion in the company since the turn of the century, came in 1924 as part of the strategy to defend the Guardian against charges of foreign influence or ownership. In 1921, the officers raised the question of mutualization with the Executive Committee, which authorized them to explore the idea with the state insurance department. While favorably disposed, the superintendent suggested the move be deferred, since three officers stood to benefit unduly. The three officers—Cillis, Hansen, and Heye—had purchased the 38 percent of the stock that had been confiscated as belonging to aliens by the U.S. government during the war. In 1924 the board of directors voted in favor of a mutualization plan that paid $150 per share—300 percent of par value—which would net the three officers $2,500 each in profit, a considerable sum in those days.[72] Perhaps to mollify the state insurance department, however, instead of taking this profit, the officers contributed the money to establish an employee welfare fund. Chartered by New York State in 1926, the Guardian Life Welfare Trust was intended to help company staff in times of dire need. The original $7,500 contribution from Cillis, Hansen, and Heye, grew to $21,000 by 1930 from interest and voluntary contributions, and was chartered to reach a maximum of $250,000. Although the motives for establishing the trust were either paternalistic or connected with the desires of the state superintendent of insurance, the effect was to establish what was probably the Guardian's first formal fringe benefit. Unlike previous offers of help to needy staff, this fund was impersonal in its operation and did not rely on the capriciousness or benevolence of management; it applied equally to all covered individuals.[73]

Mutualization was approved in 1924 and 1925 by all voting stockholders and a majority of voting policyholders. It also appealed to the field force, since the elimination of stock dividends would reduce expenses, increase policy dividends, and thus boost sales. "The mutualizing of the company," wrote the agency supervisor from South Carolina, "certainly puts us in a position to be leaders in net costs."[74] In January 1925 the state superintendent of insurance approved the mutual plan, and by May, when all but ten shares had been surrendered, the Guardian became a mutual company.[75]

Epilogue

This history began with three questions that seemed especially fitting to help consider the evolution of the Germania Life and its transformation into the Guardian. With the story now told, it is possible to return to the questions in an explicit way and suggest some final conclusions about the company's first sixty years.

The first question asked whether the appeal to the German and German-American markets had more than a short-term advantage for the company. As noted in the text, the Germania's focus on a large and self-conscious ethnic group provided it with an immediate and receptive domestic market, not only in New York City but in cities and small towns scattered across the country. It also offered the potential for expansion among German émigré communities abroad, and even the establishment of operations in the German states themselves. To an analyst observing the scene in 1870, this marketing strategy must have seemed sound, for the total number of Germans and persons of German origins worldwide was large and growing, and the Germans contained a large affluent element that could provide a lucrative business. These were the positive factors that Hugo Wesendonck and his colleagues saw when they started the company. There were also drawbacks, however, since the ethnic market, though large, was by definition much smaller than the general market. An analyst in 1870 might have predicted that someday the focus on the German and German-American markets might actually work to limit the company's growth, which raises the second question posed in the Prologue: Why did the Germania fail to become one of the giants in its industry?

During the 1870s the American economy entered one of its most severe contractions, pulling down with it many life insurance companies. The Germania survived, as discussed in chapter 5, as a result of cost-cutting moves and changes in its field force, but surely another factor working in its favor was the loyalty of its policyholders in both the United States and abroad. This loyalty was a great reserve of strength, which must have confirmed the wisdom of concentrating marketing efforts on one particular ethnic group. What no one could foresee was the enormous growth in the domestic life insurance industry between 1880 and 1910, which dwarfed the steady growth of the Germania in its ethnically defined markets. In 1865 the Germania had about $15 million in policies in effect and ranked twelfth among U.S. companies. Five years later, after a doubling of policies in force, the company had actually fallen in rank to nineteenth, although during the hard times of the 1870s, when other companies faltered severely, the Germania rose to the ninth rank by 1880. In the good economic conditions of the 1880s and early 1890s, however, the Germania's essentially conservative stance could not produce the kind of explosive growth enjoyed by many companies, such as the Prudential or New York Life. Although between 1880 and 1885 the Germania increased its insurance by nearly one-third, it slipped to twelfth place; and by 1890, after another growth in policies by barely one-third, it slipped to fifteenth. Between 1895 and 1900 its ranking fell to nineteenth, while its policies grew by about one-fifth, to $82 million. Between 1900 and 1910 the company's policies rose by more than 50 percent, to $126 million, while its ranking steadied at twenty-first. By comparison with these steady but modest rates of growth in sales, the Metropolitan Life, which in 1875 ranked eighteenth with $25 million of policies in force, by 1885 had moved up to seventh with $111 million; and by 1905 ranked second with $1.597 billion in policies. Between 1865 and 1910, the Germania grew eightfold, from $15 million in policies in force to $126 million, while during the thirty years between 1875 and 1905 the Metropolitan was growing sixty-threefold.[1]

Meanwhile, the scope of German immigration to the United States was changing, to the detriment of the Germania. Increasingly, from the mid-1880s immigrants to the United States were from non-German parts of Europe. For most of the nineteenth century, immigrants from the German states made up a large proportion of newcomers to the United States. Between 1849, when Hugo Wesendonck and his wife arrived in America, and about 1885, German immigrants represented anywhere from 30 to 50 percent of newcomers in most years. In 1854 they were approximately 215,000 out of 428,000 newcomers; in 1870, about 118,000 out of 387,000. Their contribution to the flourishing German-American community was discussed in an early chapter. The peak of German immigration, in absolute numbers, came in 1882, when 215,000 Germans arrived out of a total of 789,000 immigrants— about 32 percent. By 1890 the Germans' number and proportion of total immigration had declined sharply, to 92,000 and 20 percent. The decline continued during the next twenty-five years, so that by 1900 German immigrants were only 4 percent of the half million new-comers, and by 1905 about 3 percent of the slightly more than one million immigrants.[2]

The decline in German immigration sharply reduced the infusion of ethnic awareness and culture that the German-American community had been receiving for decades. It raised the likelihood that the com-munity would gradually lose its German self-identification, as it gradu-ally became absorbed into the dominant culture. Such a shift in self-identity would have profound implications for any company, such as the Germania, that based its appeal on ethnic identity. The company made a few attempts to enlarge its appeal, but without the single-minded commitment that might have brought success. As noted ear-lier, during the economic hard times of the 1870s Hugo Wesendonck made a short-lived attempt to recruit some non-German agents into the field force, but nothing came of it. Another attempt occurred in the 1880s with the creation of the industrial insurance branch, which aimed at the less affluent sector of the German-American community. Industrial insurance was transforming the Metropolitan into a giant; it was making Prudential into a vast enterprise. For the Germania, how-ever, it fizzled. In his testimony before the Armstrong Committee President Cornelius Doremus noted that industrial insurance suc-ceeded only when it received the full commitment of the company, and twenty years earlier the Germania's Committee on Agents had made a similar statement after closing down the industrial insurance branch. Why had the Germania failed to give it the needed support?

In his Armstrong Committee testimony Doremus spoke with dis-taste of the passion for bigness that had gripped the domestic life insurance industry. In Germany conditions were much more to his liking, for there policyholders were ignorant of the practice of rebating, and, in addition, showed great loyalty to their insuror. Year after year, the German policyholders renewed their Germania policies, allowing the company to keep commissions and costs low and returns high. Doremus clearly felt more comfortable with the German situation than the American. Like Hugo Wesendonck, Doremus preferred a small but loyal clientele to a large but fickle one.

This kind of approach, which sacrificed size for stability, does not seem to have worked to the disadvantage of policyholders. The rampant growth of the big companies during the period 1880–1905 was not producing economies of scale that were passed on to policyholders. If anything, the rapid growth often worked to the disadvantage of policyholders, as companies used their rising sales to underwrite even more sales efforts, rather than to reduce costs to current holders of policies. During the Armstrong Committee hearings the new president of the Equitable, Paul Morton, made a remarkable statement to the company's policyholders, which was virtually an admission of guilt. The Equitable's new administration, he stated, would not seek to have "the biggest company in the world," but "to make it the best, and safest." He went on: "Conservative lines will be followed. It will be the policy not to solicit or secure new business at the expense of the present policyholders, and in case it is determined that business in any section of the world is unprofitable that field will be abandoned." Cornelius Doremus must have read this statement in the *New York Sun* of 18 December 1905, with some relish.

Although the Germania's refusal to seek rapid growth rested on a belief in the disadvantages of bigness, there was a danger that the company might become so small, relative to its peers, that it would become especially vulnerable to external crises. One such crisis would be the loss of its European business, which would diminish an already small company.

To its credit, when the crisis hit, during World War I, the Germania's leadership acted decisively in disassociating the company from Germany, and in extricating itself from the European business. That success did not, however, provide a solution to the problem that immediately presented itself: how to become a truly American company that marketed without reference to an ethnic appeal. That is the third question posed in the Prologue.

For sixty years the company had prospered by working a substantial, although marginal, market segment; after 1920 it would have to find a replacement market, and it would have to do so lacking the great financial clout and advertising impact of a giant company. It was not a regional company, so it could not build on a geographical appeal; and its policy offerings were, if anything, rather conservative by industry standards. It retained a base of loyal policyholders, mostly German-American, but these were less a source for growth than a hedge against further decline. Even so, the Guardian continued its fall in ranking among American life insurance companies—to twenty-ninth by 1937. Simple extrapolation would have dropped the company into the basement of rankings by the 1950s or 1960s, but instead the Guardian rebounded, after World War II, to become by 1985 the twentieth largest company in its industry. Evidently, sometime after 1937 the company found a successful marketing approach, aided no doubt by the general prosperity of the period after World War II.

From this study of the company's first sixty years, it is possible to suggest some factors that might have contributed to its improved success during the second sixty. The Germania had very successfully appealed to professionals and small businessmen among Germans and German-Americans; perhaps it was able easily to transfer this facility when it turned to the broader domestic market. Again, the company may have found its "hands on" management style—a legacy from Wesendonck—some compensation for its small size and low visibility in the broad national market. Its core of loyal agents, with whom the company had good relations for most of its history, may have provided an unexpected source of strength in the new selling areas, and it is possible that clients, in turn, responded favorably to a company small enough to offer individual attention. Beyond these general observations, however, it is impossible to go. Until the research and analysis have been done that would provide definitive answers, the final question posed in the Prologue must await the second volume of the Guardian's history.

Appendix
Members of the Germania
Board of Directors, 1860–1920

This appendix provides brief descriptive entries for the 106 men who sat on the board of directors from the beginning of the company in 1860 until 1920, when the company began divesting itself of its European operations. The entries include every director whose term began during or before 1920.

The intent is to provide for each director the following information, where available: 1) full name; 2) dates of service as director, with an indication in parentheses if the service was on the special board in Berlin, which oversaw European operations; 3) places and dates of birth and death; 4) occupation (e.g., importer, lawyer); 5) occupational affiliations (corporations, partnerships, etc.); 6) additional comments relating to the director's personal, civic, or business affairs.

The information presented has been selected from much fuller material contained in dossiers compiled under the direction of Mr. John C. Angle, of the Guardian Life Insurance Company, as well as company board minutes. Years of board service begin with actual service, not date of election. Board members for whom standard historical reference works provide good accounts have received only a brief treatment in the appendix; the same is true for directors who are discussed at length in the text. Personal names that appear in the records in both German and anglicized forms have been anglicized only when cited that way in Germania/Guardian printed materials.

THOMAS ACHELIS, 1894–1911. B. Germany, 1840; d. Bremen, Germany, 1911. Importer/exporter, dry goods; Frederick Vietor & Achelis. *See also* his nephew, George F. Vietor.

ERNEST AHLEMANN, 1910–18 (European board). King's Counsel (Justizrat) in Berlin, 1915–20. Stock seized by Alien Property Commission.

LEWIS E. AMSINCK, 1860–88. Importer; L. E. Amsinck & Co. (in partnership with brother Gustav). Vice consul for Portugal in New York City.

WILLIAM AUFERMAN, 1862–65.

GEORGE CURTIS AUSTIN, 1918–33. B. Saluvia, Penn., 1863. Lawyer; Turner McClure & Rolston, 1887–93; Seward, Guthrie, Morawetz & Steele, 1893–95; Austin, McLanahan & Merrit. Nominated to board by Alien Property Commission. Elected to New York State assembly, 1895.

EWALD BALTHASAR, 1894–1902. B. Barmen, Germany, 1834; d. New York City, 1902. Silk manufacturer; partner in banking firm of Hallgarten & Co.

HERMAN RICHARD BALTZER, 1869–93. B. Stettin, Germany, 1827; d. New York City, 1893. Banker; Marcuse & Baltzer, early 1860s (*see* Hermann Marcuse); 1869–70, partner with William G. Taaks; Baltzer & Lichtenstein, by 1880.

WILHELM VON BECKER, 1908–18 (European board). B. 1835; d. 1918. City councillor, Halberstadt, Germany; mayor of Zeitz; mayor of Halberstadt, 1868–75; mayor of Düsseldorf, 1876–86; mayor of Cologne, 1886–1907; privy counsellor (with title of Excellency), 1907. Ennobled, 1911; became vice president of the Herrenhauses, Prussian Diet, 1907. Stock seized by Alien Property Commission.

AUGUST BELMONT, 1863–69. B. Alzer, Germany, 1816; d. New York City, 1890. Banker, diplomat; August Belmont & Co.; consul general to the United States for Austria, 1844–50; U.S. minister to The

Netherlands, 1853–57; chairman, National Democratic Committee, 1864–72. Helped raise and equip a German-American regiment in New York City during the Civil War.

ISAAC BERNHEIMER, 1860–93. B. Bavaria, 1812; d. Saratoga, N.Y., 1893. Merchant and real-estate investor; Bernheimer Bros. (clothing manufacturers). Sponsor of original petition for American Hebrew College.

FREDERICK AUGUST (FRITZ) VON BERNUTH, 1870–1917. B. Lennep, Germany, 1834; d. New York City, 1917. Importer and merchant; Hardt, von Bernuth & Co. (dry goods). Von Bernuth was brother-in-law to his partner, Hardt, who was also a member of the Germania board of directors.

FRANCIS BOLTING, 1880–94. B. Prussia, 1820; d. Orangetown, N.Y., 1894. Merchant.

CHARLES AUGUSTUS BOODY, 1920–26. B. Brooklyn, N.Y., 1870; d. Brooklyn, N.Y., 1926. Banker; clerk, First National Bank of New York, 1887–89; joined Peoples Trust Co. in 1889; became president in 1907.

DR. ERNST VON BORSIG, 1911–18 (European board). B. Germany, 1869; d. Berlin, 1933. Industrialist; the Borsig Works (coal, steel, locomotives). Stock seized by Alien Property Commission.

ERNST BREDT, 1865–91. B. Barmen, Germany, 1826; d. New York City, 1891. Importer and dye manufacturer; E. Bredt & Co.; director, German Savings Bank.

CHARLES BREUSING, 1860–61. B. Germany, 1825; d. New York City, 1863. Owned a music store that he later sold to B. Beer and Gustav Schirmer.

MAX BÜRGERS, 1900–1902. D. Berlin, 1902. Financier.

HENRY A. CAESAR, 1892–1918. B. Brooklyn, 1856; d. New York, 1939. Factor, silk importer, commission merchant, private banker;

H. A. Caesar & Co. At age fourteen sent to boarding school in Germany for four years. *See also* Ewald Fleitmann.

ELIE CHARLIER, 1860–71. B. France, 1826; d. Paris, 1896. Teacher. Founded Charlier Institute, a preparatory school in New York.

HUBERT CILLIS, 1891–1925. B. Cologne, Germany, 1848; d. Boston, Mass., 1925. Actuary, banker; third president of the Germania Life Insurance Company, 1915–1921; president, German Savings Bank, 1915–25. A founding member in 1889 of the Actuarial Society of America; president of the Mayor's Citizens Advisory Committee, 1917–19, which resolved matters involving aliens of German origin during World War I. Trustee of the German Society.

WILLIAM M. CRUIKSHANK, 1918–19. B. 1870; d. Garden City, N.Y., 1963. Realtor; William Cruikshank's Sons Real Estate. Trustee under the will of Theodore Roosevelt; member, Real Estate Board of New York. Appointed director by the Alien Property Commission.

ALBERT F. D'OENCH, 1894–1918. B. St. Louis, Mo., 1852; d. New York City, 1918. Architect; Bernhard Simon, 1887–1900; D'Oench & Yost, 1901–18. Designer of the Germania Life Insurance Company's Union Square home-office building in New York City. Served as New York City building superintendent, 1884–87, under Mayor William R. Grace, his father-in-law.

CORNELIUS DOREMUS, 1890–1918. B. New York City, 1842; d. New York City, 1918. Insurance executive; second president of the Germania Life Insurance Company, 1898–1915, having begun there in 1860 as an office boy.

HAMILTON EASTER, 1880–88. B. Ireland, 1810; d. Baltimore, Md., 1895. Dry-goods merchant; Hamilton Easter & Sons.

CHARLES JEROME EDWARDS, 1918–19. B. Wayne Co., N.Y., 1866; d. Brooklyn, N.Y., 1925. Insurance and banking; general manager, Equitable Life Assurance Company of New York; vice president, Roosevelt Savings Bank; president, Life Underwriters Association of New York. Appointed director by the Alien Property Commission.

HENRY G. EILSHEMIUS, 1883–92. B. Germany, 1817; d. New York City, 1892. Wine merchant; director, Germania Fire Insurance Co. (not related to Germania Life); member, the German Club.

SELIG S. FISHER, 1880–84. B. Bavaria, 1827; d. New York City, 1884. Wholesale cloth dealer.

EWALD FLEITMANN, 1893–1906. B. Schwerte, Westphalia, 1846; d. New York City, 1906. Importer and commission merchant; Fleitmann & Co. (silks and dry goods). His wife, Catherine Caesar, was sister to Henry A. Caesar, also a director of the Germania Life; his daughter Johanna married another director, Louis Watjen.

FREDERICK T. FLEITMANN, 1915–35. B. New York city, 1856; d. Berlin, 1935. Textile importer; Fleitmann Textile Corp. Cousin to Ewald Fleitmann, also a Germania Life director; trustee, Central Savings Bank (formerly German Savings Bank).

JOHN FUHRER, 1919–29. B. Cologne, Germany, 1852; d. Stamford, Ct., 1930. Actuary. Joined Germania Life in 1874 and succeeded Hubert Cillis as actuary in 1898.

CARL GOEPEL, 1902–31. B. 1847 or 1848; d. New York, 1931. Banker; first vice president and (as of 1918) trustee, Central Savings Bank (formerly German Savings Bank).

EMIL GREEFF, 1871–76. Greeff & Co., New York City.

JOHN P. GRIER, 1918–19. B. Peoria, Ill., 1868; d. New York City, 1939. Broker; partner, Smith Barney & Co. until 1924. Appointed director by the Alien Property Commission.

C. GODFREY GUNTHER, 1860–85. B. New York City, 1822; d. New York City, 1885. Fur merchant; Christian C. Gunther & Sons; mayor of New York City, 1864–65.

T. LOUIS HANSEN, 1919–27. B. Denmark, 1875; d. Montclair, N.J., 1927. Clerk, Germania Life, beginning in 1896. In 1910 became head of Germania's newly created Agency Department; then assistant to Vice

President Max Wesendonck; superintendent of agencies; agency manager and vice president; and, finally, vice president.

JOHN HEINRICH HARDT, 1860–89 (European board). B. Lennep, Germany, 1822; d. Baden-Baden, 1889. Dry-goods importer; Hardt, von Bernuth & Co. Brother-in-law of Frederick August von Bernuth, another director of the Germania Life.

HENRY HARMS, 1875–80. B. Hanover, Germany, 1820; d. Hudson County, N.J., 1893. Sugar refiner; Wintjen, Harms & Co.

CHARLES HAUSELT, 1873. B. Bavaria, 1828; d. New York City, 1890. Leather merchant; Doerr & Reinhart of Worms-on-the-Rhine. President of the German Society, 1880–90.

MAX HEIDELBACH, 1867–75. B. Germany, 1819; d. New York City, 1875. Clothier (1860s) and banker; Heidelbach, Frank & Co., New York City (1874).

OTTO HEINZE, 1884–91. B. Saarfeld, Germany, 1831; d. Lawrence, Long Island, 1891. Hosiery merchant; Henschen & Unkart; later founded Heinze, Lowy & Co. His daughter married George W. Watjen (uncle of Louis Watjen, a Germania director).

JULIUS HESS, 1866–83. B. 1829; d. 1911. Importer (?); Julius Hess & Co., New York City.

EDWARD VON DER HEYDT, 1860–90 (European and American boards). B. Elberfeld, Germany, 1828; d. Berlin, 1890. Merchant and private banker; J. W. Schmidt & Co. (New York City); then established a Berlin branch. A founding director of the Germania, he was consul for Prussia in New York City; became a baron in 1874.

CARL T. HEYE, 1917–46. B. Quakenbruck, Germany, 1871; d. White Plains, N.Y., 1946. Insurance; may have worked briefly in the Berlin office of the Germania; came to United States in 1889 and joined Actuarial Department; assistant secretary, 1896, and secretary, 1902; became fourth president of Germania Life Insurance Company, 1921–1946. Trustee and secretary, Lenox Hill Hospital.

LOUIS ADOLF VON HOFFMAN, 1860–86. B. Saxony, 1828. Banker; L. von Hoffman & Co.

CHARLES ADAMS HOLDER, 1919–25. B. New York City, 1872; d. New York City, 1955. Physician, diplomat, banker; private medical practice, 1897–1909; Foreign Service posts in Norway, France, Cologne, London, Washington, D.C., 1909–19; vice president at Guarantee Trust.

LOUIS HUESMANN, 1871–76. B. Oldenburg, Germany, c. 1816; d. Hoboken, N.J., c. 1877. Importer; Huesmann & Co.

WILLIAM R. INNES, 1918–19. B. Poughkeepsie, N.Y., 1859; d. New York City, 1920. Manufacturer; vice president and director, Chicago and South Bend Railroad; director, Union Dime Savings Bank; director, New York Life. Appointed to board by Alien Property Commission.

LOUIS JAY, 1860–72. B. Germany, 1827 or 1828. Importer; Jay & Co., New York City.

FREDERICK KAPP, 1860–84 (European and American boards). B. Westphalia, 1824; d. Berlin, 1884. Lawyer, politician, author, journalist; Zitz, Kapp & Froebel (New York law firm); editor, *New Yorker Abendzeitung*; New York State commissioner of immigration, 1867–70. Returned to Germany in 1870 and was elected to three terms in the Reichstag.

EDWARD KAUPE, 1860–62. B. Germany, 1813. Importer.

PETER KAUTH, 1860–64. B. Hamburg, Germany, 1823; d. New York City, 1884. Coal merchant.

CARL KLOENNE, 1902–14 (European board). Director, Deutsche Bank, Berlin, 1905–15. Germania stock seized by the Alien Property Commission in 1917.

GEORGE H. KUNOTH, 1873–79. B. Germany (?), 1831; d. Hoboken, N.J., 1879. Silk merchant (?); Kutter, Luckemeyer & Co., New York

City. The original executors of his estate, Gustave Kutter and Edward Luckemeyer, were also Germania Life directors.

GUSTAVE KUTTER, 1860–65. B. Germany, 1829; d. New York City (?), 1876. Importer; Loeschigke & Wesendonck of New York City and Bonn; senior member, Kutter, Luckemeyer & Co.

ADOLF KUTTROFF, 1913–34. B. Suiz, Germany, 1846; d. Woodland, Staten Island, N.Y., 1936. Merchant and importer; Pickhardt, Kuttroff, & Co. (dyestuffs and chemicals); director, General Dyestuff Corp.; trustee, Central Savings Bank. Member, the German Society; president, board of trustees, Lenox Hill Hospital, 1910–14.

JEREMIAH LAROCQUE, 1860–68. B. 1822; d. New York City, 1868. Lawyer; Bowdan, Larocque & Barlow; Shipman, Larocque & Choate.

JOHANNES LIENAU, 1860–71. B. 1823; d. Hackensack, N.J., 1883. Importer; M. Lienau & Co.

GEORGE A. VON LINGEN, 1895–1902. B. Germany (?), 1838; d. Baltimore, Md., 1907. Shipping; Schumacher & Co., New York City.

EDSON SCHUYLER LOTT, 1920–45. B. Yates Co., N.Y., 1856; d. New York City, 1945. Insurance; president, United States Casualty Co.

EDWARD LUCKEMEYER, 1860–73. B. Elberfeld, Germany, 1830; d. Paris, 1907. Importer; Kutter, Luckemeyer & Co. From 1860s through early 1880s was business partner of Otto Wesendonck. Sister Agnes (Mathilde) married Otto Wesendonck. *See also* George H. Kunoth and Gustave Kutter.

CHARLES LULING, 1860–77. B. Bremen, Germany, 1819 or 1821; d. New York City, 1877. Merchant and banker; Charles Luling & Co., partner in D. H. Watjen & Co. in Bremen.

CHARLES BLAIR MACDONALD, 1918–19. B. Ontario, Canada, 1856; d. Southampton, N.Y., 1939. Stockbroker; president and director of Barahona Co. Appointed director by the Alien Property Commission. First U.S. Amateur Golf Champion.

HERMANN MARCUSE, 1860–1900 (European and American boards). B. Germany (?), 1824; d. Germany, 1900. Private banker; Marcuse & Baltzer (New York). Returned to Germany by 1874. *See also* Herman Richard Baltzer.

CARL MICHALOWSKY, 1916–18 (European board). Director, Deutsche Bank, Berlin, 1920. Germania stocked seized by Alien Property Commission.

DAVID THOMAS MOORE, 1918–19. B. Brooklyn, N.Y. ca. 1872; d. New York City, 1951. Stockbroker; D. T. Moore & Co. Appointed director by Alien Property Commission.

RICHARD MUSER, 1883–93. B. Westphalen, Germany, 1843; d. Suffern, N.Y., 1893. Lace importer; trustee, New York Life.

EMIL OELBERMANN, 1880–94. D. Cologne (?), ca. 1897. Dry-goods merchant; E. Oelbermann & Co.; Oelbermann, Dommerich & Co.; president, German-American Insurance Co. (1880s–1890s).

OSWALD OTTENDORFER, 1860–62. B. Zwittau, Austria-Hungary, 1826; d. New York, 1900. Publisher; *New-Yorker Staats-Zeitung.* President, the German Society; president, the German Hospital and Infirmary (Lenox Hill Hospital); endowed Ottendorfer Branch Library of New York public library system.

ALBRECHT PAGENSTECHER, 1883–1921. B. Osnabruck, Germany, 1839; d. Cornwall-on-Hudson, N.Y., 1926. Paper manufacturer (first to manufacture pulp paper in North America); Hudson River Pulp & Paper Co.; International Paper Co.; Laurentide Pulp Co. His father-in-law, Bernhard Westermann, was a director of the Germania.

FRANCIS KEY PENDLETON, 1920–30. D. New York, 1930. Lawyer; New York City corporation counsel, 1907–10; New York Supreme Court justice, 1910–20; private practice, 1920–30. Grandson of Francis Scott Key.

ALFRED ROELKER, 1874–1915. B. Aufnabruch, Germany, 1837; d. New York City, 1915. Merchant and banker; Louis Windmuller &

Roelker, New York City; president, German Savings Bank; director, German American Bank; director, Germania Fire Insurance Co.

CARL L. F. ROSE, 1876–91. B. Hameln, Prussia, ca. 1832; d. New York City, 1891. Leather exporter; Toel, Rose & Co., New York City. Brother of Hermann Rose.

HEINRICH F. O. ROSE, 1901–18 (European board). D. Germany, 1918. Cousin of Hermann Rose. Germania stock seized by Alien Property Commission.

HERMANN ROSE, 1860–1910 (European and American boards). B. Hameln, Prussia, 1825; d. Berlin, 1910. Merchant; established Berlin branch of the Germania Life. *See* Carl L. F. Rose and Heinrich F. O. Rose.

CHARLES SANDER, 1880–86 (European board).

HENRY SCHAEFER, 1920–24. B. 1857; d. New York City, 1924. Commodity trader; Siegfried, Gruner & Co. (cotton, coffee, sugar); director, Corn Exchange Bank and Hagedorn & Co.

MAXIMILLIAN SCHAEFER, 1860–77. B. Wetzlar, Germany; d. United States (?), 1904. Brewer; F. & M. Schaefer Brewing Co.

JOHN FREDERICK SCHEPELER, 1860–69. Importer; partner of John D. Schepeler & Leon Rosenplanter; consul, probably for El Salvador, during the late 1860s.

CHARLES ADOLF SCHIEREN, 1904–15. B. Neuss, Germany, 1842; d. Brooklyn, N.Y., 1915. Inventor and manufacturer; Charles A. Schieren & Co. (leather belting); organizer and president, Hide & Leather Bank; president, Germania Savings Bank of Brooklyn; mayor of New York City, 1894–96.

DANIEL SCHNAKENBERG, 1912–35. B. Bremen, Germany, 1852; d. New York City, 1935. Insurance and cotton brokering; founder and president, Hagedorn & Co. (marine insurance); trustee, German Savings Bank; director, German American Bank; director, Corn Exchange Bank. Treasurer, the German Society.

ADOLPH SCHNIEWIND, 1863–65. B. Elberfeld, Germany, 1826; d. Düsseldorf, 1891. Textile manufacturing and insurance; Schniewind Brothers; special agent for the Germania Life's metropolitan district and superintendent of agencies. In Germany worked for the Germania Life in the Rhine Province.

WILLIAM SCHRAMM, 1894–1902. B. Krefeld, Germany; d. Bay Shore, Long Island, 1917. Merchant and importer. First cousin of Max Wesendonck and nephew of Hugo Wesendonck.

HUGO SCHUMANN, 1898–1913. B. Gotha, Germany, 1842; d. Brooklyn, N.Y., 1913. Insurance broker; president, Germania Fire Insurance Co.

CARL SCHURZ, 1892–1902. B. Liblar, Germany, 1829; d. New York City, 1906. Soldier, diplomat, author.

FREDERICK SCHWENDLER, 1860–90. B. Frankfurt-am-Main, Germany, 1819 or 1820; d. Orange, N.J., 1890. Importer and insurance executive; first vice president of the Germania Life.

JOSEPH SELIGMAN, 1860–80. B. Bairrsdorf, Bavaria, 1819; d. New Orleans, La., 1880. Financier and importer; J. & W. Seligman & Co.; Seligman & Stettheimer.

GUSTAV A. L. STELLWAG, 1864–83. B. Prussia, ca. 1840; d. New York City, ca. 1883. Dry-goods importer; Kessler & Co., New York.

LEONARD J. STIASTNY, 1860–81. B. Mannheim, Baden, 1830; d. Hoboken, N.J., 1881. Importer and dry-goods merchant; Bauendahl & Co. (became L. J. Stiastny Co.).

JULIUS A. STURSBERG, 1903–1906. B. Baden, Germany, 1852; d. New York City, 1929. Brick and woolens manufacturing and investing; American Enameled Brick and Tile Co.; president, Livingston Worsted

Co.; director, South Porto Rico Sugar Co.; director, Herman Stursberg Realty Co.

ALBERT TAG, 1915–28. D. New York City, 1928. Banker; president, German American Bank (later Continental Bank & Trust Co.), 1914–28; trustee, Central Savings Bank (formerly German Savings Bank).

CASIMIR TAG, 1892–1913. B. New York City, 1847; d. Brooklyn, N.Y., 1913. Banker; Charles F. Tag & Son; president, German American Bank. Son of Charles F. Tag.

CHARLES FREDERICK TAG, 1864–93. B. ca. 1824; d. Hudson Co., N.Y., 1893. Tobacco merchant; Charles F. Tag & Son; director, Equitable Gas and Light Co. of New York.

GUSTAV THEISEN, 1865–73. B. 1822. Merchant and consul.

WILLIAM STEWARD TOD, 1903–12. B. ca. 1864; d. New York City, 1924. Banker; trustee, U.S. Trust Co.

GEORGE FREDERICK VIETOR, 1869–73. B. Brooklyn, N.Y., 1839; d. New York City, 1910. Dry-goods importer and merchant; Frederick Vietor & Achelis. His uncle, Thomas Achelis, was also a director.

DAVID WALLERSTEIN, 1860–80. B. Bavaria, 1821 or 1822; d. New York City, 1880. Leather importer.

WILLIAM ISRAEL (or ISAAC) WALTER, 1918–19. B. New York City, ca. 1862; d. 1944. Cotton-goods manufacturer; Bernheimer & Walter. Nominated to board by Alien Property Commission.

LOUIS WATJEN, 1907–54. B. Dobbs Ferry, N.Y., 1876; d. New York City, 1955. Importer/exporter; Watjen, Toel & Co. (became Louis Watjen Inc.); trustee, Central Savings Bank (formerly German Savings Bank). Married Johanna Fleitmann, daughter of Germania Life director Ewald Fleitmann. *See also* Otto Heinze.

HUGO WESENDONCK, 1860–1900. B. Elberfeld, Germany, 1817; d. New York City, 1900. Founder and first president, Germania Life Insurance Company, 1860–1897. Director, German American Bank; director, German Savings Bank (Central Savings Bank after 1918). Director, German Hospital & Infirmary (Lenox Hill Hospital); director, German Society.

MAX A. WESENDONCK, 1890–1932. B. Düsseldorf, Germany, 1845; d. Paris, 1932. Senior agency officer and special director in charge of agencies, Germania Life Insurance Company; in 1898 he became second vice president and was promoted to the vice presidency in 1915 (resigned in 1920); special representative for Credit Lyonnais. Son of Hugo Wesendonck. First cousin of William Schramm, also a director.

OTTO WESENDONCK, 1868–1896 (European board). B. Elberfeld, Germany, 1815; d. Berlin, 1896. Silk importer; financier. Brother of Hugo Wesendonck; father of Karl von Wesendonk; brother-in-law of Edward Luckemeyer, all Germania directors.

KARL VON WESENDONK, 1897–1918 (European board). B. Zurich, Switzerland, 1857; d. Locarno, Switzerland, 1934. Physicist; University of Berlin. Germania stock seized by Alien Property Commission. Son of Otto and Agnes Mathilde Wesendonck. (Karl's mother succeeded in having the family ennobled, in a decree of 1900 that allowed Karl to add a hereditary "von" to his name. To distinguish himself further from other Wesendoncks Karl deleted the c from his name—Wesendonk.)

BERNHARD WESTERMANN, 1860–88. B. Germany, 1817; d. Wiesbaden (while visiting), 1889. Book merchant, B. Westermann & Co. Father-in-law to Albrecht Pagenstecher, also a director.

JOHN WESTFALL, 1860–71. B. Germany, 1813; d. Brooklyn, N.Y., 1871. Liquor importer; partner of brother Diederich Westfall.

MELVIN STOW WHITNEY, 1860–64. B. Maine, 1812; d. New York City, 1865. Merchant.

WILLIAM WOODWARD, 1918–19. B. New York City, 1876; d. New York City, 1953. Banker; president, Hanover National Bank; director, Federal Reserve Bank of New York; trustee, Union Trust Co. of New York; trustee, Greenwich Savings Bank. Nominated to board by Alien Property Commission.

Notes

1. Origins

1. Bishop, *Capital Formation through Life Insurance*, pp. 14, 15.
2. Stalson, *Marketing Life Insurance*, pp. 46–49, 126–28.
3. Ibid., p. 317.
4. Ibid., pp. 285–86.
5. North, *Growth and Welfare*, pp. 20, 22.
6. *Pottsville Standard*, 26 June 1869.
7. Nelli, *Private Insurance Business*, p. 74.
8. Nadel, "Kleindeutschland," pp. 1, 81.
9. Dolan, *Immigrant Church*, p. 39; Nadel, "Kleindeutschland," p. 100.
10. Wittke, *Refugees of Revolution*, pp. 54–55.
11. *The Story of Lenox Hill Hopsital*, pp. 1–2; Ernst, *Immigrant Life*, p. 56; Der Deutsche Rechtsschutz Verein, certificate of incorporation, 8 March 1876.
12. Manson, "Foreign Element," p. 582; Ernst, *Immigrant Life*, p. 270.
13. German Liederkranz of the City of New York, charter, sec. 1; Liederkranz, *History of the Liederkranz of the City of New York 1847 to 1947 and of the Arion New York* (1948), pp. 16–17, 31, 35.
14. Dolan, *Immigrant Church*, p. 110; Wittke, *Refugees of Revolution*, p. 304; "Free German School," *Belletristisches Journal*, 16 September 1859; Ernst, *Immigrant Life*, pp. 141–42.
15. Manson, "Foreign Element," p. 584.
16. Nadel, "Kleindeutschland," pp. 170–71.
17. The Guardian Life Insurance Company of America, Loose-leaf binder, office of the chairman of the board.
18. *Story of Lenox Hill Hospital*, p. 2; Wittke, *Refugees of Revolution*, pp. 54–55; Ernst, *Immigrant Life*, p. 270; *Belletristisches Journal*, 23 December 1859; *Belletristisches Journal*, 20 January 1860.
19. German Liederkranz of the City of New York, charter, sec. 1.; Liederkranz, *History*, pp. 91–94.
20. Jeffry M. Diefendorf, "The Germania Life Insurance Company: The German Background," unpublished paper, 1982; Albrecht, "Hugo Wesendonck."
21. Lemke, "Hugo Wesendonck"; Albrecht, "Hugo Wesendonck."
22. Albrecht, "Hugo Wesendonck"; Diefendorf, "Germania Life," p. 6.

23. *Geschichte der Deutschen Gesellschaft,* p. 631; Pfund, *German Society,* pp. 9–10; Sei-densticker, *Geschichte des Mannerchors,* p. 38.

24. Miller, *German Hospital,* pp. 17–18, 22.

25. Huch, "Anschluss der Deutschen Philadelphias," pp. 13–31.

26. Lemke, "Hugo Wesendonck."

2. *Opening Moves*

1. Charter and By-Laws of the Germania Life Insurance Company, 1860, art. II.

2. Stalson, *Marketing Life Insurance,* p. 303.

3. Minutes of the Board of Directors of the Proposed Germania Life Insurance Company, 28 March 1860.

4. Minutes of the Committee on Agencies, 30 September 1863.

5. On Seligman, see Dumas Malone, ed., *Dictionary of American Biography* (New York: Scribner's, 1943), vol. 16, pp. 571–72.

6. Minutes of the Committee on Agencies, 21 April 1860.

7. Hugo Wesendonck and Frederick Schwendler, form letter to prospective agents and physicians, 30 April 1860.

8. Report of the Committee on Agencies of the Germania Life Insurance Company, [6 June 1860].

9. Ibid.

10. Angle, "First Consulting Actuary," pp. 1, 8; Letter from Abtellung Zivilstandsamt to Professor Hans Loeffel, 15 February 1983, Guardian Archives.

11. Report of the Committee on Premiums of the Germania Life Insurance Company, [6 June 1860].

12. Minutes of the Meeting of the Directors of Germania Life Insurance Company, 6 June 1860.

13. Minutes of the Board of Directors of the Germania Life Insurance Company, 14 June 1860.

14. Charter and By-laws of the Germania Life Insurance Company, 1860, p. 25. The Board appointed Gustav Kutter, Louis A. von Hoffman, Melvin S. Whitney, John F. Schepeler, Louis Jay, and Frederick Kapp to this committee. (Minutes of the Board of Directors of the Germania Life Insurance Company, 14 June 1860.)

15. Charter and By-laws of the Germania Life Insurance Company, 1860, p. 26. David Wallerstein, Hermann Rose, Edward Luckemeyer, and Joseph Seligman constituted the first Committee on Insurance. (Minutes of the Board of Directors of the Germania Life Insurance Company, 14 June, 1860.)

16. Charter and By-laws of the Germania Life Insurance Company, 1860, p. 26. The first members of this committee were Bernhard Westermann, Isaac Bernheimer, Oswald Ottendorfer, and Charles Breusing. (Minutes of the Board of Directors of the Germania Life Insurance Company, 14 June 1860.)

17. Charter and By-laws of the Germania Life Insurance Company, 1860, p. 26. This committee was composed of Leonard J. Stiastny, Charles Luling, and Hermann Marcuse. (Minutes of the Board of Directors of the Germania Life Insurance Company, 14 June 1860.)

18. Minutes of the Board of Directors of the Germania Life Insurance Company, 14 June 1860.

19. Report of the Special Committee, 31 December 1860; Expense Book for 1860–62.

20. Report of the Special Committee, 31 December 1860.

21. Minutes of the Committee on Insurance, 15 June 1860.

22. Minutes of the Committee on Insurance, 9 July 1860. An immediate annuity is one in which the insured makes one lump premium payment and the benefits begin immediately.

23. Minutes of the Committee on Insurance, 9 July 1860.

24. Minutes of the Committee on Insurance, 22 August 1860.

25. Minutes of the Finance Committee, 27 June 1860; Address of the President to the Company's Managers, 1901, p. 9.

26. Minutes of the Finance Committee, 11 July 1860.

27. Report of the President, 31 December 1860; Report of the Special Committee, 31 December 1860.

28. Potter, *Impending Crisis*, pp. 25–50, 407–13, 485, 471, 491.

29. Minutes of the Finance Committee, 13 May 1862.

30. Minutes of the Board of Directors of the Germania Life Insurance Company, 17 May 1862; Minutes of the Finance Committee, 20 May and 11 June 1862.

31. Minutes of the Finance Committee, 11 June 1862; Minutes of the Board of Directors of the Germania Life Insurance Company, 9 July 1862; Minutes of the Finance Committee, 30 August 1862.

32. Germania Life Insurance Company Annual Report for 1862; Germania Life Insurance Company Annual Report for 1863; Minutes of the Finance Committee, 17 August 1864.

33. Johnson and Malone, eds., *Dictionary*, vol. 2, pp. 169–170; ibid., vol. 10, p. 259; ibid., vol. 16, pp. 466–70, pp. 571–72.

34. Minutes of the Finance Committee, 4 June 1864. For a discussion of the federal financing effort see Rein, *Union Financing*, pp. 22–60; and Dewey, *Financial History*, pp. 306ff.

35. Minutes of the Board of Directors of the Germania Life Insurance Company, 13 July 1864; Minutes of the Finance Committee, 17 August and 9 September 1864.

36. Minutes of the Finance Committee, 29 March and 27 April 1865.

37. Minutes of the Board of Directors of the Germania Life Insurance Company, 12 April 1865; Minutes of the Finance Committee, 27 April 1865; Germania Life Insurance Company Annual Report for 1867.

3. Creating an Agency System

1. Minutes of the Committee on Agencies, 30 September 1863.

2. Stalson, *Marketing Life Insurance*, p. 382. Hyde later became president of The Equitable Life Assurance Society.

3. Minutes of the Committee on Agencies, 27 June and 27 July 1860.

4. Minutes of the Committee on Agencies, 6 July 1860.

5. Ibid.

6. Ibid.

7. Minutes of the Committee on Agencies, 30 August 1860; Minutes of the Committee on Insurance, 22 August 1860.

8. Minutes of the Committee on Agencies, 6 July 1860.

9. Ibid. At a later meeting the Committee on Agencies added the requirement that agents provide enough information about each applicant so that there would be no question about the identity of the person examined by the medical examiner. (Minutes of the Committee on Agencies, 30 August 1860.)

10. Clough, *American Life Insurance*, p. 85; Williamson and Smalley, *Northwestern Mutual Life*, p. 74; Hudnut, *New York Life Insurance Company*, p. 29.

11. Entz, "Synopsis," pp. 24–25.

12. Minutes of the Committee on Agencies, 10, 20, and 27 July and 16 August 1860.

13. Minutes of the Committee on Agencies, 6 and 20 July and 16 August 1860.

14. Minutes of the Committee on Agencies, 19 November 1860.

15. Germania Life Insurance Company Annual Report for 1861.

16. Germania Life Insurance Company Annual Report for 1862.

17. Orville F. Grahame, "The Guardian Goes to Missouri," typescript, ca. 1938, p. 8.

18. Minutes of the Committee on Agencies, 30 September 1863.

19. Ibid. According to the minutes of this meeting, 82 percent of the insurance sold to date had been solicited through the home office.

20. Minutes of the Committee on Agencies, 30 September 1863.

21. Minutes of the Committee on Agencies, 27 June 1860.

22. James, *Metropolitan Life*, p. 34; quotation, Minutes of the Committee on Agencies, 30 September 1863.

23. Minutes of the Committee on Agencies, 27 July 1860.

24. Minutes of the Committee on Agencies, 6 August 1860.

25. Minutes of the Committee on Agencies, 19 November 1860.

26. Minutes of the Committee on Agencies, January 1861.

27. Minutes of the Committee on Agencies, 30 September 1863.

28. Minutes of the Committee on Agencies, 30 September 1863.

29. Ibid; Minutes of the Committee on Agencies, January 1861.

30. Minutes of the Committee on Agencies, 30 September 1863.

31. Minutes of the Committee on Agencies, 19 February 1862 and 21 April and 30 September 1863; Stalson, *Marketing Life Insurance*, pp. 373–74.

32. Germania Life Insurance Company Annual Report for 1860.

33. Minutes of the Committee on Agencies, 30 September 1863.

34. Germania Life Insurance Company Annual Report for 1863.

35. Ibid.

36. Report of the Special Committee on the Recommendation in the Year Financial Report: On Commissions and Agencies, 13 July 1864.

37. Ibid.

38. Germania Life Insurance Company Annual Report for 1864.

39. Minutes of the Committee on Agencies, 7 October 1864.

40. Minutes of the Committee on Agencies, 10 April 1865.

41. Minutes of the Committee on Agencies, 20 May and 12 July 1865.

42. Minutes of the Committee on Agencies, 9 October and 12 December 1866.

43. Minutes of the Committee on Agencies, 18 January 1868.

44. Minutes of the Committee on Insurance, 19 February 1862.

45. Minutes of the Committee on Insurance, 27 May 1862.

46. Minutes of the Committee on Insurance, 10 September 1862.

47. Minutes of the Board of Directors of the Germania Life Insurance Company, 8 October 1862.

48. "History of Guardian Life on West Coast—Contribution to Expansion," unsigned carbon typescript, 1956.

49. Minutes of the Committee on Insurance, 27 May 1862.

50. Minutes of the Board of Directors of the Germania Life Insurance Company, 12 July 1865; Clough, *American Life Insurance*, pp. 80–82.

51. Minutes of the Committee on Insurance, 9 October 1865; Minutes of the Board of Directors of the Germania Life Insurance Company, 11 October 1865.

52. Minutes of the Committee on Agencies, 21 October 1865 and 29 June and 9 October 1866.

53. Minutes of the Board of Directors of the Germania Life Insurance Company, 29 March 1869.

54. Minutes of the Committee on Agencies, 9 January 1867; Minutes of the Board of Directors of the Germania Life Insurance Company, 10 April 1867; Minutes of the Committee on Agencies, 18 January 1868.

55. Minutes of the Board of Directors of the Germania Life Insurance Company, 12 July 1865.

4. Return to Europe

1. Stalson, *Marketing Life Insurance*, p. 439.

2. "Baron von der Heydt," *New York Times*, 8 July 1890; Minutes of the Committee on Agencies, 10 April 1865 and 29 June 1866; Minutes of the Board of Directors of the Germania Life Insurance Company, 11 July 1866.

3. Minutes of the Committee on Insurance, 15 November 1866; Minutes of the Committee on Agencies, 12 December 1866.

4. Minutes of the Board of Directors of the Germania Life Insurance Company, 10 April 1867.

5. Minutes of the Committee on Agencies, 9 July 1867; Minutes of the Finance Committee, 9 July 1867; Minutes of the Board of Directors of the Germania Life Insurance Company, 10 July 1867.

6. Minutes of the Board of Directors of the Germania Life Insurance Company, 9 October and 14 December 1867.

7. Minutes of the Finance Committee, 21 March 1868; Minutes of the Committee on Agencies, 4 April 1868.

8. Minutes of the Board of Directors of the Germania Life Insurance Company, 8 April 1868.

9. Minutes of the Committee on Agencies, 10 October 1868.

10. Minutes of the Committee on Agencies, 9 January 1869.

11. Ibid.

12. Minutes of the Board of Directors of the Germania Life Insurance Company, 13 January 1869.

13. Minutes of the Board of Directors of the Germania Life Insurance Company, 16 January 1869.

14. Minutes of the Board of Directors of the Germania Life Insurance Company, 29 March 1869. The board also passed two resolutions designed to reduce expenses: it requested that General Attorney Rose and his assistant "propose fixed salaries in lieu of the present excessive commissions"; and it asked the special board in Berlin to "relinquish the percentage on premiums as unprecedented in this Company, inconsistent with the nature of a Life Insurance institution."

15. Minutes of the Board of Directors of the Germania Life Insurance Company, 14 April 1869.

16. Minutes of the Board of Directors of the Germania Life Insurance Company, 14 July 1869.

17. Ibid. At the same time, the board authorized an increase in the commission paid to

Paris agents, provided that they employ "courtiers" at their own expense, and further that the allowance made to the Paris office for advertising be spent on mailings instead.

18. Ibid.

19. Minutes of the Committee on Agencies, 9 July 1870.

20. Bond, *War and Society*, pp. 13–39.

21. Minutes of the Board of Directors of the Germania Life Insurance Company, 26 July 1870.

22. Ibid.

23. Minutes of the Board of Directors of the Germania Life Insurance Company, 5 August 1870; Minutes of the European Board at Berlin, 6 August 1870.

24. Minutes of the Committee on Agencies, 6 December 1870; Minutes of the European Board at Berlin, 10 March 1871 (All quotations from the minutes of the European Board are taken from translations by Dagmar Stern); Minutes of the Committee on Agencies, 12 July 1871.

25. Minutes of the Committee on Agencies, 2 March 1872; Minutes of the Board of Directors of the Germania Life Insurance Company, 6 March 1872.

26. Minutes of the Board of Directors of the Germania Life Insurance Company, 1 June 1872.

27. Minutes of the Committee on Agencies, 6 October 1873; Minutes of the Board of Directors of the Germania Life Insurance Company, 8 October 1873.

28. Minutes of the European Board at Berlin, 13 March 1874; Minutes of the Committee on Agencies, 7 October 1879; Minutes of the Board of Directors of the Germania Life Insurance Company, 8 October 1879.

29. Minutes of the European Board at Berlin, 18 March 1880.

30. Minutes of the European Board at Berlin, 23 April 1874.

31. Minutes of the Board of Directors of the Germania Life Insurance Company, 13 July 1870 and 12 April 1871; Minutes of the Finance Committee, 13 May 1871.

32. Minutes of the Committee on Agencies, 8 January 1873.

33. Minutes of the Board of Directors of the Germania Life Insurance Company, 9 July 1873; Minutes of the European Board at Berlin, 13 March 1874; quotation, Minutes of the Board of Directors of the Germania Life Insurance Company, 8 April 1874.

34. Minutes of the Finance Committee, 26 May 1874; Minutes of the Board of Directors of the Germania Life Insurance Company, 4 June 1874; Minutes of the Finance Committee, 9 June 1874.

35. Minutes of the European Board at Berlin, 12 June 1874; Minutes of the Board of Directors of the Germania Life Insurance Company, 8 July 1874; Minutes of the European Board at Berlin, 14 September 1874.

36. Minutes of the European Board at Berlin, 5 October 1875; Minutes of the Committee on Agencies, 6 October 1873; Minutes of the European Board at Berlin, 17 March 1879.

37. Minutes of the European Board at Berlin, 16 March 1878.

38. Minutes of the European Board at Berlin, 10 October 1872.

39. Minutes of the Committee on Agencies, 8 January 1873.

5. *Depression and Recovery*

1. Fels, *American Business Cycles*, p. 83.

2. Stalson, *Marketing Life Insurance*, p. 429; Buley, *American Life Convention*, pp. 91–92.

3. New York State Insurance Department, *11th Annual Report* (1870), vol. 2, pp. ix–x.

4. Stalson, *Marketing Life Insurance*, p. 426; Minutes of the Committee on Agencies, 8 April 1872.

5. Buley, *American Life Convention*, p. 90.

6. New York State Insurance Department, *14th Annual Report* (1873), p. xxxi; New York State Insurance Department, *24th Annual Report* (1883), p. xiii; U.S. Department of Commerce, Bureau of the Census, *Historical Statistics*, p. 1057; Stalson, *Marketing Life Insurance*, p. 428.

7. The Germania Life Insurance Company, "Exhibit of Policies, 1860–1914" (unpublished); Minutes of the Committee on Agencies, 7 January 1870.

8. Minutes of the Committee on Agencies, 7 January 1870.

9. Minutes of the Committee on Agencies, 7 January 1870, 6 December 1870, and 10 October 1871.

10. Minutes of the Committee on Agencies, 7 January and 25 February 1870.

11. Minutes of the Committee on Agencies, 7 January 1870; Minutes of the Board of Directors of the Germania Life Insurance Company, 11 February 1871.

12. Minutes of the Board of Directors of the Germania Life Insurance Company, 12 April 1871.

13. Minutes of the Committee on Agencies, 19 December 1871.

14. Minutes of the Committee on Agencies, 9 October 1870; Stalson, *Marketing Life Insurance*, p. 385.

15. Minutes of the Committee on Agencies, 12 July 1871.

16. Minutes of the Committee on Agencies, 9 April 1873 and 12 November 1874.

17. Minutes of the Committee on Agencies, 13 December 1874, 11 October 1876; quotation, Minutes of the Committee on Agencies, 5 January 1877.

18. Minutes of the Committee on Agencies, 30 September 1863.

19. Minutes of the Committee on Agencies, 10 October 1871 and 12 April 1875.

20. Germania Life Insurance Company Annual Report for 1861.

21. Minutes of the Board of Directors of the Germania Life Insurance Company, 9 April and 9 July 1862.

22. Germania Life Insurance Company Annual Report for 1862.

23. Germania Life Insurance Company Annual Report for 1863.

24. Ibid.

25. Report of the Special Committee re recommendations in the year-end financial report for 1863, 13 July 1864.

26. Minutes of the Committee on Agencies, 9 April 1873.

27. Minutes of the Committee on Agencies, 12 November and 6 July 1874; *The Spectator*, 13 (August 1874), p. 484.

28. Minutes of the Committee on Agencies, 11 October 1876.

29. Circular from Hugo Wesendonck to the company's agents and general agents, 19 December 1876.

30. Minutes of the Committee on Insurance, 12 April 1875.

31. Circular from Hugo Wesendonck to the company's medical examiners, 1 November 1877.

32. Minutes of the Committee on Agencies, 10 January 1882.

33. Minutes of the Committee on Agencies, 12 April 1880; Minutes of the Board of Directors of the Germania Life Insurance Company, 14 April 1880.

34. Minutes of the Committee on Agencies, 11 October 1881.

35. Ibid.

36. Minutes of the Committee on Agencies, 11 July 1883.

37. Minutes of the Committee on Agencies, 9 January 1884.

38. Minutes of the Committee on Agencies, 8 April, 8 July, and 8 October 1884.

39. Minutes of the Committee on Agencies, 10 April 1883 and 8 July 1884.

40. Minutes of the Committee on Agencies, 14 January 1885; Agreement between the Germania Life Insurance Company and Nicol Van der Velde, 15 March 1888; Minutes of the Committee on Agencies, 13 January 1886 and 30 December 1887.

41. Minutes of the Committee on Agencies, 9 January 1889; Minutes of the Board of Directors of the Germania Life Insurance Company, 25 January 1893; Minutes of the Committee on Agencies, 14 January 1891.

42. Minutes of the Committee on Agencies, 9 January 1889, 11 April 1888, and 10 October 1888. The manager of the Helena agency was F. S. Doremus, son of Cornelius Doremus (the secretary and later president of the Germania).

43. Minutes of the Board of Directors of the Germania Life Insurance Company, 25 and 30 January 1893.

44. Minutes of the Committee on Agencies, 25 July 1894.

45. Minutes of the Committee on Agencies, 24 January 1894.

46. New York State Superintendent of Insurance, Annual Report for 1891, part II, pp. xlii—xliii.

47. Henry Baldwin Hyde to Hugo Wesendonck, 4 November 1892; Minutes of the Committee on Agencies, 24 January 1894.

48. Minutes of the Finance Committee, 3 May 1893; Minutes of the Committee on Agencies, 25 July 1894.

49. Minutes of the Advisory Committee, 27 February 1895.

50. Minutes of the Committee on Agencies, 24 April 1895 and 27 October 1897.

6. New Offerings and Investments

1. Minutes of the Committee on Insurance, 6 October 1879; Minutes of the Committee on Agencies, 12 October 1880.

2. Stalson, Marketing Life Insurance, pp. 462–66.

3. Minutes of the Board of Directors of the Germania Life Insurance Company, 8 October 1879; Minutes of the Committee on Insurance, 20 October, 3 November, and 1 December 1879; Germania Life Insurance Company Memo Book, 1886; Germania Life Insurance Company Annual Report for 1877; Germania Life Insurance Company Annual Report for 1880.

4. Minutes of the Committee on Agencies, 13 July 1880.

5. Minutes of the Committee on Agencies, 12 October 1880.

6. Ibid.

7. Minutes of the Committee on Agencies, 11 January and 12 April 1881.

8. Minutes of the Committee on Agencies, 10 January 1882.

9. Ibid.

10. Minutes of the Committee on Agencies, 9 January 1884 and 14 January 1885.

11. Minutes of the Committee on Agencies, 13 January 1886 and 12 January 1887.

12. Stalson, Marketing Life Insurance, pp. 310, 318–19.

13. Minutes of the Committee on Insurance, 17 February 1872; Minutes of the Committee on Agencies, 2 March 1872; Minutes of the Board of Directors of the Germania Life Insurance Company, 6 March 1872.

14. Minutes of the Board of Directors of the Germania Life Insurance Company, 8 October 1873.

15. Stalson, *Marketing Life Insurance*, pp. 317, 501.

16. Minutes of the Board of Directors of the Germania Life Insurance Company, 10 January 1883, 11 July 1888, and 26 October 1892.

17. Williamson and Smalley, *Northwestern Mutual Life*, p. 101; Stalson, *Marketing Life Insurance*, pp. 487–88.

18. Minutes of the Committee on Insurance, 26 May 1873; Minutes of the European board at Berlin, 10 October 1873.

19. Germania Life Insurance Company, Policy Information and Rate Book, 1874.

20. Minutes of the Board of Directors of the Germania Life Insurance Company, 4 June, 8 July, and 14 October 1874; Minutes of the Committee on Insurance, 13 October 1874.

21. Minutes of the Committee on Insurance, 22 April 1878.

22. Germania Life Insurance Company, "Dividend Tontine Policies," 1889, pp. 6–7; Minutes of the Committee on Agencies, 9 October 1889 and 22 April 1891.

23. Stalson, *Marketing Life Insurance*, pp. 490–92, 552.

24. Minutes of the Committee on Insurance, 15 February 1875; Minutes of the Board of Directors of the Germania Life Insurance Company, 14 April and 13 October 1875.

25. Minutes of the Board of Directors of the Germania Life Insurance Company, 9 October 1878 and 9 April 1879.

26. Minutes of the Committee on Insurance, 7 January 1885; Germania Life Insurance Company, "Bond Policies Incontestable and Self-nonforfeitable," 1885; Minutes of the Board of Directors of the Germania Life Insurance Company, 13 April 1887; Minutes of the Committee on Agencies, 13 January 1886.

27. Minutes of the Advisory Committee, 26 August 1896; Minutes of the Board of Directors of the Germania Life Insurance Company, 28 October 1896.

28. Minutes of the Finance Committee, 9 April 1890; Germania Life Insurance Company, "Loan Values" [1890].

29. Germania Life Insurance Company, "Business Instructions for Agents," 1889; Minutes of the Advisory Committee, 29 May 1895 and 6 January 1897.

30. Minutes of the Board of Directors of the Germania Life Insurance Company, 12 March 1890 and 14 November 1891.

31. Minutes of the Advisory Committee, 2 August 1899; "Gold Bonds for Beneficiaries," *The Chronicle*, 10 October 1901, p. 198; "Germania Issues Attractive Gold Bond Policies," *The Standard*, 12 October 1901, p. 332.

32. Minutes of the Committee on Insurance, 27 October 1909.

33. Ibid.

34. Carl Heye, "Seventy Years at the Guardian," unpublished typescript [1930], p. 9.

35. Minutes of the Finance Committee, 8 and 15 July 1868 and 24 July and 20 September 1869.

36. Minutes of the Finance Committee, 14 October 1873, 29 January and 26 February 1877, and 9 January 1878.

37. Minutes of the Finance Committee, 2 July 1877 and 8 and 22 October 1877.

38. Minutes of the Finance Committee, 15 November 1880 and 21 February and 25 July 1881.

39. Minutes of the Finance Committee, 18 September 1882; Minutes of the Board of Directors of the Germania Life Insurance Company, 11 April 1883.

40. Minutes of the Finance Committee, 28 May, 11 June, and 25 June 1883; Report of the Special Committee for 1897.

41. Minutes of the Finance Committee, 15 and 17 February 1872, 23 December 1873, and 6 January 1874.

42. Minutes of the Finance Committee, 10 July 1876.

43. Minutes of the Board of Directors of the Germania Life Insurance Company, 12 July 1876.

44. Minutes of the Finance Committee, 15 May 1882 and 28 April 1884.

45. "Questionnaire to employees regarding the Company's history," 1937.

46. Minutes of the Finance Committee, 14 April 1886, 23 December 1887, and 4 February and 19 April 1888.

47. Address of the President to the Company's Managers, 1901, p. 22.

48. Minutes of the Advisory Committee, 30 March 1896.

49. Address of the President to the Company's Managers, 1901, pp. 22–23.

50. Minutes of the Finance Committee, 14 and 15 May 1888 and 27 February 1889.

7. Consolidation in Europe

1. Minutes of the Board of Directors of the Germania Life Insurance Company, 12 July 1882.

2. Stalson, *Marketing Life Insurance*, p. 823.

3. Minutes of the Board of Directors of the Germania Life Insurance Company, 2 March 1889; Minutes of the European Board at Berlin, 23 May 1889; Minutes of the Committee on Agencies, 10 July 1889.

4. Minutes of the European Board at Berlin, 9 January and 18 March 1875. All quotations from the minutes of the European Board are taken from translations by Dagmar Stern.

5. Minutes of the Finance Committee, 13 January and 26 April 1875.

6. Minutes of the Board of Directors of the Germania Life Insurance Company, 14 April 1875 and 12 July 1876; Minutes of the European Board at Berlin, 14 September 1876 and 17 January 1877.

7. Minutes of the Finance Committee, 21 March and 9 April 1902; Minutes of the Board of Directors of the Germania Life Insurance Company, 23 April 1902.

8. Minutes of the Finance Committee, 18 June, 2 July, and 23 July 1902; Minutes of the Board of Directors of the Germania Life Insurance Company, 22 April 1903.

9. Minutes of the European Board at Berlin, 17 January and 15 October 1877.

10. Minutes of the Committee on Agencies, 8 January 1878; Minutes of the Board of Directors of the Germania Life Insurance Company, 9 January 1878.

11. Minutes of the Board of Directors of the Germania Life Insurance Company, 10 January and 11 April 1883. Occasionally, the European board delayed introducing liberalizations made by the home office. In the mid-1880s, the European board debated the advisability of adding the incontestability clause adopted by the Germania in 1883 for American policies. Because it thought incontestability would encourage applicants to conceal previous illnesses, the European board was hesitant about its introduction. However, when Mutual of New York introduced its "sweeping easements," the board had no choice but to institute the practice (Minutes of the European Board at Berlin, 21 October and 17 December 1885).

The practices of German companies forced the Germania to liberalize its position on war risks. In 1888, the European branch urged the reconsideration of the Germania's policy, noting that the Gotha, perhaps the leading company in Germany, assumed war risks without extra premiums for those who "in obedience to the existing service law, engage in actual war" and for professional soldiers who were noncombatants, and offered war-risk insurance at extra premium to professional combatants. The board agreed to let the branch insure soldiers, but only according to the terms and restrictions that the Gotha "has adopted, or may hereafter adopt." When the European branch objected that it was impracticable to depend on the "constantly changing rules" of another insurance company, the board rescinded its restriction (Minutes of the Board of Directors of the Germania Life Insurance Company, 9 March 1888 and 2 March 1889).

12. Minutes of the Committee on Agencies, 6 December 1870.

13. Clough, *American Life Insurance*, p. 71.

14. Minutes of the Board of Directors of the Germania Life Insurance Company, 12 January 1870.

15. Minutes of the Board of Directors of the Germania Life Insurance Company, 12 January 1870.

16. Minutes of the Finance Committee, 12 January 1870.

17. Minutes of the Board of Directors of the Germania Life Insurance Company, 12 January 1870.

18. Minutes of the European Board at Berlin, 13 December 1872; Minutes of the Committee on Agencies, 8 January 1873.

19. Minutes of the Board of Directors of the Germania Life Insurance Company, 8 January 1873.

20. Minutes of the European Board at Berlin, 28 January 1873.

21. Minutes of the Finance Committee, 8 October 1873; Minutes of the Board of Directors of the Germania Life Insurance Company, 8 October 1873.

22. Minutes of the Board of Directors of the Germania Life Insurance Company, 4 January 1891 and 24 January 1894.

23. Keller, *Life Insurance Enterprise*, p. 108; Buley, *Equitable*, pp. 282, 423–28.

24. "President Cleveland on the Prussian Question—Comment of the German Press," *The Weekly Underwriter*, 7 December 1895, p. 302.

25. See, for example, "Barriers Abroad," *The Chronicle*, 18 September 1902, p. 149.

26. Conze, "German Empire," pp. 274–91, 289.

27. "Communications. The Germania Life in Prussia," *The Weekly Underwriter*, 7 December 1895, p. 301.

28. Minutes of the Board of Directors of the Germania Life Insurance Company, 26 October 1898.

29. "Germany's New Insurance Law," *The Chronicle*, 7 November 1901.

30. Minutes of the Board of Directors of the Germania Life Insurance Company, 24 July 1901.

31. Minutes of the Finance Committee, 14 August 1901; Minutes of the Board of Directors of the Germania Life Insurance Company, 23 July 1902.

32. Minutes of the Finance Committee, 27 December 1906; Minutes of the Board of Directors of the Germania Life Insurance Company, 24 April 1907.

33. Minutes of the European Board at Berlin, 21 October 1885.

34. Minutes of the Board of Directors of the Germania Life Insurance Company, 14 July 1886; Minutes of the Finance Committee, 13 October 1886.

35. Minutes of the Board of Directors of the Germania Life Insurance Company, 13 October 1886 and 10 April 1889.

36. Minutes of the Advisory Committee, 21 July, 15 September, and 26 October 1897.

37. Minutes of the Board of Directors of the Germania Life Insurance Company, 27 January 1897.

38. Recollections of John E. Albert for the "Questionnaire to employees regarding the Company's History," 1937.

39. Ibid.

8. New Leadership, New Challenges

1. Carl Heye, "Seventy Years at the Guardian," unpublished typescript [1930], p. 8.

2. *New York Tribune*, 10 June 1890.

3. "Germania Life's Impregnable Position," *The Chronicle*, 20 June 1901, p. 292.

4. Minutes of the Board of Directors of the Germania Life Insurance Company, 24 April 1901.

5. Minutes of the Board of Directors of the Germania Life Insurance Company, 8 October 1879.

6. Minutes of the Board of Directors of the Germania Life Insurance Company, 13 July 1881.

7. Minutes of the Board of Directors of the Germania Life Insurance Company, 23 April 1890.

8. Minutes of the Board of Directors of the Germania Life Insurance Company, 10 January 1883, and 28 October 1891. In 1891 the board modified the procedure for selecting its members by creating a nominating committee. All nominations were to be referred to this committee, which would notify the board when it was prepared to make its recommendation.

9. Address of the President to the Company's Managers, 1901, p. 28; Minutes of the Board of Directors of the Germania Life Insurance Company, 24 April 1901; "The Germania Life Insurance Company of New York: Testimony Given before the Joint Committee of the Senate and Assembly of the State of New York, Dec. 20th–21st, 1905," (Germania Life Insurance Company of America, [1906]), p. 9.

10. Minutes of the Board of Directors of the Germania Life Insurance Company, 24 April 1901; quotation, *The Weekly Underwriter*, 8 February 1902, p. 81.

11. Minutes of the Committee on Agencies, 24 November 1894.

12. Minutes of the Board of Directors of the Germania Life Insurance Company, 26 March 1902.

13. Minutes of the Board of Directors of the Germania Life Insurance Company, 10 June 1902.

14. Minutes of the Board of Directors of the Germania Life Insurance Company, 13 December 1902.

15. Contents of letters summarized by Professor Hans L. Trefousse, Brooklyn College, in letter to John C. Angle, 15 April 1982.

16. Minutes of the Board of Directors of the Germania Life Insurance Company, 13 December 1902.

17. New York State Insurance Department, "Examination for 1909," p. 17; Minutes of the Finance Committee, 8 November 1911. In a subsequent examination, conducted in 1913, the auditors noted that Doremus was purchasing bonds in a manner that did not conform to the New York insurance laws (New York State Insurance Department, "Examination for 1913," p. 16).

18. E. J. Moorhead, "Sketches," pp. 51–83; Minutes of the Board of Directors of the Germania Life Insurance Company, 31 December 1915.

19. Stalson, *Marketing Life Insurance*, pp. 877–78; *Best's Insurance Reports—Life/Health* (Oldwick, N.J.: A. M. Best, 1984), p. vii.

20. Buley, *American Life Convention*, vol. 1, p. 212.

21. Ibid., p. 213.

22. "Testimony," p. 24.

23. Ibid., p. 29.

24. Buley, *American Life Convention*, vol. 1, p. 213.

25. "Testimony," p. 38.

26. "Washington Life Inquiry," *New York Sun*, 20 December 1905.

27. Buley, *American Life Convention*, vol. 1, p. 212.

28. "Testimony," p. 40.

29. Ibid., p. 41.

30. Keller, *Life Insurance Enterprise*, pp. 195–96, 257.

31. Stalson, *Marketing Life Insurance*, p. 551.

32. "Testimony," p. 1.

33. "Exhibit of Policies, 1860–1914" (unpublished); Minutes of the Committee on Agencies, 24 April 1901; "The Germania Life's Banquet," *The Chronicle*, 6 June 1901, p. 269.

34. "Safety of Assured His Theme," *The Chronicle*, 25 July 1901, p. 43.

35. Ibid.

36. Minutes of the Finance Committee, 5 June 1901.

37. Minutes of the Committee on Agencies, 22 January 1902; "Exhibit of Policies."

38. Minutes of the Committee on Agencies, 22 April 1908 and 27 October 1909.

39. Minutes of the Committee on Agencies, 22 April 1908, 27 April 1910, and 26 April 1911.

40. Minutes of the Committee on Agencies, 23 January 1907; New York State Insurance Department, "Report on the Examination of the Germania Life Insurance Company of New York, N.Y. as of December 31, 1909 Together with a Report, dated January 3, 1911 on the Company's Dividend System," (1911), pp. 8–9.

41. C. Heye, "Seventy Years," p. 8.

42. N. E. Berry to Carl Heye, 8 August 1916.

43. Minutes of the Finance Committee, 27 January 1915.

44. "March 1916, 'Hansen Month,'" *Service*, March 1916, p. 10; "Cillis Month," *Service*, October 1916, p. 1; "To the Company's Representatives," *Service*, April 1917, p. 1.

45. N. E. Berry to Carl Heye, 8 August 1916; Carl Heye [?] to Hubert Cillis, 23 September 1916, in "Albany, Cincinnati, and St. Louis meetings."

46. Minutes of the Board of Directors of the Germania Life Insurance Company, 31 December 1915; Minutes of the Committee on Insurance, 25 October 1916.

47. Minutes of the Board of Directors of the Germania Life Insurance Company, 25 October and 27 December 1916.

48. "Institutes Health Service," *The Weekly Underwriter*, 1 May 1915, p. 493; Germania Life Insurance Company, "How to Lengthen Your Life: A Modern Insurance Service," 1916; Hubert Cillis to the Germania's managers and cashiers, "Circular re: Health Reclamation Service," 10 May 1918.

49. Minutes of the Board of Directors of the Germania Life Insurance Company, 16 December 1916.

50. New York State Insurance Department, "Examination for 1913;" Minutes of the Finance Committee, 7 June 1898.

51. Minutes of the Finance Committee, 21 June 1899; Minutes of the Finance Committee, 2 August 1899, 25 April 1900, and 9 October 1901.

52. Heye, "Seventy Years," p. 8; Minutes of the Finance Committee, 30 March 1898.

53. Minutes of the Board of Directors of the Germania Life Insurance Company, 27 April 1898; Minutes of the Finance Committee, 8 June 1898; "Testimony," pp. 20–23.

54. Minutes of the Finance Committee, 24 June 1908.

55. Minutes of the Finance Committee, 24 June 1908 and 3 March 1909.

56. Minutes of the Finance Committee, 5 April, 7 July, and 7 October 1909 and 23 March 1910; Minutes of the Sub-Committee of the Finance Committee, 1 June 1909.

57. Minutes of the Finance Committee, 22 July, 5 April, and 22 December 1909; Minutes of the Building Committee, 15 April and 1 February 1910, and 20 July 1911; Minutes of the Finance Committee, 23 April 1913.

58. "Facts and Opinions," *The Weekly Underwriter*, 13 May 1911, p. 386.

9. New Ideas in Management

1. Recollections of employees M. J. Peterson, Sophie Bulow, and Margaret Orth to the "Questionnaire to employees regarding the Company's History," 1937.

2. Stalson, *Marketing Life Insurance*, pp. 578–80, 585, 590, 595.

3. "Guardian to Have Prospect Bureau," *Eastern Underwriter*, 19 March 1920, p. 5; "An Announcement from the Educational Department," *Service*, 31 December 1923, p. 3; "Columbia Scholarships," *Guardian Family News*, January 1922, p. 5; Ibid., February 1922, p. 3.

4. Minutes of the Board of Directors of the Germania Life Insurance Company, 24 July 1918.

5. Minutes of the Committee on Agencies, 23 July 1919; "Inter-City Conference of Guardianites," *Service*, 1 December 1924, pp. 2–3.

6. Merrill, *Classics*, pp. 1–8; Henry Metcalfe, "The Science of Administration," in Merrill, p. 37; Henry R. Towne, "The Engineer as an Economist," in Merrill, pp. 49–50; Frederick W. Taylor, "What Is Scientific Management?", in Merrill, pp. 67–71.

7. Harry Arthur Hopf, "Management and the Optimum," in Merrill, *Classics*, p. 327.

8. Ibid., p. 337.

9. Ibid., pp. 357–63.

10. Hagedorn, *White Collar Management*, pp. 16–18.

11. "About *Service*," *Service*, 2 January 1922, p. 1.

12. Hagedorn, *White Collar Management*, p. 19.

13. Ibid., pp. 19–20.

14. Ibid., pp. 22–23.

15. Ibid., p. 20, n. 31.

16. Ibid., pp. 20–22.

17. Ibid., pp. 25–33.

18. The following discussion draws on a company file, "In re: efficiency suggestions" [1913–1915].

19. Hagedorn, *White Collar Management*, p. 14.

20. Hopf, "Management and the Optimum," in Merrill, *Classics*, p. 363.

21. "The Germania Life Insurance Company of New York: Testimony given before the Joint Committee of the Senate and Assembly of the State of New York, December 20th–21st, 1905" (Germania Life Insurance Company of America, [1906]), pp. 26, 53; Cornelius Doremus to Heinrich Rose, 21 June 1912.

22. Cornelius Doremus to Hubert Cillis, 18 August 1913; "Memorandum in re Communications Had With NewYorker Germania Lebens-Versicherungs-Gesellschaft," 12 August 1913.

23. "Memorandum in re Communications Had With NewYorker Germania Lebens-Versicherungs-Gesellschaft," 12 August 1913.

24. Cornelius Doremus to Hubert Cillis, 18 August 1913.

25. Ibid.

26. Stalson, *Marketing Life Insurance*, p. 823.

27. Minutes of the Finance Committee, 17 December 1913.

28. Response of M. J. Peterson to "Questionnaire to employees regarding the Company's History," 1937.

10. War and the End of the Germania

1. "Statement, 12 August 1914" in company memos re problems of business in Europe around World War I.

2. "War Does Not Bother United States Insurance Companies," *New York Evening Sun*, 25 September 1914.

3. "German Insurance Loans New Problem," *The New York Evening Sun*, 25 October 1914, p. 7; Minutes of the Finance Committee, 29 July 1914, 13 January 1915, 9 September 1915, and 8 March 1916.

4. Minutes of the Board of Directors of the Germania Life Insurance Company, 28 October 1914, 27 October 1915, 26 April and 26 July 1916, 24 January and 22 August 1917, and 22 August 1918.

5. Luebke, *Bonds of Loyalty*, pp. 45, 67–68.

6. Ibid., pp. 60–66, 68–69.

7. Wittke, *German-Americans*, pp. 141–42, 179–87.

8. Minutes of the Finance Committee, 29 December 1915.

9. Minutes of the Finance Committee, 18 October 1916.

10. Hubert Cillis to field staff, circular re European business during World War I, 6 April 1917.

11. Circular letter re annual statement in German, 17 May 1917.

12. Minutes of the Nominating Committee, 18 April 1917.

13. Minutes of the Finance Committee, 18 April 1917; "The Kind of Co-operation That Counts," *Service*, June 1917, p. 3; Germania Life Insurance Company, "First Year of the War and How Modern Insurance Serves, April 1917–April 1918," 1918.

14. Carosso, *Investment Banking*, pp. 224–25; Minutes of the Finance Committee, 16 May 1917; R. H. Treman, deputy governor of Federal Reserve Bank of New York, to Hubert Cillis, 10 May 1917 in *Service*, May 1917, frontispiece.

15. Minutes of the Finance Committee, 3 and 17 October 1917; "Plotts on Front Page," *Service*, November 1917, p. 10.

16. Minutes of the Finance Committee, 3 April, 1 May, and 18 September 1918.

17. Minutes of the Finance Committee, 23 October 1918.

18. "Speech at the First Field Convention," Carl Heye's files, 1917.

19. "Expressions of the Company's Managers who attended the New Orleans Convention on the change of name question," 12 November 1917, company files, pp. 2, 3, 6.

20. Carl Heye, "Seventy Years at the Guardian," unpublished typescript, [1930], p. 10.

21. "Analysis of the Proposed Change of Name Situation," internal confidential memorandum, n.d., pp. 1–5.

22. Ibid., pp. 5–6.

23. [T. Louis Hansen?], untitled typescript, 24 October 1917; pp. 6–7, 9.

24. Hubert Cillis to Jesse S. Phillips, 22 November 1917; Hubert Cillis to Jesse S. Phillips, 24 November 1917.

25. "Memorandum in re Special Meeting to be held on December 5 '17;" Minutes of the Board of Directors of the Germania Life Insurance Company, 5 Deember 1917.

26. "Germania Life Company to Bear American Name," *New York Herald*, 6 December 1917. See also "To Get Rid of 'Germania'," *The World*, 6 December 1917.

27. "Guardian Life Month," *Service*, April 1918, frontispiece.

28. "Analysis of the Proposed Change of Name Situation," internal confidential memorandum, n.d., pp. 2–3; [T. Louis Hansen?], untitled typescript, 24 October 1917; p. 6; Hubert Cillis to The Guardian Life Insurance Company of America, European Branch, Berlin, 7 July 1919.

29. Stalson, *Marketing Life Insurance*, p. 436; Minutes of the Finance Committee, 6 July 1875 and 12 October 1887; Minutes of the Board of Directors of the Germania Life Insurance Company, 12 October 1887; Minutes of the Committee on Agencies, 22 July 1891.

30. Minutes of the Board of Directors of the Germania Life Insurance Company, 22 October 1902 and 22 April 1908; Minutes of the Finance Committee, 24 July 1907.

31. Minutes of the Finance Committee, 5 and 19 June 1912.

32. Minutes of the Finance Committee, 13 August, 24 November, and 3 December 1913.

33. Minutes of the Finance Committee, 8 March 1916.

34. Minutes of the Board of Directors of the Germania Life Insurance Company, 5 December 1917; Hubert Cillis to the Guardian Life Insurance Company of America, European Branch, Berlin, 7 July 1919, trans. p. 3.

35. "The Guardian Life Promotions," *Insurance Index*, 8 January 1921, p. 6.

36. "Alien Property Custodian," p. 2, National Archives, RG 131, Entry 2.

37. Alien Property Custodian, Corporation Management Department, Docket Record, the Guardian Life Insurance Company of America, National Archives, RG 131, Entry 95; Hubert Cillis to the Guardian Life Insurance Company of America, European Branch, Berlin, 7 July 1919, trans. p. 3.

38. Minutes of the Board of Directors of the Guardian Life Insurance Company of America, 24 April 1918.

39. Dulon & Roe to the Guardian Life Insurance Company, 27 April 1918.

40. Minutes of the Board of Directors of the Guardian Life Insurance Company of America, 10 May and 22 August 1918.

41. "To Be Sold by the Alien Property Custodian 1548 Shares of Stock of Guardian Life Insurance Company," announcement; "Auction sale of Guardian Capital Stock, 1919," Carl T. Heye's files; Hubert Cillis to the Guardian Life Insurance Company of America, European Branch, Berlin, 7 July 1919, trans., p. 4.

42. Crosby, *Epidemic and Peace*, p. 207; "Small Dividends Should Cause No Dissatisfaction," *Chicago Evening Post*, 30 December 1918; Hubert Cillis, "Memorandum on Dividends," 12 December 1918; Hubert Cillis to the company's representatives, 20 December 1919, in "influenze epidemic (1918)—effect on dividends 1918–1919," Carl T. Heye's files.

43. Minutes of the Finance Committee, 19 February 1919.

44. Hubert Cillis to the Guardian Life Insurance Company of America, European Branch, Berlin, 7 July 1919.

45. Minutes of the Board of Directors of the Guardian Life Insurance Company of America, 23 July 1919; "Memorandum from Executive Officers to the Nominating Committee," in Minutes of the Nominating Committee, 29 October 1919.

46. Minutes of the Board of Directors of the Guardian Life Insurance Company of America, 23 December 1919; Minutes of the Nominating Committee, Report to the Board of Directors, 23 December 1919.

47. Minutes of the Finance Committee, 6 August 1919.

48. Minutes of the Finance Committee, 9 November 1921.

49. Minutes of the Board of Directors of the Guardian Life Insurance Company of America, 23 July 1919 and 23 December 1919; Nominating Committee, report to the Board of Directors, 23 December 1919.

50. Minutes of the Executive Committee, 20 December 1920 and 16 March 1921.

51. Minutes of the Executive Committee, 17 March, 28 May, and 21 July 1920 and 19 January and 22 June 1921.

52. Minutes of the Board of Directors of the Guardian Life Insurance Company of America, 23 December 1919; Minutes of the Finance Committee, 23 November 1921.

53. Minutes of the Board of Directors of the Guardian Life Insurance Company of America, 28 December 1921 and 27 December 1922.

54. Minutes of the Finance Committee, 11 November 1921; Minutes of the Board of Directors of the Guardian Life Insurance Company of America, 25 January 1922.

55. Minutes of the Board of Directors of the Guardian Life Insurance Company of America, 25 January 1922.

56. T. Louis Hansen to Carl Heye, 15 February 1922.

57. Minutes of the Executive Committee, 26 July 1922; Carl Heye, memorandum to the board of directors, 23 October 1922.

58. Minutes of the Executive Committee, 25 October 1922 and 17 January 1923; T. Louis Hansen, untitled report on liquidation negotiations, 15 October 1923, p. 7, in "correspondence with Mr. Hansen re: transfer of German business, 1923," Carl T. Heye's files.

59. Minutes of the Executive Committee, 25 April 1923; Memorandum in re European Situation, 6 June 1923, in "in re sale of Austria-Hungary business," Carl T. Heye's files.

60. T. Louis Hansen, untitled report on liquidation negotations, 15 October 1923, p. 7.

61. As further protection "against the very remote contingency" of a failure of both the Phoenix and the Munich which might require the Guardian to liquidate the balance of the German business then still outstanding, the company replaced the German assets transferred to the Phoenix. The transfer included all company securities, but the Guardian retained ownership of its office buildings. (Minutes of the Executive Committee, 24 October and 21 November 1923.)

62. Minutes of the Executive Committee, 26 March and 16 July 1924.

63. Minutes of the Executive Committee, 18 May 1927.

64. Minutes of the Board of Directors of the Guardian Life Insurance Company of America, 26 October 1927; New York State Insurance Department, "Evaluation of the Guardian Life Insurance Company of America," 1929, pp. 3CL–4CL or 117–18.

65. T. Louis Hansen, untitled report on liquidation negotiations, 15 October 1923, p. 6.

66. Carl Heye to Valentine Howell, 9 October 1933, in "Revalorization, 1923–1936," Carl T. Heye's files; New York State Insurance Department, "Evaluation of the Guardian," 1932.

67. Carl Heye to Albert Conway, New York State superintendent of insurance, 18 June 1930, in "letters to and from the Superintendent of Insurance, 1930–1," Carl T. Heye's files.

68. Albert Conway, New York State superintendent of insurance, to The Guardian Life Insurance Company of America, 27 June 1930, in "letters to and from the Superintendent of Insurance, 1930–1," Carl T. Heye's files.

69. Sullivan & Cromwell to Guardian Life Insurance Company, 5 March 1931.

70. Minutes of the Board of Directors of the Guardian Life Insurance Company of America, 22 April 1931; "Entitlement Plan for the Division of Assets of Guardian Life Insurance Company of America Published in the *German Reich* and *Prussian Staatsanzeiger* 12 December 1931," typescript.

71. Minutes of the Board of Directors of the Guardian Life Insurance Company of America, 25 April 1934; Minutes of the Executive Committee, 16 September and 28 October 1931.

72. Minutes of the Executive Committee, 20 July 1921; Carl Heye, "Seventy Years at the Guardian," pp. 12–13; Minutes of the Board of Directors of the Guardian Life Insurance Company of America, 25 November 1924.

73. Carl Heye, "Seventy Years at the Guardian," pp. 12–13.

74. Minutes of the Board of Directors of the Guardian Life Insurance Company of America, 17 December 1924 and 28 January 1925; quotation, Samuel A. Irby to Carl Heye, 19 December 1924.

75. Minutes of the Board of Directors of the Guardian Life Insurance Company of America, 28 January 1925; Minutes of the Executive Committee, 20 May 1925.

Epilogue

1. Stalson, *Marketing Life Insurance*, pp. 787–99, passim.

2. U.S. Bureau of the Census, *Historical Abstracts of the United States-Colonial Times to 1957* (Washington, 1960), pp. 56–57.

Bibliography

Primary Sources

COMPANY MATERIALS

Annual Reports
Exhibit of Policies, 1860–1914
Expense Book, 1860–62
Minutes of the Advisory Board
Minutes of the Board of Directors
Minutes of the Committee on Agencies
Minutes of the Committee on Insurance
Minutes of the European Board at Berlin
Minutes of the Finance Committee
Minutes of the Special Committee
Report of the President
Service
Miscellaneous: circulars, correspondence, memoranda, pamphlets, reports of ad hoc
    committees, responses to internal surveys, speeches.

PUBLIC DOCUMENTS

New York State Insurance Department. "Examination of the Germania Life Insurance
    Company for Dec. 12, 1909." 1911.
——. "Examination of the Germania Life Insurance Company for 1913." [1914].
——. "Evaluation of the Guardian." 1929.
——. "Evaluation of the Guardian." 1932.
——. Annual Reports.
U.S. Alien Property Custodian. Corporation Management Dept. Docket Record. "The
    Guardian Life Insurance Company of America." National Archives. RG 131.

NEWSPAPERS

Belletristisches Journal. 1859–60.
Chicago Evening Post. 1918.
Chronicle. 1901–1902.

Eastern Underwriter. 1920.
Insurance Index. 1921.
New York Evening Sun. 1905, 1914.
Spectator. 1874.
Standard. 1901.
Weekly Underwriter. 1895, 1911, 1915.

Secondary Sources

Abbott, Lawrence F. *The Story of NYLIC: A History of the Origin and Development of the New York Life Insurance Company from 1845 to 1929.* New York: New York Life Insurance Company, 1930.
Albrecht, Wolfgang. "Hugo Wesendonck, 1817–1900." Translated by Dagmar Stern. In *Wuppertaler Biographien.* Vol. 7. Wuppertal, 1967.
Angle, John C. "America's First Consulting Actuary." *The Actuary* 15:8 (October 1981): 1, 8.
Bishop, George A. *Capital Formation through Life Insurance: A Study in the Growth of Life Insurance Services and Investment Activities.* Homewood, Ill.: Richard Irwin, 1976.
Bond, Brian. *War and Society in Europe, 1870–1970.* Leicester: University of Leicester Press, 1983.
Buley, R. Carlysle. *The American Life Convention, 1906–1952: A Study in the History of Life Insurance.* New York: Appleton-Century-Crofts, 1953.
——. *The Equitable Life Assurance Society of the United States, 1859–1964.* New York: Appleton-Century-Crofts, 1967.
Carosso, Vincent P. *Investment Banking in America: A History.* Cambridge: Harvard University Press, 1970.
Clough, Shepard. *A Century of American Life Insurance: A History of the Mutual Life Insurance Company of New York, 1843–1943.* New York: Columbia University Press, 1946.
Conze, Werner. "The German Empire." In *The New Cambridge Modern History,* edited by F. H. Hinsley, vol. 11, pp. 274–91. Cambridge: Cambridge University Press, 1962.
Crosby, Alfred W., Jr. *Epidemic and Peace, 1918.* Westport, Ct.: Greenwood Press, 1976.
Dewey, Davis Rich. *Financial History of the United States.* New York: Longmans, Green, 1934.
Dolan, Jay P. *The Immigrant Church: New York's Irish and German Catholics, 1815–1865.* Baltimore: Johns Hopkins University Press, 1975.
Entz, John Frederic. *Synopsis of a Variety of Tables, New Features, and Improvements in Life Insurance, Endowments and Annuities Proposed to the New York Life Insurance and Trust Co. of New York.* New York: Evening Post Steam Presses, 1872.
Ernst, Robert. *Immigrant Life in New York City, 1825–1863.* Port Washington, N.Y.: Ira J. Friedman, 1949.
Faust, Albert Bernhardt. *The German Element in the United States.* New York: Steuben Society of America, 1927.
Fels, Rendigs. *American Business Cycles, 1865–1897.* Chapel Hill: University of North Carolina Press, 1959.
Geschichte der Deutschen Gesellschaft von Pennsylvanien. Philadelphia: Neubrud von Graf & Breuninger, 1917.
Hagedorn, Homer J. "White Collar Management: Harry Arthur Hopf and the Rationalization of Business." Ph.D. dissertation, Harvard University, 1955.

History Committee, *History of the Liederkranz of the City of New York, 1847 to 1947, and of the Orion, New York.* New York: Drechsel Printing, 1948.

Huch, C. F. "Anschluss der Deutschen Philadelphias an die republikanische Partei im Jahre 1856." *Mitteilungen des Deutschen Pionier-Vereins von Philadelphia* 21 (1911): 13–31.

Hudnut, James M. *History of the New York Life Insurance Company 1895–1905.* New York: New York Life Insurance Company, 1906.

——. *Semi-Centennial History of the New-York Life Insurance Company 1845–1895.* New York: New York Life, 1895.

James, Marquis. *Metropolitan Life: A Study in Business Growth.* New York: Viking Press, 1947.

Keller, Morton. *The Life Insurance Enterprise, 1885–1910: A Study in the Limits of Corporate Power.* Cambridge, Mass.: Belknap Press, 1963.

Kesslinger, J. M. *Guardian of a Century.* New York: Guardian Life Insurance Company of America, 1960.

Lemke, Theodor. "Hugo Wesendonck." Translated by Gertrude Barber. In *Geschichte des Deutschthums von New York von 1848.* New York: Verlag von Theodor Lemke, 1891.

Luebke, Frederick C. *Bonds of Loyalty: German-Americans and World War I.* DeKalb: Northern Illinois University Press, 1974.

Manson, George J. "The 'Foreign Element' in New York City. I. The Germans." *Harper's Weekly* (4 August 1888).

May, Earl C. and Will Oursler. *The Prudential: A Story of Human Security.* Garden City, N.Y.: Doubleday, 1950.

McMorrow, Mary Elizabeth. "The Nineteenth-Century German Political Immigrant and the Construction of American Culture and Thought." Ph.D. dissertation, Graduate Faculty of the New School for Social Research, 1982.

Merrill, Harwood F., ed. *Classics in Management.* Rev. ed. New York: American Management Association, 1970.

Miller, Albert G. *History of the German Hospital of Philadelphia and Its Ex-Resident Physicians.* Philadelphia: J. B. Lippincott, 1906.

Moorhead, E. J. "Sketches of Early North American Actuaries." *Transactions, Society of Actuaries* 37 (1985): 51–83.

Nadel, Stanley, "Kleindeutschland: New York City's Germans, 1845–1880." Ph.D. dissertation, Columbia University, 1981.

Nelli, Humbert O. *The Private Insurance Business in the United States Economy.* Research paper no. 48, Department of Insurance and the Bureau of Business and Economic Research School of Business Administration, Georgia State College, 1967.

North, Douglass C. *Growth and Welfare in the American Past: A New Economic History.* Englewood Cliffs, N.J.: Prentice-Hall, 1966.

O'Connor, Richard. *The German Americans.* Boston: Little, Brown, 1968.

Pfund, Harry. *A History of the German Society of Pennsylvania.* Philadelphia: German Society of Pennsylvania, 1964.

Potter, David M. *The Impending Crisis, 1848–1861.* New York: Harper & Row, 1976.

Rein, Bert W. *An Analysis and Critique of the Union Financing of the Civil War.* Amherst, Mass.: Amherst College Honors Thesis No. 12, 1962.

Seidensticker, Oswald. *Geschichte des Mannerchors in Philadelphia 1835–1885: Zur Funtzigjahrigen Jubelfeier am 15. December 1885.* Philadelphia: Verlag des Mannerchors, 1885.

Stalson, J. Owen. *Marketing Life Insurance: Its History in America.* Homewood, Ill.: Richard Irwin, 1969.

Stern, Fritz. *Gold and Iron. Bismarck, Bleichroder and the Building of the German Empire.* New York: Alfred Knopf, 1977.

The Story of Lenox Hill Hospital. n.p., 1947.

Trefousse, Hans L. *Carl Schurz, A Biography.* Knoxville: University of Tennessee Press, 1982.

——, ed. *Germany and America: Essays on Problems of International Relations and Immigration.* Brooklyn: Brooklyn College Press, 1980.

U.S. Bureau of the Census. *Historical Statistics of the United States: Colonial Times to 1970.* Washington, D.C.: Government Printing Office, 1975.

Von Skal, George. *History of German Immigration in the United States and Successful German-Americans and Their Descendants.* New York: Smiley, 1908.

Williamson, Harold F. and Orange A. Smalley. *Northwestern Mutual Life: A Century of Trusteeship.* Evanston, Ill.: Northwestern University Press, 1957.

Wittke, Carl. *German-Americans and World War I.* Columbus, Ohio: Ohio State Archaeological and Historical Society, 1936.

——. *The German-Language Press in America.* Lexington, Ky.: University of Kentucky Press, 1957.

——. *Refugees of Revolution: The German Forty-Eighters in America.* Philadelphia: University of Pennsylvania Press, 1952.

——. *We Who Built America: The Saga of the Immigrant.* Rev. ed. Cleveland: Press of Case Western Reserve University, 1967.

Zucker, A. E., ed. *The Forty-Eighters.* New York: Columbia University Press, 1950.

Index